Word for Windows Answers: Certified Tech Support

Mary Campbell

Osborne **McGraw-Hill**

Berkeley • New York • St. Louis • San Francisco
Auckland • Bogotá • Hamburg • London
Madrid • Mexico City • Milan • Montreal
New Delhi • Panama City • Paris • São Paulo
Singapore • Sydney • Tokyo • Toronto

Osborne **McGraw-Hill**
2600 Tenth Street, Berkeley, California 94710, USA

For information on software, translations, or book distributors outside of the U.S.A., please write to Osborne McGraw-Hill at the above address.

Word for Windows Answers: Certified Tech Support

1234567890 DOC 9987654

ISBN 0-07-882031-6

Publisher Lawrence Levitsky	**Illustrator** Marla Shelasky
Project Editor Mark Karmendy	**Series Design** Marla Shelasky
Computer Designer Peter F. Hancik	**Quality Control Specialist** Joe Scuderi

Contents
at a
Glance

Contents

15 Forms 389

Foreword

Few things are as frustrating as having a computer problem that you can't solve. Computer users often spend hours trying to find the answer to a *single* software question! That's why the tech support experts at Corporate Software Incorporated (CSI) have teamed up with Osborne/McGraw-Hill to bring you the **Certified Tech Support Series**—books designed to give you all the solutions you need to fix even the most difficult software glitches.

At Corporate Software, we have a dedicated support staff that handles over 200,000 software questions every month. These experts use the latest hardware and software technology to provide answers to every sort of software problem. CSI takes full advantage of the partnerships that we have forged with all major software publishers. Our staff frequently receives the same training that publishers offer their own support representatives and has access to vendor technical resources that are not generally available to the public.

Thus, this series is based on actual *empirical* data. We've drawn on our support expertise and sorted through our vast database of software solutions to find the most important and frequently asked questions for Word for Windows. These questions have also been checked and rechecked for technical accuracy and are organized in a way that will let you find the answer you need quickly—providing you with a one-stop tech support solution to your software problems.

No longer do you have to spend hours on the phone waiting for someone to answer your tech support question! You are holding the single, most authoritative collection of answers to your software questions available—the next best thing to having a tech support expert by your side.

We've helped millions of people solve their software problems. Let us help you.

Randy Burkhart
Senior Vice President, Technology
Corporate Software Inc.

Acknowledgments

I would like to thank all the staff at Corporate Software who enthusiastically committed so much time and knowledge to this effort. So many of them spent time on weekends and after hours to search their data banks for the best questions and answers. They also spent untold hours reviewing manuscript and pages and responding to all of our requests for help. Without all of their hard work, this book would not exist. I would like to personally thank each of the following people for their assistance:

Alex W., Ann-Marie H., Blair V., Brian C., Daniel B., David Ch., David Co., Donald B., Donald R., Lala M., Rob S., Steven R., and William C.

Special thanks to:

Nancy E., Joseph M., Kristen E., Howard K., Kim A., Jan R., Christian P., Jennifer L., Lisa K., and Louis C.

The staff at Osborne was also an important part of this book. Without exception, everyone did more than their share to insure that we met all the important deadlines. I would like to extend special thanks to: Larry Levitsky, Publisher, for the idea to do the series and all of his work with Corporate Software to make the idea a reality; Kelly Vogel, Editorial Assistant, who helped to organize all the components of the project; Cindy Brown, Managing Editor, whose handling of this project was as flawless as ever; Mark Karmendy, Project Editor, who managed the editorial process and helped to polish the manuscript; and all of the Production staff, who each did everything possible to make this book the best source of technical support available.

I would also like to give special thanks to my assistants, Gabrielle Lawrence and Elizabeth Reinhardt. They contributed extensively to the book's contents and art work, and proofread the final manuscript to help catch technical and grammatical errors.

Introduction

There is no good time to have a problem with your computer or the software you are using. You are anxious to complete the task you started and do not have time to fumble through a manual looking for an answer that is probably not there anyway. You can forget about the option of a free support call solving your problems, since most software vendors now charge as much as $25 to answer a single question. *Word for Windows Answers: Certified Tech Support* can provide the solution to all of your Word problems. It contains the most frequently asked Word questions along with the solutions to get you back on track quickly. The questions and answers have been extracted from the data banks of Corporate Software, the world's largest supplier of third-party support. Since they answer over 200,000 calls a month from users just like you, odds are high that your problem has plagued others in the past and is already part of their data bank. *Word for Windows Answers: Certified Tech Support* is the next best thing to having a Corporate Software expert at the desk right next to you. The help you need is available seven days a week, any time you have a problem.

Word for Windows Answers is organized into 17 chapters. Each chapter contains questions and answers on a specific area of Word, and we have tried to organize them so that you'll find the simplest questions at the beginning, progressing to intermediate and advanced questions as you move through the chapter.

With this organization, you will be able to read through questions and answers on particular topics to familiarize yourself with them before the troubles actually occur. An excellent index makes it easy for you to find what you need even if you are uncertain which chapter would cover the solution.

Throughout the book you will also find the following elements to help you sail smoothly through your Word tasks, whether you are a novice or a veteran user:

- **Frustration Busters:** Special coverage of Word topics that have proven confusing to many users. A few minutes spent reading each of these boxes can help you avoid problems in the first place.

- **Tech Tips and Notes:** Short technical helps that provide additional insight to a topic addressed in a given question.

- **Tech Terrors:** Pitfalls you will want to steer clear of.

Top Ten Tech Terrors

In this first chapter, we've culled the ten most likely technical "traumas" you may run into with Word for Windows and presented step-by-step solutions to them. These are problems that *thousands* of users have encountered. They've turned to the consultant expertise at Corporate Software for help, and so can you!

In fact, you can probably avoid these problems altogether simply by reviewing this list as a preventive measure. If for some reason, however, you still run into any of them, you'll know just how to fix them.

Recently, I got the error message "Cannot save or create the file. Make sure the disk is not full or write protected." when I tried to save a file. Why am I suddenly experiencing this problem?

This error message appears because a program called SHARE.EXE, which lets DOS and other programs work with the same file at the same time, either is not loading or not operating properly. There are several methods you can use to correct this problem. Method #1 will work 99 percent of the time.

Method #1
Examine your AUTOEXEC.BAT file to make sure that SHARE loads with the appropriate settings. First, start the System Configuration Editor:

1. Switch to the Program Manager.
2. Choose <u>R</u>un from the <u>F</u>ile menu.
3. Type **SYSEDIT** in the <u>C</u>ommand Line text box.
4. Click OK.

The System Configuration Editor displays the contents of four files: AUTOEXEC.BAT, CONFIG.SYS, WIN.INI, and SYSTEM.INI. Each file appears in its own window, as shown in Figure 1-1. Examine the contents of your AUTOEXEC.BAT file to make sure it contains this line:

```
C:\DOS\SHARE.EXE /L:500 /F:5100
```

If SHARE loads with different switches, edit the line to match the one shown above, make certain the line appears at the top of the AUTOEXEC.BAT, and save the file. Exit all of your applications, including Windows, and then restart your system to see the effect of your changes.

If the error message recurs after you modify the AUTOEXEC.BAT file and reboot, edit the AUTOEXEC.BAT file again. This time, change the line that loads SHARE to set the /L switch to 1000 instead of 500.

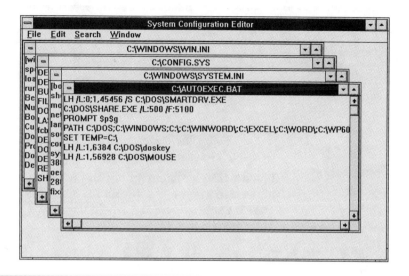

FIGURE 1-1   The System Configuration Editor

Method #2
Open the System Configuration Editor (as described in Method #1) and activate the CONFIG.SYS window. Edit the FILES and BUFFERS parameters so that the numbers are no lower than 60 and 30, respectively. The lines should now read:

```
FILES=60
BUFFERS=30
```

or higher, if deemed necessary.

Method #3
The applications you run on your computer store temporary files in a *temp directory*. Verify that this directory exists on your system, that your operating system knows where it's located, and that it is empty:

1. Exit Windows to display the DOS prompt.

2. At the DOS prompt, type **SET** and press ENTER.
   DOS displays several lines, similar to the ones shown here:

```
COMSPEC=C:\DOS\COMMAND.COM
PROMPT=$p$g
PATH=C:\DOS;C:\WINWORD;C:\WINDOWS;C:\WORD
TEMP=C:\DOS
windir=C:\WINDOWS
```

1. If a TEMP= line appears, switch to that directory and delete any files in it that have a .TMP extension.

2. If no TEMP= statement displays when you type **SET**, you need to insert a line in your AUTOEXEC.BAT file that reads **SET TEMP=*directory***, where *directory* is the name of the temp directory.

Tech Tip: You may want to periodically delete any .TMP files from your drive. Before you do so, exit Windows and any other programs. (You shouldn't delete temporary files while programs are active because they may rely on them.) Then, switch to the root directory (usually C:\), type **DIR *.TMP /S** , and press ENTER. Delete any files that appear.

Method #4

Double-check that there is enough free space on your hard drive to store the file you are attempting to save. Generally, you need at least three times the size of the document available if it contains any graphics.

Method #5

If you encounter this message while attempting to save a master document, save each subdocument individually before saving the master document as a whole.

Method #6

Upgrade to Word for Windows, version 6.0a. If you are running Windows or Windows for Workgroups in enhanced mode, Word 6.0a automatically loads a program called VSHARE. VSHARE performs the same functions as SHARE.EXE, but doesn't need to be loaded in the AUTOEXEC.BAT file. (You only need SHARE.EXE if you are running Windows or Windows for Workgroups in standard mode.)

You can upgrade to Word 6.0a by downloading a file called PATCH.EXE from CompuServe, or WORD60A.EXE from the Microsoft Download Service (206-936-6735).

2 I developed a number of templates in Word for Windows 2.0 and would like to use them in Word for Windows 6.0. Do I have to recreate them?

Before you can use your Word for Windows 2.0 templates in Word 6.0, you must convert them to the new format. For each template you want to use:

1. Choose Open from the File menu.

2. Select Document Templates (*.dot) from the List Files of Type drop-down list box.

3. Use the Directories list box to switch to the directory containing the Word for Windows 2.0 templates.

4. Select the desired Word for Windows 2.0 template in the File Name list box and choose OK to open it.

5. Choose Save As from the File menu. By default, Word for Windows 6.0 saves the template file in the WINWORD\TEMPLATE directory.

6. To convert the file to the new 6.0 format, choose Word at the prompt.

Tech Tip: If you have any trouble saving or using the templates in the new format, contact Microsoft for a list of the features you can expect to successfully convert from Word for Windows 2.0 templates. Some features in these templates are obsolete and do not function properly in Word 6.0. This list highlights the problems you may encounter.

3 Even though I had the automatic save feature turned on, Word didn't save all the changes I made to my document! Why not?

When you set up Word to automatically save your document at regular intervals, it periodically makes a copy of your document and adds a .ASD extension. However, it doesn't retain any changes you make during the intervening period. In addition, the .ASD files are only temporary; when you save or close the document, they are deleted. You should always save your document before closing it by choosing

the Save command on the File menu, even if you are using the automatic save feature.

The .ASD files are designed to let you recover work in the event of a system crash or power failure—in other words, an emergency. For example, imagine that you've been working on a sales report all afternoon with the automatic save feature turned on. Suddenly, your building experiences a "black out" that cuts the power to your system. Hours of work down the drain! But when the power is restored, you reboot and restart Word. To your relief, Word updates your sales report file to match the last .ASD file created. Although it may not rescue the changes you made during the last few minutes before the crash, the automatic save feature greatly reduces the amount of time you now have to spend getting the sales report back into shape.

To turn on the automatic save feature or adjust how often Word saves your documents:

1. Choose Options from the Tools menu.

2. Click the Save tab.

3. Select the Automatic Save Every check box.

4. Enter an interval in the Automatic Save Every [ ] minutes text box. (We recommend every fifteen minutes, especially if you work quickly.)

5. Choose OK to return to the document with your new settings in effect.

Tech Tip: To find out or change where these .ASD files are stored, choose Options from the Tools menu and then click the File Locations tab. Look for AutoSave Files in the File Types list box. The directory following this entry is where these files are saved. Highlight this entry and choose Modify to change this location.

 Because I knew I didn't have enough room on the C drive, I decided to install Word on the D drive. Why does the Word Setup program still warn me that there is not enough room on the C drive?

You are probably getting this message because Windows is installed on the C drive of your computer. Word includes a group of "applets" or supplementary applications (Equation Editor, WordArt, and Graph) and some filters that Word and other Microsoft applications share. These "applets" and filters are installed in the WINDOWS\MSAPPS directory, which is probably located on drive C. Word displays this message because you do not have enough disk space for these programs and filters. If this is the case, you have two choices:

- Make room on the C drive to install the applets and filters.
- Perform a Custom/Complete Installation, and specify not to install these programs and filters.

If, however, Windows is installed on the D drive, you should check that there are no references to drive C in the MSAPPS section of your WIN.INI file. You can view this file by using the System Configuration Editor (as described in the first question in this chapter). If such references exist, the Setup program for Word is unsuccessfully trying to install some of the applets or filters to drive C. In this case, edit the references in the WIN.INI file to refer to the D drive instead.

Tech Tip: It is extremely important that your temp directory has sufficient space to store the temporary files created during an installation. Before you start Word's Setup program, make sure that the drive on which your temp directory is located has at least 6 to 8 MB of available space above and beyond what the program itself requires. This rule also applies if your temp directory is stored on a RAM drive; however, Microsoft does not recommend using a RAM drive for installation purposes.

 I already have Word for Windows 2.0 on my computer and just bought Word for Windows 6.0. Do I have to remove 2.0 or can I run both versions?

You can run both versions of Word for Windows on the same computer as long as you take certain precautions.

First, you must install Word 6.0 in a different directory than the one in which Word 2.0 is stored. For example, you might install Word 6.0 in a directory called WINWORD6 and leave Word 2.0 in the WINWORD directory.

Second, the main application file for Word 2.0 and for Word 6.0 have the same name: WINWORD.EXE. You must rename one of these files to successfully run both versions on the same computer. For example, you might rename the WINWORD.EXE file stored in the Word 2.0 directory to WINWORD2.EXE. Once you rename this file, you must tell Windows where to find it by following these steps:

1. Select the program item in the Program Manager for the version of Word whose file name you changed. Press ALT+ENTER or choose <u>P</u>roperties from the <u>F</u>ile menu to open the Program Item Properties dialog box:

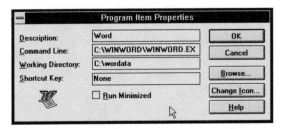

2. Edit the contents of the <u>C</u>ommand Line text box to refer to the new file name. For example, if you renamed your Word 2.0 application file, edit the line to read **C:\WINWORD\WINWORD2.EXE** and then choose OK to save the change.

In this example, Windows will run WINWORD.EXE to start Word 6.0 and WINWORD2.EXE to open Word 2.0.

I run Word 2.0 on my home computer but I use Word 6.0 at work. Why can't my home computer read the files I bring home from work?

Word 6.0 uses a different file format than Word 2.0. For compatibility, Word 6.0 comes with a special converter that lets it open files saved in Word 2.0. Because Word 2.0 preceded Word 6.0, it obviously doesn't have such a built-in converter to read files created in this new release. You can, however, save your Word 6.0 documents in the Word 2.0 format by following these steps:

1. Display the document in Word 6.0 that you want to use on your home computer.

2. Choose Save <u>A</u>s from the <u>F</u>ile menu.

3. Select Word for Windows 2.0 from the Save File as <u>T</u>ype drop-down list box.

4. Enter a name for the file in the File <u>N</u>ame text box.

5. Specify the directory in which you want to save the file in the <u>D</u>irectories list box and then choose OK.

Microsoft has also made available a converter that lets Word 2.0 open Word 6.0 documents. To request a copy, contact Microsoft Product Support as listed in your Word Users' Manual.

7 I want to create personalized form letters but I can't figure out how to create the file that contains the variable data. What's the easiest way to do this?

You produce form letters in Word by merging a *main document*, which contains the text and formatting that you want to appear in every letter, with the contents of a second file, called a *data source*. The data source stores all of the unique information that appears in each copy of the letter in *fields*. When you perform the merge, the contents of the fields replace *merge field codes* in the main document.

For example, you might have a data source with the names and addresses of the participants attending a conference. You could combine this data source with a main document—such as a letter, envelope label, or name tag—to generate a personalized item for each attendee. Alternatively, you can individually select a subgroup of attendees for which you want to produce documents.

You might want to use the following fields to store information about the conference attendees:

First Name
Last Name
Street Address
City
State
Zip Code
Phone Number
Company

Follow these steps to identify the main document and the appropriate fields:

1. Choose Mail Merge from the Tools menu to display the Mail Merge Helper dialog box shown here:

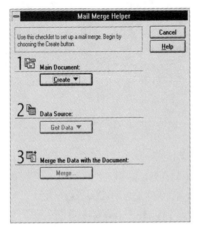

2. Under Main Document, click Create and then select one of the document types listed.

3. In the message box that appears below, specify whether you want to use the contents of the active window or a new document as the main document. Pick Active Window if the current window displays the document you want to use; otherwise, click New Main Document.

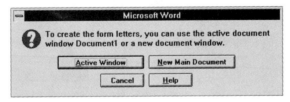

4. Click Get Data under Data Source.

5. Choose Create Data Source.

6. When the Create Data Source dialog box appears, select the names of the fields you want to include in the data source file.

Tech Tip: If you already have a file you want to use as the data source, choose Open Data Source, then select the appropriate file name.

7. The Field <u>N</u>ames in Header Row list box displays the set of field names that appear in the data source. You can:

- Add new field names by typing them in the <u>F</u>ield Names text box and clicking <u>A</u>dd Field Name.
- Remove field names by highlighting them and clicking <u>R</u>emove Field Name.
- Reorder field names by highlighting them and clicking the Move buttons to the right of the Field <u>N</u>ames in Header Row list box.

8. When you are finished selecting and arranging the field names, choose OK to store them in the data source.

9. In the Save Data Source dialog box, enter a name for the data source file in the File <u>N</u>ame text box and then choose OK.

10. Choose Edit <u>D</u>ata Source to open a Data Form dialog box like the one shown in Figure 1-2. This dialog box includes a text box for each of the fields you selected in the Create Data Source dialog box.

11. Enter the data for the first data record—in this case, the first person—and then click <u>A</u>dd New to add it to the data source.

12. Repeat the preceding step for each record, or person, until all the data is entered and then choose OK.

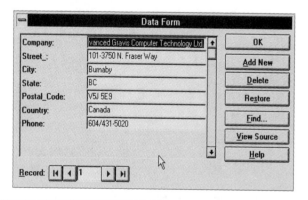

FIGURE 1-2   Enter data for a Word data source in the Data Form dialog box

Word 6.0 stores the data source information in a file with the name you specified in step 5. To view the data, you can open this file as you would any other in Word 6.0. The data you entered in the Data Form dialog box appears in a table format, as shown in Figure 1-3.

Tech Tip: See Chapter 11, "Merges," for more information about merging Word documents.

How do I merge my data source with the main document?

Before you merge the main document and the data source, verify the following:

- You have stored all of the data you want to use in the data source file.

- You inserted the merge fields in the main document in the locations at which you want the variable data to appear in the final document.

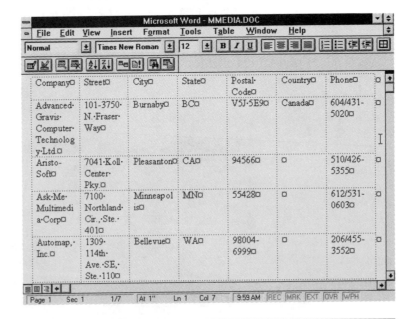

FIGURE 1-3   A Word data source document

To merge the data source with the main document:

1. Display the main document in the active window.
2. Click one of the merge buttons on the Mail Merge toolbar to merge the two documents and specify where the output appears:

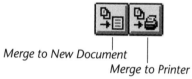

Merge to New Document

Merge to Printer

Alternatively, click the Mail Merge button to display the Mail Merge dialog box. Specify where to send the output of the merge, how to treat blank lines created by missing field entries, which records you want to merge, and other options. Choose OK to perform the merge.

I want to delete some document files. Can I do this without leaving Word?

To delete files from within Word:

1. Choose Find File from the File menu.
2. If the Search dialog box appears, as shown here, enter criteria in the Search For area of the dialog box to find a group of files that includes the ones you want to delete, and then choose OK.

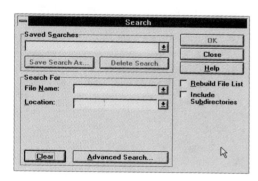

If you have used this feature before, Word displays the last group of files you selected. In this case, choose the Search button to display the Search dialog box and then search for the appropriate group of files.

Tech Tip: See Chapter 8, "File Management," for more information about using the Find File feature to create and use searches.

3. Select the files you want to delete in the Listed Files list box.

4. Select Commands and then Delete; alternatively, you can press the DEL key.

5. Select Yes to confirm that you want to delete the selected file or files.

6. Choose Close to exit the Find File dialog box.

10 How can I set a different font as the default?

To reset the default font used by new documents created in Word 6.0, you need to change the default font in the template upon which they are based. Unless you've specified otherwise, Word 6.0 uses the NORMAL.DOT template when it creates new documents. To edit this template:

1. Choose Font from the Format menu.

2. Select the desired font using the Font, Font Style, and Size list boxes on the Font tab.

3. Select Default.

4. If you want to use this font as the default for all new documents created with the template, select Yes at the prompt.

Tech Tip: The default font setting is saved as part of the current template. If you are working in a document created with a template other than NORMAL.DOT, the new default font affects only documents based on this other template.

Setup

It's easy to install Word 6.0 for Windows—just let the Word Setup program do it for you! All you have to do is insert the first Setup disk into your A drive (or whichever drive is appropriate for the type of disk you're using), choose Run from the Program Manager's File menu, type **A:\SETUP** in the Command Line text box (substitute another letter for A, if appropriate), and click OK. Setup takes it from there! Once installed, you can start Word by simply double-clicking its program item in the Program Manager.

FRUSTRATION BUSTERS!

Word offers so many features that you may find you need to make a few changes to maximize your system resources. To improve performance, you may want to try one or more of the following, depending on which Word features you are using:

- Close any Word documents with which you are not currently working.

- Divide a large document into smaller ones.

- Close other active applications.

- Remove any RAM drives, unless you have at least 8MB of RAM.

- Increase the amount of RAM on your computer.

- Add a Windows accelerator card, if your monitor's resolution is better than 800 x 600 or you are using a 256-color mode.

- Make sure your Windows swap file is a permanent swap file, except if you are using a compressed drive.

- Use a disk cache, such as SMARTDrive.

- Reduce the numbers that appear the SMARTDRV statement in your AUTOEXEC.BAT file, unless you have at least 8MB of RAM.

- Change the number of buffers set in your CONFIG.SYS file to a higher or lower number.

- Set the Desktop wallpaper to None in the Desktop dialog box, which you access from the Windows Control Panel.

What does my computer need to run Word for Windows 6.0?

To run Word for Windows 6.0, you computer must meet the following minimum hardware and operating system requirements:

Recommended RAM	4MB
Disk space for minimum setup	6MB
Disk space for full setup	26MB
Operating system	Windows 3.1 or higher

You should also make certain that the drive on which Windows itself is installed has at least 6MB of disk space available for the applets and filters, which are also used by other Microsoft products. These requirements reflect the *minimum* configuration you need to install and use Word for Windows 6.0; exceeding these requirements will make Word run faster and better.

How can I set up Word so that it always makes a backup copy of my document when I save it?

You can tell Word to automatically create a backup copy of your original document whenever you save it. Word saves the revised document with the regular .DOC extension; it saves the original document using the same name with a .BK! extension. Figure 2-1 depicts this process. If you want to work with your original document instead of the edited one (for example, if you're not satisfied with the modifications you made), you can simply open the backup copy instead. You can see these files in the Open dialog box by selecting All Files (*.*) from the List Files of Type drop-down list box.

To automatically create backup copies of your original documents whenever you save the edited versions:

1. Choose Options from the Tools menu.
2. Click the Save tab.
3. Select the Always Create Backup Copy check box under Save Options, then choose OK.

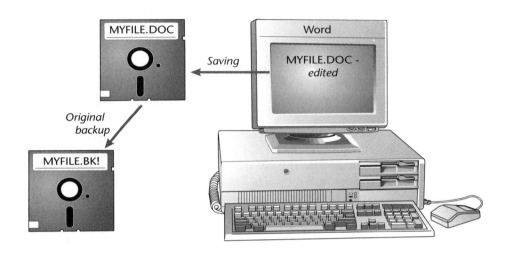

FIGURE 2-1   Word automatically saves a backup copy

Can Word automatically save documents for me while I'm working?

Yes, you can tell Word to automatically create *temporary* backup files while you are working. These files, which have an .ASD extension, let you recover any changes you've made to a document in the event of a system crash. Otherwise, you may lose your most recent modifications to any open documents. These files can be lifesavers if your system shuts down abnormally, for example, due to a power failure. After you reboot, you should immediately resave the salvaged documents by using the Save command on the File menu or the Save button on the Standard toolbar.

To implement the AutoSave option so that Word automatically saves your documents as you work:

1. Choose Options from the Tools menu.

2. Click the Save tab.

3. Select Automatic Save check box.

4. Enter the interval you want to occur between automatic saves in the Minutes text box.

5. Choose OK.

Tech Terror: Unlike .BK! files, Word deletes .ASD files when you save or close the associated documents. Therefore, do not depend on them as your only backup versions!

You can specify an interval from 1 to 120 minutes. By default, the automatic save feature is turned on with a 10 minute interval.

Word stores the .ASD files in a specific directory. To identify or change the location of these files:

1. Choose Options from the Tools menu.

2. Click the File Locations tab.

3. Note the location listed after AutoSave Files in the File Types list box.

4. If you want to change the location, select AutoSave Files and then click Modify.

5. Specify a new directory, then click OK twice.

When I installed Microsoft Word, I spelled my company's name wrong at the prompt. Is there any way to fix it?

The Setup program stores the user information in an encrypted format on the installation disks. It automatically enters the same user and company names if you use these disks to install Word 6.0 on another computer. Once you enter your name and company information during installation, the only way to change it is by obtaining a new set of Word disks, uninstalling the current Word files, and then reinstalling the product with the new disks.

The user information you input during installation is completely separate from the data that appears on the User Info tab in the Options dialog box. Word uses this user name, initials, and mailing address when it performs certain functions, such as marking revisions, labeling annotations, protecting documents, and printing envelopes and labels. To change this information:

1. Choose Options from the Tools menu.

2. Click the User Info tab.

3. Type the replacement information in the appropriate text boxes.

4. Click OK.

During installation, Word changed a line in my AUTOEXEC.BAT file to read "C:\DOS\SHARE.EXE /L:500 /F:5100." Do I need this line and, if so, why?

This statement must appear in your AUTOEXEC.BAT file to run Word 6.0. This line loads the SHARE program, which lets more than one program access the same file at a time. These new settings load SHARE with settings that support the new OLE 2. *Object Linking and Embedding (OLE)* allows in-place editing of embedded objects. It also lets both source and client applications use the same object, such as a graphic, text, or some other type of data.

Why doesn't the Word toolbar button start Excel now that I upgraded from Excel 4 to Excel 5? What can I do to fix this?

You've probably installed the new version of Excel in a different directory. The button is still looking for Excel in the old directory, where it can't be found. To fix this:

1. Start Excel by double-clicking the program item in the Program Manager.

2. With Excel running in the background, click the Excel button on the Microsoft toolbar in Word.

This process "retrains" the button to use the new version of Excel. The next time you click the button, it will launch the new version of Excel.

I'm installing Word for Windows 6.0, but I don't see an option to install it to a network file server. Why?

Microsoft updated the Setup program for Word for Windows 6.0 to more closely match the network Setup for Windows 3.1. Now, you must run the Administrative Setup to the file server before you can install Word on a workstation. To install Word 6.0 to a file server, you need to start Setup using the /A switch. To do so:

1. Choose <u>R</u>un from the Program Manager's <u>F</u>ile menu.
2. Type **A:\SETUP /A** (substitute a different drive, if appropriate) in the <u>C</u>ommand Line text box.
3. Choose OK.

When you perform the installation process, Setup offers an option to install to a file server. You can simply enter the server's directory when Word prompts you about where to install the program files.

I already have Word for Windows 2.0 on my computer and just bought Word for Windows 6.0. Do I have to remove Word 2.0 or can I run both versions?

You can run both versions of Word for Windows on the same computer as long as you take certain precautions.

First, you must install Word 6.0 in a different directory than the one in which Word 2.0 is stored. For example, you might install Word 6.0 in a directory called WINWORD6 and leave Word 2.0 in the WINWORD directory.

Second, the main application file for Word 2.0 and for Word 6.0 have the same name: WINWORD.EXE. You must rename one of these files to successfully run both versions on the same computer. For example, you might rename the WINWORD.EXE file stored in the Word 2.0 directory to WINWORD2.EXE. Once you rename this file, you must tell Windows where to find it by following these steps:

1. Select the program item in the Program Manager for the version of Word whose file name you changed. Press ALT+ENTER or choose <u>P</u>roperties from the <u>F</u>ile menu to open the Program Item Properties dialog box:

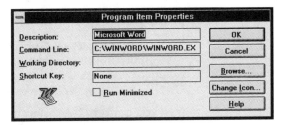

2. Edit the contents of the <u>C</u>ommand Line text box to refer to the new file name. For example, if you renamed your Word 2.0 application file, edit the line to read

   C:\WINWORD\WINWORD2.EXE

   and then choose OK to save the change.

In this example, Windows will run WINWORD.EXE to start Word 6.0 and WINWORD2.EXE to open Word 2.0.

When I start Word, it displays various error messages about my Normal template. Could it be corrupted?

You can test the validity of the Normal template by starting Word 6.0 using the /A switch. This starts Word using a standard default template, without any add-ins or additional templates attached. To test your template:

1. Exit Word and switch to the Program Manager.

2. Choose <u>R</u>un from the <u>F</u>ile menu.

3. Type **C:\WINWORD\WINWORD.EXE /A** in the <u>C</u>ommand Line text box. (If Word for Windows is not installed in the WINWORD directory, substitute the appropriate directory.)

4. Click OK.

If Word starts successfully and no error messages display, you can assume that the Normal template itself is damaged. In this case, use the File Manager to open the WINWORD\TEMPLATE directory, rename or delete the NORMAL.DOT file, and then restart Word. If you start Word 6.0 using the /A switch or without the Normal template, it automatically resets all the defaults to those that Word 6.0 had when you first installed it.

The Normal template stores all your global styles, macros, default settings, and screen setups. If the template is corrupt, you may need to recreate any items that you added or customized. Alternatively, if you rename NORMAL.DOT, you may be able to use Word's Organizer to copy styles, macros, toolbars, and AutoText entries from the corrupt template file to the new NORMAL.DOT that Word automatically creates.

When I try to open Word 6.0, I receive the message "Word has caused a General Protection Fault in module WINWORD.EXE" and the program won't start. How can I run Word?

There are a number of steps you can take to troubleshoot the cause of this error. First, check whether your Normal template is corrupt:

1. Choose <u>R</u>un from the <u>F</u>ile menu in the Program Manager.

2. Type **C:\WINWORD\WINWORD.EXE /A** and click OK. (If Word for Windows is installed in a different directory, substitute it in the path you enter.)

If Word opens without displaying any error messages, your NORMAL.DOT template file is corrupt. To recreate this template:

1. Start the File Manager.

2. Select NORMAL.DOT in the TEMPLATE subdirectory of the directory that contains your Word for Windows program files.

3. Choose Re<u>n</u>ame from the <u>F</u>ile menu, type a new name for this file, and then click OK.

4. Start Word.

When Word cannot locate NORMAL.DOT, it automatically creates a new template and reverts back to the original default settings.

If the General Protection Fault error message persists, change your display driver to VGA. Some video drivers are known to cause this problem. You may also need to reinstall your printer driver. To check your display:

1. Double-click the Windows Setup icon in the Program Manager's Main program group.

2. Choose Change Systems Settings from the Options menu.

3. Select VGA in the Display drop-down list box and then click OK.

4. Select Current if Windows detects an existing driver on your system.

5. Exit Windows and then restart it to use the new display setting.

To reinstall your printer driver:

1. Start the File Manager and open the WINDOWS\SYSTEM subdirectory.

2. Identify and select the name of the printer driver file, which indicates the printer type and ends with a .DRV extension. (For example, the printer driver for a Hewlett-Packard LaserJet III printer is HPPCL5A.DRV and the printer driver for a Postscript printer is PSCRIPT.DRV.)

3. Change Rename from the File menu.

4. Enter the same file name with a different extension.

5. Click OK.

6. Open the Windows Control Panel, which is located in the Program Manager's Main program group.

7. Double-click the Printers icon, or choose Printers from the Settings menu.

8. Select the default printer in the Installed Printers list box and then click Remove.

9. Choose Add and reselect your printer. (If you are using a printer that does not appear on the list, select Install Unlisted or Updated Printer at the top of the list and

then use either the file provided on disk by the printer's manufacturer or one obtained from Microsoft's Download Service.)

10. Choose Install.

11. When the prompt appears, insert the appropriate Microsoft Windows Disk. If the Windows disk is in drive A, click OK. If the Windows disk is in drive B, type **B:**, and then click OK.

12. Select Set as Default Printer when your printer appears in the Installed Printers list box.

13. Choose Close and then exit the Control Panel.

At this point, you eliminated the most probable causes for the General Protection Fault and Word should start correctly.

When I perform a Typical installation, what components are not included?

These components are not installed during a Typical setup:

- Dialog Editor
- ODBC files
- Technical Support Help
- Microsoft Graph
- Microsoft Equation Editor
- The LETTERS and MACRO subdirectories, which contain the business letter templates and macro files, respectively: CONVERT.DOT, LAYOUT.DOT, MACRO60.DOT, and TABLES.DOT
- Two text converters: Word for Windows 2.0 and RFT-DCA
- Six graphics filters: Micrografx Designer/Draw, Kodak Photo CD, CGM, PCX, CompuServe GIF, and AutoCAD DXF

Also, during a Typical installation, Word prompts you to confirm that you want to install WordBasic Help and WordPerfect Help before it does so.

Tech Tip: It is extremely important that your temp directory has sufficient space to store the temporary files created during an installation. Before you start Word's Setup program, make sure that the drive on which your temp directory is located has at least 6MB to 8MB of available space above and beyond what the program itself requires.

I want to add a component of Word that I did not originally install. Is there any way to add it without reinstalling the whole program?

Follow these steps to install a single component of Word without reinstalling the entire program:

1. Start Setup. You can either run Setup using Setup Disk 1 or, if you ran a Typical or Complete Installation, by double-clicking the Word Setup program item (found in the program group with Word for Windows 6.0 icons) in the Program Manager.

2. The Setup program detects any installed components and provides you with three choices: Add/Remove, Install Again, and Remove All.

3. Click Add/Remove to display the Maintenance Mode dialog box shown in Figure 2-2.

4. Indicate the components to add or remove by selecting or clearing the appropriate check boxes.

Each time you elect to add a component, the Setup program updates the Space Required statistic; similarly, if you indicate that you want to remove an item, Setup adjusts the Space Available figure. If you do not see a check box for the specific component you want to install, highlight the appropriate category and click Change Option. Setup opens a dialog box in which you can select additional options.

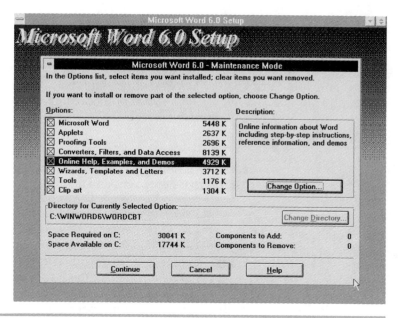

FIGURE 2-2   Adding or Removing Word components in the Maintenance
Mode dialog box

Tech Terror: If you clear a check box for a
component that is already installed, Setup
deletes it from your hard disk. If this
accidentally occurs, simply repeat this
procedure described here to reinstall it.

5. When you have finished selecting the components you
want to add or remove, click Continue.

6. At the Setup prompts, insert the disks required to install
the specific components.

**I knew I didn't have enough room on the C drive, so I
decided to install Word on the D drive. Why does the
Word Setup program still warn me that there is not
enough room on the C drive?**

You are probably getting this message because Windows is
installed on the C drive of your computer. Word includes a

group of "applets" or supplementary applications (Equation Editor, WordArt, and Graph) and some filters that Word and other Microsoft applications share. These "applets" and filters are installed in the WINDOWS\MSAPPS directory, which is probably located on drive C. Word displays this message because you do not have enough disk space for these programs and filters. If this is the case, you have two choices:

- Make room on the C drive to install the applets and filters.

- Perform a Custom/Complete Installation, and specify not to install these programs and filters.

If, however, Windows is installed on the D drive, you should check that there are no references to drive C in the MSAPPS section of your WIN.INI file. You can view this file by using the System Configuration Editor (as described in the first question in Chapter 1). If such references exist, the Setup program for Word is unsuccessfully trying to install some of the applets or filters to drive C. In this case, edit the references in the WIN.INI file to refer to the D drive instead.

Can I have Word 6.0 automatically open a particular document every time it starts?

You can change the properties of the Word 6.0 program item in the Program Manager to specify a document to open whenever you start the program. To specify the file:

1. Select the Word 6.0 program item in the Program Manager.

2. Choose Properties from the Program Manager's File menu, or press ALT+ENTER.

3. Add the path and file name of the document to the end of the contents of the Command Line text box. For example, you might add **D:\DOCUMENT\CSI.DOC** to make the entry read C:\WINWORD\WINWORD.EXE D:\DOCUMENT\CSI.DOC.

4. Choose OK to save the new properties.

Now, whenever you start Word 6.0, the document you entered in the command line automatically displays.

You can also create several different icons for Word and have each one open a different document upon start-up. For example, you might have one icon that opens CSI.DOC and another that opens OSBORNE.DOC. You can use the File Manager as a shortcut to create multiple icons:

Tech Tip: Be sure to provide the complete path to the document; otherwise, Word may not be able to locate the file.

1. Open the Windows File Manager.

2. Resize the File Manager window, if necessary, so that you can also see the Program Manager program group window to which you want to add the new icons.

3. Drag the Word document file from the File Manager window to the program group window.

A Word icon appears in the program group with the document's name beneath it. Repeat this procedure to create additional icons. This method can be extremely helpful if you have particular documents with which you work frequently.

When I tried to install Word Assistant, I got a message that Word was not installed on my computer, even though it is. Why?

It's possible that Word Assistant just wasn't getting the right signals to indicate that Word was installed. There are two steps you can take to rectify this problem:

■ Display the WINWORD6.INI file in the Notepad or another text editor. Verify that the programdir= statement indicates a valid path to the WINWORD.EXE file.

■ Make certain that the executable program file is called WINWORD.EXE. If you changed the name to make it possible to run two versions of Word on the same system, you may need to change the name back.

I liked the way you could edit the WIN.INI file in Word 2.0. Is there anyway to do this in Word 6.0?

Yes, you can use Word 6.0 to enter commands in the WIN.INI file in the same way as you did in Word 2.0. To do so, follow these steps to run a macro that is included with Word 6.0:

1. Choose Macro from the Tools menu.

2. Select Word Commands in the Macros Available In drop-down list box.

3. Select ToolsAdvancedSettings in the Macro Name list box, or enter it in the text box.

4. Choose Run.

5. Use the Advanced Settings dialog box shown in Figure 2-3 to edit the WIN.INI file the same way you did in Word 2.0.

Tech Tip: You can also change most of the program options by choosing Options from the Tools menu and indicating your selections on the appropriate tabs.

Advanced Settings
Modify startup settings stored in WINWORD6.INI and WIN.INI

Categories: Microsoft Word

Startup Options:

```
USER-DOT-PATH=C:\WINWORD\TEMPLATE\
WORKGROUP-DOT-PATH=
INI-PATH=C:\WINWORD\
DOC-PATH=C:\WORDATA\
TOOLS-PATH=C:\WINWORD\
PICTURE-PATH=C:\WINWORD\CLIPART\
AUTOSAVE-PATH=C:\WINWORD\
STARTUP-PATH=C:\WINWORD\STARTUP\
PROGRAMDIR=C:\WINWORD
```

Option: USER-DOT-PATH

Setting: C:\WINWORD\TEMPLATE\

OK   Cancel   Help   Delete   Set

FIGURE 2-3   Using the Advanced Settings dialog box to modify the WIN.INI file directly

In Word 2.0, I set my default working directory by changing the properties of the Word program item. This doesn't work for Word 6.0. How do I set the working directory?

With Word 6.0, you set the working directory from within the program itself by following these steps:

1. Choose Options from the Tools menu.
2. Click the File Locations tab.
3. Select Documents in the File Types list box.
4. Click Modify.
5. Enter the path of the working directory in the Location of Documents text box, or select the directory by using the Directories and Drives list boxes.
6. Click OK then Close to return to your document.

While setting up Word, I received this error message: "While registering OLE servers, Setup had a problem with REG.DAT, SHELL.DLL or disk space." What's wrong and how can I fix it?

There are two reasons why this error message may display:

■ Your WINDIR variable is invalid or missing. The WINDIR variable defines which directory Windows uses to hold temporary files.

■ Your .REG files have no association. Windows can only recognize the application information if the .REG files have the correct association. This association lets you open and print files from the File Manager. It also provides full functionality of OLE.

To check whether a WINDIR variable exists and is valid:

1. Choose Run from the Program Manager's File menu.
2. Enter **SYSEDIT** in the Command Line text box, then click OK.

3. When the System Configuration Editor opens, move to the window that displays your AUTOEXEC.BAT file, if necessary.

4. Check the Path statement to make sure that it includes the Windows directory. For example, your Path statement might look like this:

```
path c:\;c:\windows;c:\dos
```

If necessary, add the correct Windows directory to the Path statement.

5. Save any changes to the AUTOEXEC.BAT file by choosing Save from the System Configuration Editor's File menu.

6. If you made any changes to the AUTOEXEC.BAT file, reboot your computer so they can take effect.

To check your .REG files' associations:

1. Choose Search from the File Manager's File menu.

2. Enter ***.REG** in the Search For text box.

3. Enter **C:** in the Start From text box.

4. Select the Search All Subdirectories check box and click OK.

5. Select one of the .REG files in the Search Results window.

6. Choose Associate from the File menu.

7. Registration Entries should appear in the Associate With text box. If it doesn't, create the association by selecting Registration Entries (regedit.exe) from the list box, then clicking OK.

After checking and correcting these two items, rerun Setup.

When I try to install Word 6.0, Setup displays a long error message telling me that I need to report a file to Microsoft Product Support Services. How do I install Word?

This message results from a minor error in the Word program code. The primary cause for this error is that the WINDIR environmental variable, which sets the Windows directory, does not include a drive letter in its path. For example, if WINDIR is set to WINDOWS instead of C:\WINDOWS, you may encounter this error. Windows automatically sets the WINDIR variable, based on the Path statement in your AUTOEXEC.BAT file. If the Path line exceeds 128 characters, you may also encounter this error.

The best solution to this problem is to obtain the Word 6.0a update by contacting Microsoft. You can upgrade to Word 6.0a by downloading a file called PATCH.EXE from CompuServe, or WORD60A.EXE from the Microsoft Download Service (206-936-6735).

If you need to install Word before you receive the update, you can try to work around the problem by modifying your AUTOEXEC.BAT file. Follow these steps to examine and edit the Path statement in your AUTOEXEC.BAT file to eliminate this error message:

1. Choose Run from the Program Manager's File menu, type **SYSEDIT** in the Command Line text box, and then click OK to start the Windows System Configuration Editor.

2. Move to the window that displays the AUTOEXEC.BAT file, if necessary.

3. Check the line that loads SHARE to make sure it loads using the correct settings. The line should read:

```
c:\dos\share.exe /1:500 /f:5100
```

4. Make sure that the Set Temp= line specifies a valid directory with a minimum of 6MB of space.

5. Check that the Path statement lists your Windows directory, including the drive letter. For example, the Path statement might look like:

```
Path c:\;c:\windows;c:\dos
```

6. Remove any lines in both the CONFIG.SYS and AUTOEXEC.BAT files that are not absolutely required to boot your computer and run Windows.

7. Save your edited CONFIG.SYS and AUTOEXEC.BAT files by choosing Save from the File menu.

8. Exit Windows, reboot your computer, and then rerun Setup.

Can I get the Quick Preview to display automatically when I start Word?

You can tell Word to present the Quick Preview menu, shown in Figure 2-4, every time the program opens. The Quick Preview feature helps you learn about Word. It may have appeared automatically the first few times you started the application. To display Quick Preview whenever you start Word:

1. Select the Word program item in the Program Manager.

2. Choose Properties from the File menu, or press ALT+ENTER.

3. At the end of the contents of the Command Line text box, add a space and then type

/mHelpQuickPreview

Now, when you open Word by double-clicking the program item, the Help Quick Preview menu appears.

FIGURE 2-4   Exploring Word's features in the Quick Preview menu

When I installed Word for Windows 6.0, Setup didn't include the tutorial. Why not?

You probably are using Windows NT or OS/2 version 2. The tutorials that ship with Word for Windows 6.0 cannot run under these operating systems. Because Setup recognizes Windows NT or OS/2 on your system, it neither creates the WORDCBT (computer-based training) directory nor installs the tutorial files. Setup does not alert you about this omission.

How can I ensure that network users will use my company's default network templates?

There are two ways you can ensure that all users work with your company's default network templates. The method you use to achieve this depends on whether you have already installed

Word on the workstations.

Method #1
If you have already installed Word on the workstations:

1. Choose Options from the Tools menu.
2. Click the File Locations tab.
3. Select the User Templates entry in the File Types list box.
4. Click Modify.
5. Select your Server Template Directory.
6. Click OK, then click Close.

Method #2
If you have not yet installed Word on the workstations:

1. In a spreadsheet application, such as Excel, open the SETUP.STF file, which is stored in the server's Word 6.0 directory.
2. Identify and move to the Template row.
3. Change the installation directory column so that it indicates the path to your server.
4. Save the SETUP.STF file and run the workstation installation.

 When I install Word on a network, how can I ensure that users work with the company's Normal template, but only use local versions of the other templates?

Word 6.0 derives template information from the WINWORD6.INI file, which is stored in the Windows directory. Word 6.0 searches for NORMAL.DOT and other templates in the order listed here:

Directory Searched	Associated WINWORD6.INI Statement
Workgroup template directory	WORKGROUP-DOT PATH=
User template directory	USER-DOT PATH=
Word program directory	PROGRAMDIR=
Current directory	

To have all users access the same NORMAL.DOT, you must store the file in a central location and then refer to it in the Workgroup template path. Word looks first at the Workgroup template path to find shared templates; it then examines the User template path to locate non-shared templates. If these settings are left blank, then Word uses the default template. The default used depends on how you installed Word and whether individuals have their own user directories in which non-shared template files are stored.

You can change the path of the Workgroup template so that Word uses the network version of NORMAL.DOT and then set the User template directory setting to indicate the location of any local templates, or vice versa. You can also change these parameters in advance by customizing the server's SETUP.STF file.

 I installed Word from disks, and made copies of the disks on my hard drive. I no longer have the Setup disks. When I try to install another component, Word prompts me to insert a disk in the drive from which I originally installed. What do I do?

You can change where Word looks for setup disks by modifying your SETUP.STF file, which is stored in the Setup subdirectory of your Word 6.0 program directory. To modify this file:

1. Open SETUP.STF in a spreadsheet program, such as Excel.

2. Search for the line that begins with the words "Source Directory."

3. Change the path that follows this text to the path from which you want to install Word, such as **C:\WINWORD6\DISKS**.

Tech Tip: Make sure you include the last backslash in the path!

4. Save SETUP.STF and restart the Setup program.

I don't want Word to open a new document when it starts. Can I disable this feature?

Yes, you can prevent Word from automatically opening a new document when it starts by following these steps:

1. Select the Word program item in the Program Manager.

2. Choose <u>P</u>roperties from the <u>F</u>ile menu, or press ALT+ENTER.

3. Modify the contents of the <u>C</u>ommand Line text box by adding a space and **/n** at the end of the current entry as shown below:

```
\winword\winword.exe /n
```

4. Click OK.

Can I integrate Bookshelf 1993 with Word 6.0 as I did with version 2.0?

Bookshelf's integration features are designed to work with Word for Windows 2.0. In order to use it with Word 6.0, you must manually install Bookshelf. With Word installed and functioning normally, you can perform the following steps to install Bookshelf's integration features to allow Word 6.0 to successfully communicate with Bookshelf 1993:

1. Install Bookshelf 1993. Make sure the option to install Word 2.0 for Windows Integration is *not* checked or Bookshelf will not function correctly with Word 6.0.

2. Copy the following files from the Bookshelf 1993 VIEWER\BS93WORD subdirectory on the CD-ROM to the directories listed. Replace WINDOWS with the name of your Windows program directory and WINWORD with the name of your Word 6.0 for Windows program directory, if necessary.

File	Directory
BOOKSHLF.INI	WINDOWS
BOOKSHLF.DLL	WINDOWS\SYSTEM
WORDDDE.DAT	WINWORD
DDEAPP.EXE	WINWORD

Tech Terror: These steps assume that you installed Windows in C:\WINDOW and Word for Windows in C:\WINWORD, and that the CD-ROM disk drive is drive D. If this is not how your system is set up, modify the drives and directories indicated here to match your system configuration. For example, if you installed Word for Windows to D:\WINWORD, type **D:\WINWORD** instead of **C:\WINWORD**.

Tech Tip: Make sure these files are not read only. If they are, select each one, in turn; choose the Properties command from the File menu in the File Manager; clear the Read Only check box; and then click OK

3. Choose Run from the File menu in the Program Manager, type **SYSEDIT**, and click OK.

4. Move to the window that displays the WIN.INI file and add the following text to the [Bookshelf] section:

```
Viewerpath=C:\WINDOWS\SYSTEM\MVIEWER2
Bookspath=D:\BOOKS\
Integration=2
SendToDlg=1
HelpFile=C:\WINWORD\WINWORD.HLP
```

5. Set the location of Word for Windows 6.0 in the WIN.INI file. Depending on whether Word 2.0 was previously installed, use one of these methods:

   ■ If Word 2.x for Windows was installed, scroll to the [Microsoft Word 2.0] section in the WIN.INI file. Check whether a programdir= statement exists and, if so, specifies the correct path to the Word 6.0 for Windows program directory, such as programdir=C:\WINWORD.

   ■ If Word 2.x for Windows was not previously installed, or if you cannot find the [Microsoft Word 2.0] section in the WIN.INI file, create a new section by entering these two lines:

```
[Microsoft Word 2.0]
programdir=C:\WINWORD
```

1. Choose E̲xit from the F̲ile menu, then choose Y̲es when you are asked if you want to save the modified WIN.INI file.

2. Close then restart Windows to use the new WIN.INI settings.

3. Start Word for Windows 6.0.

4. Choose O̲pen from the F̲ile menu.

5. Use the Dri̲ves and D̲irectories list boxes to switch to the VIEWER\BS93WORD subdirectory on the Bookshelf CD-ROM drive.

6. Double-click the BSHELF93.DOT document template in the File N̲ame list box.

7. Choose Save A̲s from the F̲ile menu, type **C:\WINWORD\STARTUP\BSHELF93.DOT** in the File

Name text box, and click OK to save the file in the correct
Word 6.0 directory.

8. Choose Exit from the File menu.

9. Restart Word so the changes you just made take effect.

Tech Tip: The Online Word User's Guide
included with Bookshelf 1993 is designed
exclusively for use with Word 2.x for Windows
and is not installed with this procedure.

Now that Bookshelf is installed, customize Word's menus to
work with the Bookshelf features by following these steps:

1. Choose Customize from the Tools menu, click the Menus
tab to see the dialog box shown below, and select Macros
in the Categories list box.

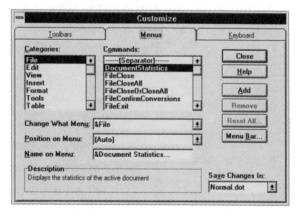

2. Add the Quote of the Day command to the View menu.

   a. Select wabQuoteOfTheDay in the Macros list box.

   b. Select &View in the Change What Menu drop-down
   list box.

   c. Select At Bottom in the Position on Menu drop-down
   list box.

   d. Type **&Quote Of The Day** in the Name on Menu
   text box.

   e. Click the Add button.

3. Add a separator to the <u>T</u>ools menu.

   a. Select —Separator— in the Mac<u>r</u>os list box.

   b. Select &Tools in the Change What Men<u>u</u> drop-down list box.

   c. Select At Bottom in the <u>P</u>osition on Menu drop-down list box.

   d. Click the <u>A</u>dd button.

4. Add the Bookshel<u>f</u> command to the <u>T</u>ools menu.

   a. Choose wabBookshelfDlg in the Mac<u>r</u>os list box.

   b. Select &Tools in the Change What Men<u>u</u> drop-down list box.

   c. Select At Bottom in the <u>P</u>osition on Menu drop-down list box.

   d. Type **Bookshel&f** in the <u>N</u>ame on Menu text box.

   e. Click the <u>A</u>dd button.

5. Add a separator to the <u>I</u>nsert menu.

   a. Choose —Separator— in the Mac<u>r</u>os list box.

   b. Select &Insert in the Change What Men<u>u</u> drop-down list box.

   c. Select At Bottom in the <u>P</u>osition on Menu drop-down list box.

   d. Click the <u>A</u>dd button.

6. Add the <u>V</u>oice Annotation command to the <u>I</u>nsert menu.

   a. Choose wabInsertVoiceAnno in the Mac<u>r</u>os list box.

   b. Select &Insert in the Change What Men<u>u</u> drop-down list box.

   c. Select At Bottom in the <u>P</u>osition on Menu drop-down list box.

   d. Type **&Voice Annotation** in the <u>N</u>ame on Menu text box.

   e. Click the <u>A</u>dd button.

7. Add the Media Pla<u>y</u>er Clip command to the <u>I</u>nsert menu.

   a. Choose wabInsertVideo in the Mac<u>r</u>os list box.

   b. Select &Insert in the Change What Men<u>u</u> drop-down list box.

    c. Select At Bottom in the <u>P</u>osition on Menu drop-down list box.

    d. Type **Media Pla&yer Clip** in the <u>N</u>ame on Menu text box.

    e. Click the <u>A</u>dd button.

8. Click the Close button to close the Customize dialog box.

You're done! If you'd like, you can also add buttons for these macros to an existing or custom toolbar.

I installed Bookshelf 1993 and configured it to integrate with Word 6.0. Now, I get a WordBasic error 5 (illegal function call) when I try to activate Bookshelf or the Bookshelf Tip of the Day menu items in Word. What's wrong?

This message indicates that there is a conflict involving the BOOKSHLF.DLL file. Either this file is not stored in the right location or the program is trying to use a duplicate copy instead. Use the File Manager to search for copies of the BOOKSHLF.DLL file. If only one exists, make sure it is stored in the WINDOWS\SYSTEM directory; if not, move it there. If there is a duplicate, for example, in the main \WINDOWS directory, simply delete it.

I just installed Bookshelf 1993 and configured it to integrate with Word 6.0. When I try to choose either <u>V</u>oice Annotation or Media Pla<u>y</u>er Clip from the <u>I</u>nsert menu, I get this WordBasic Error: "1264: server application, source file or item cannot be found." Why does this happen and what can I do to fix it?

These menu commands run macros that access the same list of objects that you can embed by choosing the <u>O</u>bject command from the <u>I</u>nsert menu. If the application media clip or sound does not appear on the list of objects you can embed, Word cannot recognize them as OLE objects. You therefore cannot

access the associated command. Check the [Embedding] section
of the WIN.INI to confirm that it includes the following lines:

```
MPlayer=Media Clip,Media Clip,mplayer.exe,picture
SoundRec=Sound,Sound,SoundRec.exe,picture
```

Check to see if the above lines are in the WIN.INI file by
doing this:

1. Choose Run from the File menu in the program Manager,
   type **SYSEDIT**, and select OK.

2. Switch to the window showing WIN.INI.

3. Find the [Embedding] section.

4. If you do not see the two lines, add them after the other
   lines in this section.

5. Choose Exit from the File menu and select Yes if you are
   prompted to save WIN.INI.

Working with Your Word Document

As you create and edit your documents, you may have questions about some of Word 6.0's basic features. This chapter addresses such issues, including how to use the keyboard, mouse, and commands to help you work most effectively and efficiently in Word. If you are new to Word, start by taking a look at the Frustration Busters, which identify the elements of the Word application window.

FRUSTRATION BUSTERS!

Word for Windows appears in a window, just like any other Windows application. The window includes various elements that make it easy to develop, modify, print, and save documents. These elements, which are shown in Figure 3-1, include:

- The *application title bar* describes the contents of the window. The title bar of the Word application window displays "Microsoft Word." Each document window's title bar identifies the file it contains. If the document window is maximized to fill the entire Word window, the document name appears in the application's title bar.

- The *document window* appears within the application window and displays the contents of the current file. You can have one or more documents open at a time. Figure 3-1 shows a maximized document window. In this case, the document title appears in the main title bar along with the application name. If a document window is not maximized, it has its own title bar, which includes the file name, its Control menu box, and its sizing buttons.

- The *menu bar* lists the names of the Word pull-down menus (for example, Edit). You open a menu either by clicking the appropriate word on the menu bar or by pressing ALT and the underlined letter (such as ALT+E). You choose a command from a pull-down menu by typing the underlined letter, moving to the command and pressing ENTER, or by clicking it once with your mouse.

- *Toolbars* contain *buttons*, each of which performs a particular Word command, macro, or feature. Toolbar buttons are like shortcuts that simplify common tasks. For example, in many cases, you can click a toolbar button once to execute a specific command, rather than clicking two or three times to perform the same action by using the menu. Figure 3-1 includes both the Standard and Formatting toolbars. You can select how many and which pre-existing toolbars to display. You can also customize and create your own toolbars.

- The *ruler* shows the current margins, tab stops, indents, and distances.

■ The vertical and horizontal *scroll bars* indicate your relative position within a document. You can move to another part of the document by either clicking the scroll bar or dragging the *scroll box*. You can choose to have none, one, or two scroll bars display on the screen.

■ The *view buttons* quickly switch between three different views. Views provide a variety of ways you can look at your document.

■ The *status bar* at the bottom of the Word application window displays information about the current document and other features. The status bar in Figure 3-1 indicates that you are on page 1 in the first section of a two-page document. It also tells you the location of the insertion point and the current time.

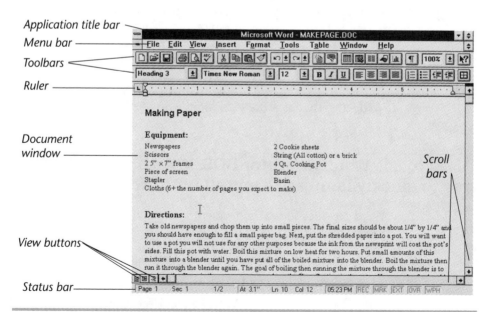

Application title bar
Menu bar
Toolbars
Ruler

Document window

Scroll bars

View buttons

Status bar

FIGURE 3-1   Word for Windows application window

How do I quit a session of Word?

There are three ways to exit Word:

- Double-click Word's Control menu box, which appears in the upper-left corner of the application window, as shown here:

Word's Control menu box

- Choose E̲xit from the F̲ile menu.
- Press ALT+F4.

When you exit Word, it closes any open documents. Word prompts you to save any document that you have modified since it was last saved. Click Y̲es to save the modified document, N̲o to retain the previous version, or Cancel to return to Word.

Every time I open Word, I see the Tip of the Day. Can I turn this option off?

To suppress the daily tip, choose the Ti̲p of the Day command from the H̲elp menu, clear the S̲how Tips at Startup check box, and click OK. Alternatively, you can clear the S̲how Tips at Startup check box the next time that you start Word.

To redisplay tips at start-up, simply reselect the check box.

I used to use WordPerfect for DOS. What's the easiest way to quickly familiarize myself with Word 6.0?

Word provides several convenient and helpful options for former WordPerfect users. To enable them:

1. Choose O̲ptions from the T̲ools menu.
2. Click the General tab.
3. Select the Help for W̲ordPerfect Users check box.

The WordPerfect Help feature displays the equivalent Microsoft Word command when you press a WordPerfect keystroke. It can even demonstrate the comparable Word feature.

4. Select the Na_vi_gation Keys for WordPerfect Users check box.

If you select this check box, you can use many of the same WordPerfect 5.*x* keystrokes while you work in Word 6.0.

5. Select the Bl_ue_ Background, White Text check box.

This option displays Word documents as white text on blue to help WordPerfect users feel right at home in the Word environment.

6. Click OK.

You can also display WordPerfect Help by double-clicking the WPH indicator in the status bar. Word displays a window like the one shown in Figure 3-2. You then select a WordPerfect command to learn how to perform the same action in Word. In addition, you can click _O_ptions to specify how WordPerfect Help displays and how it performs demos.

Tech Tip: You can also run demos from the _H_elp menu to learn how to use some of Word's features. To do so, choose the _E_xamples and Demos command from the _H_elp menu and then select the Word feature about which you want to know more. Word's extensive online Help includes step-by-step instructions for performing many of the most common tasks.

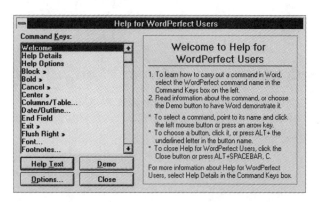

FIGURE 3-2 WordPerfect Help for using Word features

What do "WPH" and "WPN" mean on my status bar?

The "WPH" that appears in the status bar is the WordPerfect Help indicator. When the letters appear in black, it is turned on; when the letters are gray, it is turned off.

To turn WordPerfect Help on or off, you can perform either of these steps:

- Choose WordPerfect Help from the Help menu or double-click the WPH or WPN indicator, select the Options button, select or clear the Help for WordPerfect Users check box, and then click OK.

Tech Terror: If you switch to Word as an OLE 2 application to create a Word embedded object and press ESC, Word 6.0 may not function properly while WordPerfect Help is turned on. This problem is fixed with the Word 6.0a update.

- Choose Options from the Tools menu, click the General tab, select or clear the Help for WordPerfect Users check box, and then choose OK.

"WPN" indicates that the WordPerfect Navigation Keys setting is turned on. To turn off this feature, perform either of these steps:

- Choose WordPerfect Help from the Help menu or double-click the WPN or WP status bar indicator, select the Options button, clear the Navigation Keys for WordPerfect Users check box, and then click OK.

- Choose Options from the Tools menu, click the General tab, clear the Navigation Keys for WordPerfect Users check box, and then choose OK.

If both WordPerfect features are enabled, Word displays "WP" in the status bar instead of "WPH" and "WPN."

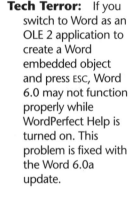

Besides the online Help in Word, where else can I find assistance?

Word comes with two forms of Help: the online Help, which you access by pressing F1 or by choosing Contents from the Help menu, and the Microsoft Word User's Guide

In addition, there are many other sources of help available to you, including the following:

- You can call the Microsoft Product Support line at (206) 462-9673 (a toll call) to get personal customer support on any problem you've encountered with any version of Word. You can also get information faxed to you.

- If you subscribe to either America Online or CompuServe, you can post your questions on the Microsoft forum. *Forums* are computer exchanges whereby many people can communicate, usually about a single subject. If you enter a question, more than likely someone will reply with information about the particular problem you are experiencing and how to solve it.

- On CompuServe, you can also receive help directly from Microsoft representatives. Simply type **GO MSWORD** to move to the MSWORD forum and input your query. Many well-known Word authors also maintain links to this forum.

- You can also access the Microsoft Knowledge Base that provides information on many Microsoft products on CompuServe by typing **GO MSKB** at any ! prompt.

- Computer book publishers offer several titles that address various aspects of using Microsoft Word. Peruse the shelves of your local computer outlet or bookstore to find one that fits your needs. For example, to learn about the full spectrum of Word features, you might consider *Word for Windows: The Complete Reference* by Mary Campbell.

- For advanced users, Microsoft Press publishes the *Microsoft Word Developer's Kit* and *Microsoft Word Resource Kit*, which comes with a disk that contains various files you can use.

- You can call Microsoft's Fast Tips Service at (800) 936-4100. This service provides recorded answers to the most common questions and problems.

- If you performed a complete installation of Word 6.0, you can choose the Technical Support command on the Help menu to view information about electronic services, telephone support, product training, consultation, and other support options available from Microsoft.

How can I tell what the various buttons on a toolbar do?

You can use the ToolTips feature to easily display a description of a given toolbar button. To enable this option:

1. Choose <u>T</u>oolbars from the <u>V</u>iew menu.
2. Select the <u>S</u>how ToolTips check box in the Toolbars dialog box.
3. Click OK.

To view a ToolTip, slowly move the mouse pointer over the right border of a toolbar button. A label appears, which indicates the button's function, as shown here:

How can I find out more about particular buttons and menu commands?

You can use the Help button at the right end of the Standard toolbar to display further information about toolbar buttons and menu commands. When you click this button, which looks like a question mark with an arrow, your mouse pointer changes to the same shape, as shown here:

You then click the button or menu command about which you want to know more. When you release the button, Word displays the Help topic that describes the particular button or command. When you're done reading the contents of the Help window, close it or press ALT+TAB to return to Word.

Tech Tip: You can also click the Help button and then highlight text in your document to find out more about its formatting. Word displays a box that indicates the formatting of the particular character and paragraph that you selected. To remove this information from the screen, simply click the Help button again.

Why do I see a list of menu commands when I click the right-hand mouse button?

Word provides shortcut menus that list the commands most commonly used with whatever object is currently selected. If a shortcut menu exists for a given item, it appears when you click the element with the right-hand mouse button. For example, this illustration shows the shortcut menu that displays when you click text with the right-hand button:

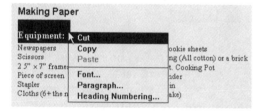

You choose a command from a shortcut menu by highlighting it and then pressing ENTER, or by clicking it with either mouse button. All of the commands listed on Word's shortcut menus are also available on Word's standard menus.

What does the text on the right-hand side of the pull-down menus mean?

These shortcut keys indicate keyboard shortcuts you can use to perform the associated menu commands. For example, to the right of the New command on the File menu, Word displays CTRL+N. This indicates that you can choose the New command without opening the File menu by simply pressing the CTRL key and the N key at the same time. When two keynames appear joined by a plus (+) sign, they are a *key combination;* you execute the action by pressing both keys at once.

Word includes a number of pre-assigned shortcut keys, as shown in Table 3-1. The shortcuts may consist of a single key, a function key, and/or a key combination.

You can view, modify, or remove these key assignments by using the Keyboard tab in the Customize dialog box, which is accessed from the Tools menu. You can also assign new shortcut keys to existing commands, macros, fonts, AutoText, styles, and common symbols. Chapter 7, "Customization, Styles, and Templates," includes several questions about altering Word's key combinations.

How can I display information about my system in Word?

Choose the About Microsoft Word command on the Help menu to display your basic registration information in a dialog box. If you then click the System Info button, another dialog box appears that lists more detailed data about your current setup, as shown in Figure 3-3. You can select items such as System, Printing, Fonts, and Proofing from the Choose a Category drop-down list box to display specific information about them. Clicking the Save button stores the information in a file called MSINFO.TXT in the WINDOWS directory. You can also print the contents by choosing the Print button. When you are finished, click the Close button and then OK.

Tech Tip: You can display the information shown in Figure 3-3 even when Word is not open. You simply run the System Info program by choosing the Run command from the Program Manager's File menu. Type **\WINDOWS\MSAPPS\MSINFO\MSINFO.EXE** in the Command Line text box and then click OK. (This assumes that the MSINFO program is installed and that your shared Word applications are stored in the WINDOWS\MSAPPS directory.)

Shortcut Key	Menu Command
ALT+F4	Close on the application window's Control menu
ALT+F5	Restore on the application window's Control menu
ALT+F10	Maximize on the application window's Control menu
CTRL+ESC	Switch To on the application window's Control menu
CTRL+A	Select All on the Edit menu
CTRL+C	Copy on the Edit menu
CTRL+F	Find on the Edit menu
CTRL+G	Go To on the Edit menu
CTRL+H	Replace on the Edit menu
CTRL+N	New on the File menu
CTRL+O	Open on the File menu
CTRL+P	Print on the File menu
CTRL+S	Save on the File menu
CTRL+V	Paste on the Edit menu
CTRL+W	Close on the document window's Control menu
CTRL+X	Cut on the Edit menu
CTRL+Y	Repeat on the Edit menu
CTRL+Z	Undo on the Edit menu
CTRL+F5	Restore on the document window's Control menu
CTRL+F6	Next Window on the document window's Control menu
CTRL+F7	Move on the document window's Control menu
CTRL+F8	Size on the document window's Control menu
CTRL+F10	Maximize on the document window's Control menu
DEL	Clear on the Edit menu
F7	Spelling on the Tools menu
SHIFT+F7	Thesaurus on the Tools menu
ALT+NUM5	Select Table on the Table menu

TABLE 3-1   Shortcut Keys for Menus

What are the differences between the views listed on the View menu?

Word offers six possible ways to look at a given document: normal view, page layout view, outline view, master document

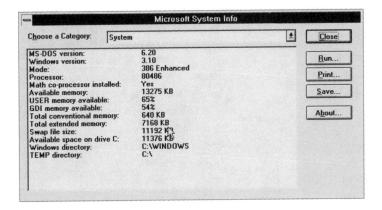

FIGURE 3-3   Microsoft System Info showing information about your computer

view, full screen view, and print preview. You access all but print preview from the View menu. The best view to use at any given moment depends on the task you wish to perform.

Figure 3-4 depicts documents displayed in four common types of views:

Outline view

Master document view

Page layout view

Normal view

FIGURE 3-4   Some of the views available for a document

Normal view is designed for use when creating and editing a document. The document appears partially, but not fully, formatted; the display speed is fast; and headers and footers do not appear.

Page layout offers a WYSIWYG (what-you-see-is-what-you-get) view of your document and is most useful when you are putting the final touches on your work. Graphics and column formatting display exactly as they will print; headers and footers appear in gray but in their correct positions. Because this view depicts greater detail, the display speed is slower.

You use *outline view* to create, format, and organize a document in outline format. You use different heading levels to arrange and indent related text. Outline view lets you collapse or expand your outline as well as reorder parts of a document by simply moving their respective headings. When you print from outline view, the output includes only the outline levels currently visible on the screen.

Master document view helps you organize, maintain, and format a large document that is divided into several related subdocuments. You can expand, collapse, insert, delete, and rearrange multiple documents as needed by using this view.

Print preview, which is accessed from the File menu, displays one or more full pages of a document at once, as you can see in Figure 3-5. It lets you see how the page(s) will appear when printed and gives you an opportunity to examine the overall formatting of a document, including the location of page breaks.

Although it appears on the View menu, *full screen* isn't a view per se. It doesn't really change how the document itself appears; instead, it removes many of the standard window elements from the screen to display as much of your document as possible at once. Full screen uses the entire screen to display just the document—it removes the title bars, menu bar, toolbars, ruler, scroll bars, status bar, and so on, from the screen. You can still use the keyboard to execute commands (from memory) while in full screen view. To exit full screen mode, click the Full Screen toolbar button that appears in the lower-right corner of the screen.

You can toggle among all but print preview by choosing commands on the View menu. To display your document using print preview, either choose the Print Preview command from the File menu or click the Print Preview button on the Standard toolbar. You can also switch to normal, page layout, or outline

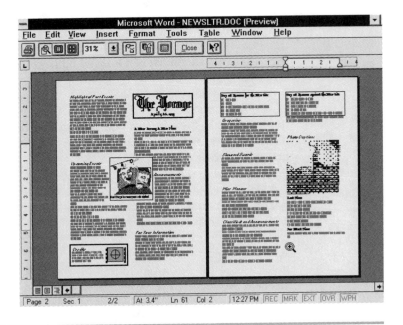

FIGURE 3-5   Two pages of a document shown in the print preview option

view by clicking the appropriate buttons to the left of the horizontal scroll bar, as shown here:

Normal View
Page Layout View
Outline View

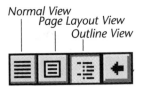

My menu bar disappeared. How do I get it back?

Most likely, you have switched to full screen view. There are three ways to return to your previous view and restore all your screen elements, including the menu bar:

■ Press ESC.

■ Press ALT+V to display the <u>V</u>iew menu and then choose F<u>u</u>ll Screen.

- If the Full Screen toolbar appears on your screen, click its only button, shown here:

When I press ENTER, my window doesn't scroll downwards until I start typing. What's wrong?

You probably have the Help for WordPerfect Users and Navigation Keys for WordPerfect Users options enabled. As in this case, Word may function slightly differently when these features are turned on. You should only select these WordPerfect features when you definitely want to use the same key combinations as in WordPerfect for DOS. Otherwise, turn off the WordPerfect assistance to solve this and any similar problems.

Tech Tip: The Word 6.0a update fixes this problem. If you frequently use WordPerfect Help, you should call Microsoft to obtain a copy of this maintenance (no charge) upgrade.

To disable this feature:

1. Choose Options from the Tools menu.

2. Click the General tab.

3. Clear the Help for WordPerfect Users and the Navigation Keys for WordPerfect Users check boxes.

4. Choose OK to return to the document.

When I first switched to full screen mode, a toolbar button appeared that I could use to return to my previous view. Somehow this toolbar has disappeared. Is there any way to redisplay it?

While you are in full screen mode, press ALT+V and then choose Toolbars from the View menu. Select the Full Screen check box in the Toolbars list box (this check box is only available when you are in full screen mode), and click OK. The Full Screen toolbar should reappear on the screen.

I accidentally had my CAPS LOCK key on. Now my text looks like "tHIS". How can I change the text without retyping my entire document?

To change the case of the text in a document without reentering it:

1. Select the text you want to change; if you want to modify the entire document, choose Select All from the Edit menu.

2. Choose the Change Case command from the Format menu.

3. Select the tOGGLE cASE option button in the Change Case dialog box and then click OK.

Word reverses the capitalization in the selected text. In other words, lowercase becomes uppercase and vice versa.

Table 3-2 illustrates the effect of the different capitalization options on this sample sentence: MicroSOFT WORD can fix mOST CAPitalization ERRORS.

You can also change the capitalization of selected text with SHIFT+F3. Pressing SHIFT+F3 cycles through title case, uppercase, and lowercase.

Capitalization Option	Effect on Sample Sentence
Sentence case	Microsoft WORD can fix most capitalization ERRORS.
lowercase	microsoft word can fix most capitalization errors.
UPPERCASE	MICROSOFT WORD CAN FIX MOST CAPITALIZATION ERRORS.
Title Case	Microsoft WORD Can Fix Most Capitalization ERRORS.
tOGGLE cASE	mICROsoft word CAN FIX Most capITALIZATION errors.

TABLE 3-2   Use the Change Case dialog box options to modify capitalization in your document

In addition, you may want to add the All Caps button to one of your toolbars. This button appears in the Format category on the Toolbars tab of the Customize dialog box. You click this button to reformat the selected text as uppercase.

Tech Tip: Word's AutoCorrect feature can fix some capitalization mistakes for you. For example, if you type **MIcrosoft**, AutoCorrect automatically changes it to Microsoft, if the word has been added to the list.

 ### I just discovered that Word is replacing existing text with the new text I type instead of just inserting it! What's wrong?

Check the status bar at the bottom of the Window. If the OVR indicator appears in black, you inadvertently switched to overtype mode. To switch back to the default insert mode, perform one of the following actions:

- Double-click OVR.
- Press INS (as long as it isn't set up to paste text).
- Choose Options from the Tools menu, click the Edit tab, clear the Typing Replaces Selection check box, and click OK. (You can change back to overtype mode by reselecting this option.)

 **Tech Tip:** The Use the INS key for Paste check box on the Edit tab of the Options dialog box determines whether pressing INS switches between overtype and insert mode (the check box is cleared), or pastes the contents of the Clipboard at the insertion point's location (the check box is selected).

 ### Can I copy and move text with my mouse?

Word provides a *drag and drop* feature that lets you easily move and copy text with the mouse. To move text, you first select it and then, when the cursor is an arrow, click it with the mouse.

Continue holding down the mouse button and move the pointer (which now looks like an arrow) to the new location where you want the text to appear. As you do so, the status bar displays the message, "Move to where?" and a vertical bar indicates where the text will be placed if you release the mouse button at that moment. When the vertical bar is at the desired location, release the mouse button to move the selection. You can even move the selection to a location in the document that is not presently on the screen by dragging the mouse beyond the top or bottom of the document window.

Tech Tip: You can use the drag and drop method to copy text between two OLE 2 compatible applications.

Copying text is just like moving text except that you hold down the CTRL key as you drag the mouse to the new location. In this case, the status bar displays "Copy to where?" and a small plus (+) sign appears next to the mouse pointer.

You can also use drag and drop to move or copy text from one document to another. To do so, open both documents, choose the Arrange All command on the Window menu to display them side by side, and then drag the selection from one window to the other. Similarly, if you split a document window into panes, you can drag and drop selections from the top pane to the bottom one, and vice versa. Dragging and dropping between panes lets you quickly move or copy text within a document when the locations are far apart.

Is there a way to quickly select all of the text from the insertion point to the end of the document?

You can press CTRL+SHIFT+END to select all of the text from the insertion point's present location to the end of the document. By the same token, you can highlight all of the text from the insertion point to the beginning of the document by pressing CTRL+SHIFT+HOME.

Is there a quick way to move back to the last edit I made?

When you press SHIFT+F5, Word moves the insertion point back to your last edit. You can press this key combination up to four times to return to the previous four edits. If you have just opened the document, pressing SHIFT+F5 moves you to the position at which the insertion point was located when you last closed and saved the file.

Is there a quick way to repeat a find?

You can press SHIFT+F4 to search for the same text for which you last looked with the <u>F</u>ind command on the <u>E</u>dit menu.

How can I quickly select words, sentences, and paragraphs?

There are several ways to quickly select words, sentences, and paragraphs in Word:

- You can select a word by double-clicking it, or pressing CTRL+RIGHT ARROW.

- You can select a sentence by holding down CTRL and clicking anywhere in the sentence.

- You can select the entire paragraph by triple-clicking (clicking three times in rapid succession) any word in the paragraph.

- You can select from the beginning of a paragraph to the current location of the insertion point by holding down CTRL+SHIFT while you press the UP ARROW key. Similarly, you select from the insertion point's position to the end of the paragraph by pressing CTRL+SHIFT+DOWN ARROW.

Is it possible to display spaces, tabs, paragraph marks, and other nonprinting characters?

Word 6.0 offers three ways to display and hide non-printing characters:

- Choose <u>O</u>ptions from the <u>T</u>ools menu and click the View tab. Under Nonprinting Characters, select or clear the <u>A</u>ll option, and then click OK to display or hide these characters, respectively. You can also individually select the nonprinting characters you would like to display on your screen by selecting or deselecting the box beside each option.

- To toggle the display of nonprinting characters on and off using the keyboard, press CTRL+* (you must use the asterisk on the 8 key, not the one on the numeric keypad).

- Click the Show/Hide button on the Standard toolbar, shown here:

When I delete the last word in a sentence, is there any way to automatically remove the space before it?

Word can intelligently add and delete spaces as you insert and remove words in your document. As you mention, when you delete the last word in the sentence, you also want to remove the space before it so that the punctuation immediately follows the remaining text. On the other hand, when you paste text to the end of a sentence, you want to insert a space before it. You can use Word's Smart Cut and Paste feature to automatically perform these tasks.

For example, suppose you want to move the phrase "that make editing text easier" from the end of the first sentence to the end of the second in the following paragraph:

```
Word for Windows has several new features that make editing
text easier. AutoCorrect and AutoText are some of the new features.
```

If you move the phrase without enabling the Smart Cut and Paste feature, the first sentence includes an unwanted space before the period while the second lacks a necessary space between the words "features" and "that," as shown here:

```
Word for Windows has several new features . AutoCorrect and
AutoText are some of the new featuresthat make editing text easier.
```

If you enable Smart Cut and Paste and then move the selection, the result is perfectly acceptable:

```
Word for Windows has several new features. AutoCorrect and
AutoText are some of the new features that make editing text easier.
```

Follow these steps to turn the Smart Cut and Paste feature on or off (it is on by default):

1. Choose the <u>O</u>ptions command from the <u>T</u>ools menu.
2. Click the Edit tab.
3. Select or clear the Use <u>S</u>mart Cut and Paste check box to enable or disable this feature, respectively.
4. Click OK.

Word keeps choosing the entire word when I drag my mouse across it. Is there a way to select the text one character at a time?

Word is currently set to select an entire word whenever you highlight part of it.
To turn off this feature:

1. Choose <u>O</u>ptions from the <u>T</u>ools menu.
2. Click the Edit tab.
3. Clear the Automatic <u>W</u>ord Selection check box.
4. Click OK.

Tech Tip: This Automatic <u>W</u>ord Selection setting also tells Word to begin checking the spelling at the beginning of the word in which the insertion point is located when you choose <u>S</u>pelling from the <u>T</u>ools menu.

How do I find paragraph marks when I search a document?

Word has a number of special characters, including the paragraph mark, for which you can search within a document. To search for a paragraph mark in Word:

1. Choose the Find command from the Edit menu.

2. To enter the paragraph code in the Find What text box, you can either type ^**p** or click the Special button and select Paragraph Mark. (The ^, or caret, symbol appears above the 6 on the keyboard.)

Table 3-3 lists the other special characters for which Word can search. In most cases, you must enter the codes exactly as they appear; in other words, this feature is case-sensitive. Also, certain special characters can be used only in the Find What text or in the Replace With text, as specified.

I need to quickly hide the contents of confidential documents I'm working on when people stop by my desk. How do I do this in Word for Windows 6.0?

The quickest way to achieve this result in Word 6.0 is to simply minimize the window which contains the confidential information. You can minimize either the document window itself or the entire Word application window.

You minimize a window by clicking its Minimize button at the right end of the title bar, as shown here:

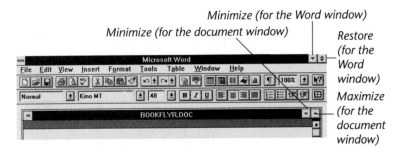

Minimize (for the Word window)

Minimize (for the document window)

Restore (for the Word window)

Maximize (for the document window)

Code to Enter	Finds/Replaces	Restrictions
^?	Any character	Find What only
^#	Any digit (0-9)	Find What only
^$	Any letter (A-Z, a-z)	Find What only
^&	Contents of the Find What text box	Replace With only
^a	Annotation mark	Find What only
^b	Section break	Find What only
^c	Clipboard contents	Replace With only
^d	Field	Find What only
^e	Endnote mark	Find What only
^f	Footnote mark	Find What only
^g	Graphic	Find What only
^l	End-of-line character created by pressing SHIFT+ENTER	
^m	Manual page break created by pressing CTRL+ENTER	
^n	Column break	
^p	Paragraph mark	
^s	Nonbreaking space	
^t	Tab character	
^w	White spaces (nonbreaking spaces; paragraph, section, and hard page breaks; tab, end-of-line, and end-of-cell characters)	
^-	Optional hyphens	
^~	Nonbreaking hyphens	
^	Caret	
^+	Em dash	
^=	En dash	
^0nnn	ANSI character, where nnn is the ANSI character code	
^nnn	ASCII character, where nnn is the ASCII character code	

TABLE 3-3   Entries to Find Special Characters

As you can see, there are two Minimize buttons: one for the Word application window and one for the document window. The button you click determines which window you minimize. Once minimized, the document or application appears as an icon, as shown here:

Tech Tip: To resize the application window from the keyboard, press ALT+SPACEBAR to display its Control menu and then choose the appropriate command. Similarly, you press ALT+HYPHEN to open the document window's Control menu, which contains commands to reduce and enlarge it . Alternatively, you can assign a shortcut key to any of the window sizing commands to execute it more quickly. See Chapter 7, "Customization, Styles, and Templates," for information about assigning shortcut keys.

Once a window is minimized, you can double-click its icon to redisplay it. Alternatively, you can click the icon once to display the Control menu. You then choose <u>R</u>estore to display the window in its pre-icon state or Ma<u>x</u>imize to expand it to its maximum size.

Tech Tip: You can press ALT+F10 to maximize the Word application window.

If you minimized a document, you can also open Word's <u>W</u>indow menu to select, and thus redisplay, an "iconized" window. Similarly, you press ALT+TAB to switch to and redisplay the Microsoft Word application window.

You click a window's Maximize button to enlarge it to the largest size possible. Once you do so, the button becomes a Restore button, which you can click to return the window to its previous size.

 ## Are there any easy ways to create common types of documents, such as memos and fax cover sheets?

Word includes ten *wizards* to help you create some of the most commonly used documents. When you use a wizard, it prompts you for personalized information, which it then uses to create the document.

Wizard Name	Documents Created
Agenda	Agendas for meetings
Award	Awards
Calendar	Monthly calendars
Fax	Cover sheets for faxes
Letter	Sample letters for common business applications
Memo	Interoffice memos
Newslttr	Newsletters
Pleading	Pleadings for legal documents
Resume	Resumes
Table	Tables

TABLE 3-4   Word Supplies Ten Wizards to Help You Create Commonly Used Documents

Table 3-4 lists the different wizards and the type of documents that each produces:

To create a document using a wizard:

1. Choose New from the File menu.

2. Select the wizard you want to use to create the document from the Template list box.

3. Click OK.

4. Once the wizard starts, reply to the prompts that it displays; the questions you see depend on which wizard you are using.

5. When you have input all the necessary information, click Finish.

Word creates the document based on the wizard you chose and the responses you entered to the questions. Figure 3-6 shows a document produced with the Newslttr wizard.

I like the Word 6.0 wizards, but do I always have to perform each step?

When you use a wizard, you can perform as many or as few steps as necessary to input your individual information and

FIGURE 3-6   A Document created with the Newslttr wizard

selections. At whatever point you wish, you can click the <u>F</u>inish button. The wizard takes it from there, using the defaults for any options you've skipped.

 When I use the Newslttr Wizard to create a Modern style newsletter, the text runs into the right border from page 2 onward. How can I make the newsletter look better?

In this case, the text in the right-hand column is too close to the right border. Follow these steps to correct this problem:

1. Choose the <u>H</u>eader and Footer command from the <u>V</u>iew menu.

2. Click the border added by the Newslttr Wizard to select it.

3. Choose Drawing Object from the Format menu and click the Size and Position tab.

4. Increase the width to at least 7.10 inches in the Width text box and then choose OK.

5. Click the Close button on the Header and Footer toolbar to return to the document.

The numbers in the middle of the status line disappeared. How do I redisplay them?

The numbers that appear after "At" and "Ln" in the status line indicate the insertion point's current position. If they are no longer visible, follow these steps to redisplay them:

1. Choose Options from the Tools menu.

2. Click the View tab.

3. Select the Draft Font check box.

4. Click the Print tab.

5. Select the Background Repagination check box.

6. Click OK.

How can I assign symbols to a shortcut key in Word?

You can assign a symbol to a shortcut key by performing these steps:

1. Choose Symbol from the Insert menu.

2. Double-check the contents of the Character list box on the Special Characters tab to make sure no preset shortcut key exists for the symbol or character you desire. (Most popular symbols have pre-assigned keys in Word.)

3. If no shortcut exists, select the symbol or special character to which you want to assign a shortcut key from the appropriate tab in the Symbol dialog box.

4. Click the Shortcut <u>K</u>ey button.

5. In the Customize dialog box that appears, press the key or key combination that you want to assign to enter it in the Press <u>N</u>ew Shortcut Key text box.

Tech Tip: After you enter a key or key combination in the Press <u>N</u>ew Shortcut Key text box, make sure this shortcut isn't already associated with another Word feature. If so, Word displays a message to this effect under the Currently Assigned To label. If you then click the <u>A</u>ssign button, Word reassigns the key or key combination to the new symbol or character instead.

6. Click the <u>A</u>ssign button.

7. Repeat these steps for each symbol or character to which you want to assign a key or key combination.

8. Click Close two times to return to the document.

 ## How do I insert a path and file name in a document?

You can add a FileName field to the document to insert the path and file name directly into it. To add this field:

Tech Tip: If you use a field to display the file name, the information is updated whenever you rename the document or move it to another location.

1. Move the insertion point to the location in the document at which you want the path and file name to appear.

2. Choose Fi<u>e</u>ld from the <u>I</u>nsert menu.

3. Select FileName in the Field <u>N</u>ames list box.

4. Type **\p** after FILENAME in the <u>F</u>ield Codes text box if you want to display the directory and path information. Alternatively, you can click the <u>O</u>ptions button, click the Field S<u>p</u>ecific Switches tab in the Field Options dialog box, make sure \p is selected in the S<u>w</u>itches list box, click the <u>A</u>dd to Field button, and then choose OK.

5. Click OK to add the field to the document.

Is there any way to move text from several locations to another position or document all at once?

You can use Word's Spike feature to move multiple text blocks or graphics, in order, either to another position in the same document or to another Word document altogether. Because the Spike feature can store text and graphics cut from one or more locations, you can use it to avoid a lot of cutting and pasting.

You can insert the Spike's contents in any location in any open Word document. Follow these steps to use the Spike to store and insert multiple items:

1. To add text or graphics to the Spike, select the item and then press CTRL+F3. Repeat this step to add additional items to the Spike without removing what is already stored there.

2. To insert the contents of the Spike at the current location, type **SPIKE**, and then press F3 or click the Insert AutoText button on the Standard toolbar, shown here. Alternatively, you can press CTRL+SHIFT+F3 to insert the contents of the Spike at the designated position and empty the Spike at the same time.

For example, suppose you want to select outlined blocks of text in the CAMPING.DOC document shown in Figure 3-7 and then insert them in a new document.

You would first select each portion of text and press CTRL+F3. When you have finished selecting the text blocks, create the new document. Type **SPIKE**, then press F3, or click the Insert AutoText button on the Standard toolbar, to insert the text, as shown here:

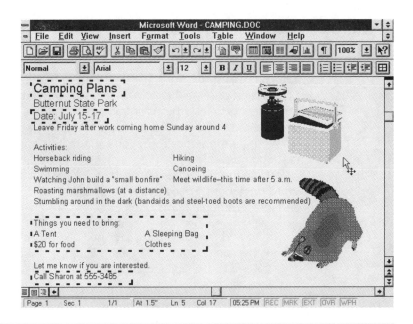

FIGURE 3-7 Selections of text to add to the Spike

Layout and Design

No matter how good the contents of your document, if it isn't appealing to the eye, your readers may simply skip over it. The better the layout, the more effective your documents are as communication media. By using such features as headers and footers, columns, different styles, and indentation, you can greatly enhance not only the readability of your output but the likelihood that it will, in fact, be read!

FRUSTRATION BUSTERS!

Generally, it makes sense to create and edit your entire document before you tackle any layout issues. By finalizing the contents first, you can address the layout design without worry that modifications will subsequently alter its appearance.

On the other hand, sometimes you may want to create a document with a standard, prescribed format, such as a business letter or a quarterly report. In this case, you can setup a standard layout in advance, either by using or modifying one of the many templates that come with Word 6.0 or by creating your own! For more information about templates, see Chapter 7, "Customization, Styles, and Templates."

After I insert a section break, my heading numbering still uses the same format. Why doesn't it change?

Heading numbering is applied to text that uses the heading styles. Style definitions do not change across section breaks, so Word increments the heading style's numbering regardless of the section. If you want to use different numbering formats in sections, you need to insert Next Page section breaks, and then use regular paragraph or line numbering. To restart the numbering, you need in insert a single unnumbered paragraph before the one that begins the next numbering sequence.

Tech Note: You can create unnumbered paragraphs between numbered ones by pressing SHIFT+ENTER, instead of ENTER. This creates a new line, but not an actual new paragraph, so the numbering is not applied.

I import a lot of text files. Is there a quick way to format them?

Word 6.0 offers a new AutoFormat feature. AutoFormat applies existing styles to your documents according to the options you specify. For example, Figure 4-1 shows a "before" and "after" of a document that was formatted with AutoFormat. After using AutoFormat, you can review and selectively accept or reject the changes it made to your document.

To use AutoFormat:

1. Open the unformatted document.

2. Either choose <u>A</u>utoFormat from the <u>F</u>ormat menu, press CTRL+K, or click the AutoFormat button, as shown here:

Click OK if Word prompts you to confirm before it formats your document. Word will only prompt you before formatting if you selected <u>A</u>utoFormat from the <u>F</u>ormat menu.

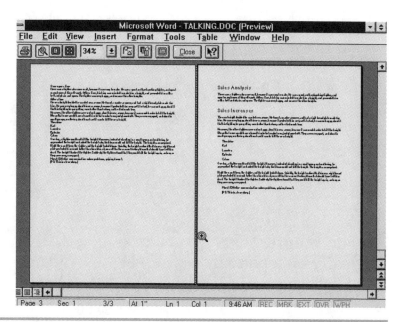

FIGURE 4-1   You can use AutoFormat to quickly format your plain documents

3. After Word formats your document, it displays the Auto-Format dialog box. You have several options at this point:

- If you click Select Review Changes, Word opens another dialog box that lets you select which formatting changes you want to reject.

- Click Accept to accept all of the formatting changes that AutoFormat made.

- Click Reject All to discard all of the changes that AutoFormat made.

- Click Style Gallery to select styles from another template, which will change the way your document looks.

You can specify exactly what AutoFormat will and won't format by modifying the settings on the AutoFormat tab in the Options dialog box. For example, you might tell Word 6.0 to leave certain existing formatting intact. To change the AutoFormat settings:

1. Choose Options from the Tools menu.

2. Click the AutoFormat tab.

3. Select or clear check boxes to indicate what you do and don't want AutoFormat to modify.

4. Click OK to return to the document.

Tech Tip: You can customize AutoFormat by choosing AutoFormat from the Format menu and then clicking the Options button.

How do I center text vertically on a page in Word 6.0?

It's easy to center text vertically on a page in Word 6.0. When you do so, Word automatically makes the top and bottom margins the same size, as shown in Figure 4-2. You may find this feature particularly appropriate for brief letters, memos, and cover pages.

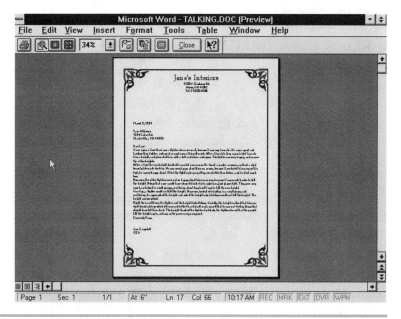

FIGURE 4-2   The top and bottom margins are the same size when you center text vertically

To center text vertically on the page:

1. Choose Page Setup from the File menu.

2. Click the Layout tab.

3. Select Center in the Vertical Alignment drop-down list box.

4. Click OK to vertically center each page of the current section.

Tech Note: If you follow the steps specified, the vertical alignment change will be applied to the current section of the document. You can also choose This Point Forward or Whole Document in the Apply to drop-down list box. If you selected text before invoking this command, your choices include Selected Text or Whole Document.

Is there an easy way to find out the formatting applied to text?

Word 6.0 offers a shortcut for determining any given text's character and paragraph formatting. To display this information:

1. Click the Help button on the Standard toolbar, so that the mouse pointer becomes a question mark.

2. Click the text whose formatting you want to check. Word displays any paragraph and font styles applied to the text as well as any direct formatting, as shown in Figure 4-3.

3. To hide the formatting information, either click the Help button again or press ESC.

Can I apply character formatting with the keyboard?

Word provides shortcut keys for applying many different types of character formatting, as listed in Table 4-1. If you want to change the formatting of existing text, select it

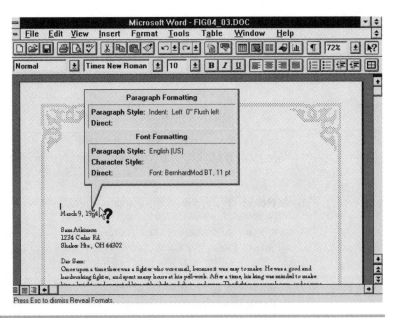

FIGURE 4-3   Word 6.0 provides an easy way to check text formatting

Formatting Effect	Key Combination
Subscripts text	CTRL+=
Decreases the font size by one point	CTRL+[
Increases the font size by one point	CTRL+]
Makes the text bold	CTRL+B
Italicizes the text	CTRL+I
Changes the font to the next smaller available font size	CTRL+<
Superscripts text	CTRL+PLUS (above the equal sign)
Changes the font to the next larger available font size	CTRL+>
Decreases the space between characters	CTRL+{
Increases the space between characters	CTRL+}
Changes the text to All Caps	CTRL+SHIFT+A
Adds a double underline	CTRL+SHIFT+D
Lets you select a new font	CTRL+SHIFT+F
Applies the Hidden format	CTRL+SHIFT+H
Changes the text to Small Caps	CTRL+SHIFT+K
Lets you select a new font size	CTRL+SHIFT+P
Converts the text to the Symbol font	CTRL+SHIFT+Q
Underlines the words but not spaces	CTRL+SHIFT+W
Reverts to the default text format	CTRL+SHIFT+Z
Adds a single underline	CTRL+U
Toggles the case from uppercase to lowercase to initial capitalization	SHIFT+F3

TABLE 4-1   Shortcut keys you can use to apply character formatting

before using the appropriate shortcut keys. If you press the key combination without first selecting any text, Word applies the formatting to whatever you next type at the insertion point's location.

How do I remove a character style from text in my document?

First, select the text whose character style you want to remove. Then, press CTRL+SPACEBAR to return the text to the default character style.

Why can't I see my character formats in outline view?

In outline view, you can specify whether Word displays character formatting. If you choose not to show formatting, Word simply shows all of the text in the Normal style character format. This generally lets you see more text at once; otherwise, the outline headings are usually formatted in a larger font size, which takes up more room on the screen. You can still tell which paragraphs are headings, though, because they remain properly indented in outline format.

To display character formatting in outline view, you simply click the Show Formatting button on the Outlining toolbar, as shown here:

Figure 4-4 shows two versions of the same outline side-by-side. The top one simply displays the text in Normal style; the bottom document reflects all of the character formatting.

Tech Terror: Don't worry! Even though you can't see the character formatting in outline view, you haven't lost it. If you click the Show Formatting button or switch to another view, the character formatting reappears.

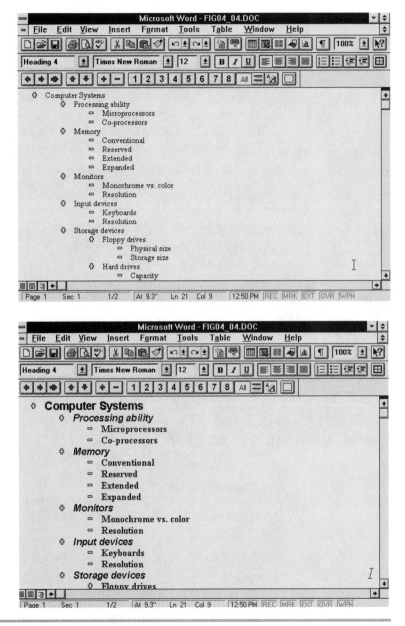

FIGURE 4-4   You can choose whether or not to display character formatting in outline view

In Word 2.0, I used shortcut keys to change the font and font size of text. Why don't they work in Word 6.0?

Word 6.0 supports two different keyboard shortcuts for changing the font and font size:

- To choose a new font, press CTRL+SHIFT+F and type the font name in the Font box on the Formatting toolbar; this is equivalent to pressing CTRL+F in Word 2.0

- To change the font size, press CTRL+SHIFT+P and enter or select the new size in the Font Size box on the Formatting toolbar; this shortcut is the same as pressing CTRL+P in Word 2.0.

If the Formatting toolbar is not displayed on the screen when you press either of these key combinations, they automatically open the Font dialog box so you can make your changes. Alternatively, you can press CTRL+D to display the Font dialog box.

Tech Tip: You can also simply highlight the contents of the Font or Font Size box with the mouse and then type your entry. In addition, you can click the associated arrow to display a drop-down list from which you can choose a different typeface or point size.

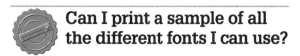

Can I print a sample of all the different fonts I can use?

Word 6.0 comes with a macro called FontSampleGenerator. This macro creates a document that displays a sample of each of the available fonts.

To access and run this macro:

1. Choose <u>M</u>acro from the <u>T</u>ools menu.

2. Click Organizer.

3. Click the Close <u>F</u>ile button under the left-hand list box.

4. Click the Open <u>F</u>ile button (which was formerly the Close <u>F</u>ile button) to display the Open dialog box.

5. Use the <u>D</u>irectories and Dri<u>v</u>es list boxes to switch to the WINWORD\MACROS directory.

6. Select MACRO60.DOT in the File <u>N</u>ame list box and then click OK.

7. The list box on the left-hand side of the Organizer dialog box now displays all of the macros available in the MACRO60.DOT template.

8. Select FontSampleGenerator in the left-hand list box.

9. Click Copy and then click Close.

10. Choose Macro from the Tools menu again.

11. Select FontSampleGenerator in the Macro Names list box.

12. Click Run. Word displays the number of fonts available and asks you which point size to use to display the samples.

13. Choose a point size and then click OK.

The macro generates a new document that contains a table with font names in the first column and samples in the second, as shown in Figure 4-5. You can print this document as you would any other and then use it as a reference when selecting a font for a document.

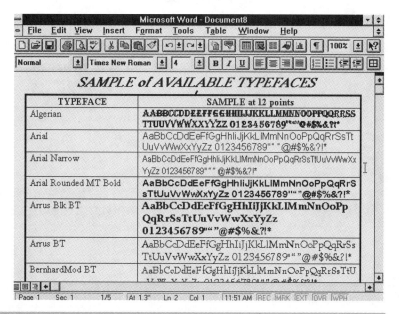

FIGURE 4-5   The FontSampleGenerator macro creates a sample of all of the available fonts

Can I put a border around a single letter or word?

You can place a border around a single letter or word by adding an Equation field with the \X switch. This switch causes the Equation field to draw a box around whatever appears in the parentheses following the switch. You can insert the field by using either the keyboard or the menu.

To add an Equation field with the keyboard:

1. Position your insertion point where you want the boxed text to appear.

2. Press CTRL+F9 to insert the field code, which looks like a pair of curly brackets.

3. Between the field codes, type **EQ \X** followed by the text you want to appear in a box in parentheses.

You can nest parentheses and use multiple \X switches to create different effects, as shown in Table 4-2.

To add an Equation field by using the menu:

1. Choose Fi_e_ld from the _I_nsert menu.

2. Select Equations and Formulas in the _C_ategories list box.

3. Select Eq in the Field _N_ames list box.

4. Enter **\X(*the text you want to appear in a box)*** in the _F_ield Codes text box.

5. Click OK.

Tech Terror: You must use the key combination to insert this special code; simply typing curly brackets doesn't work.

Code	Result
{EQ\X (C.S.I.)}	C.S.I.
{EQ\X (C.) \X(S.) \X (I.)}	C. S. I.
{EQ\X (\X (\X (C.S.I.)))}	C.S.I.

TABLE 4-2   You can nest parentheses and use multiple \X switches

Are there shortcuts that I can use to apply paragraph formats?

Word 6.0 includes a number of shortcut keys that you can use to add paragraph formatting to your document, as listed in Table 4-3. If you press a key combination without first selecting text, the formatting only affects the paragraph in which the insertion point is located. Alternatively, you can select

Formatting	Shortcut Key
Applies the Heading 1 style	ALT+CTRL+1
Applies the Heading 2 style	ALT+CTRL+2
Applies the Heading 3 style	ALT+CTRL+3
Removes a blank line before the paragraph, if one exists; otherwise, adds a blank line	CTRL+0
Applies single line spacing	CTRL+1
Applies double line spacing	CTRL+2
Applies 1.5 line spacing	CTRL+5
Centers the paragraph	CTRL+E
Fully justifies the paragraph	CTRL+J
Applies AutoFormat	CTRL+K
Left-aligns the paragraph	CTRL+L
Moves the left indent one tab stop to the left	CTRL+M
Removes any paragraph formatting that is not part of the paragraph's style	CTRL+Q
Right-aligns the paragraph	CTRL+R
Applies the List style	CTRL+SHIFT+L
Moves the left indent one tab stop to the right	CTRL+SHIFT+M
Applies the Normal style	CTRL+SHIFT+N
Activates the Style box on the Formatting toolbar, if displayed; otherwise, opens the Style dialog box	CTRL+SHIFT+S
Moves a hanging indent one tab stop to the right	CTRL+SHIFT+T
Indents all but the first line of a paragraph to the first tab stop, or moves an existing hanging indent one tab stop to the left	CTRL+T

TABLE 4-3   Shortcut keys for paragraph formatting

text that spans multiple paragraphs and then use a shortcut key to reformat them all at once.

Tech Tip: You only need to select a portion of text in a paragraph to change the formatting of the entire paragraph.

Is there a shortcut for copying paragraph formatting in Word 6.0 as there was in Word 2.0?

You can use the Format Painter feature to copy paragraph formatting from one block of text to another in Word 6.0. Paragraph formatting includes indents, line spacing, spacing before and after paragraphs, alignment, hyphenation, line numbering suppression, and other text flow options.

To copy only the paragraph formatting:

1. Click the Show/Hide button on the Standard toolbar.

2. Select the paragraph mark at the end of the paragraph whose formatting you want to copy.

3. Click the Format Painter button on the Standard toolbar, as shown here:

4. Click anywhere in the paragraph to which you want to apply this formatting.

Can I format my document when I'm in outline view?

You can format your document in certain ways while in outline view. For example, you can type and revise text as well as apply font styles such as boldface and italics. However, you cannot modify paragraph formatting in a document displayed in outline view. You must switch to normal or page layout view to adjust such formatting as indents, tab stops, alignment, and line spacing.

Indentation	Key Combination
Indents the left edge of a paragraph one or more tab stops to the right	CTRL+M
Moves the left indent of a paragraph one tab stop to the left	CTRL+SHIFT+M
Applies a hanging indent, in which the body of the paragraph is indented one tab stop further to the right than the first line	CTRL+T
Moves a hanging indent one tab stop to the left	CTRL+SHIFT+T

TABLE 4-4   You can use the keyboard to apply four types of indents

Is there a shortcut for applying indents?

There are four indent settings that you can apply from the keyboard in Word 6.0, as indicated in Table 4-4. In all cases, you either move the insertion point to the paragraph you want to indent or select multiple paragraphs before pressing the appropriate key combination. Pressing the keystrokes more than once increases or decreases the indent accordingly.

Tech Tip: When you increase or decrease a hanging indent, Word changes the indentation of the body of the paragraph, not the first line.

How do I change the indents in outline view?

To put it briefly, you can't. None of your paragraph formatting appears in outline view. In fact, the indents you do see indicate heading levels and will not display elsewhere.

If you want to modify the your document's indentation, switch to normal or page layout view by choosing the appropriate command from the <u>V</u>iew menu or clicking one of the buttons to the left of the horizontal scroll bar.

On the other hand, if you want to change the appearance of the outline itself, you must change the style to alter the indentation of heading styles, delete or apply the Hidden character format to the intervening body text, and then reformat the outline in normal or page layout view.

How can I change the position of a tab stop?

The easiest way to move a tab stop is by using the ruler. To do so:

1. If necessary, choose <u>R</u>uler from the <u>V</u>iew menu to display the ruler.

2. Select the paragraph or paragraphs in which you want to move the tab stop.

3. Drag the tab marker to the right or the left on the ruler.

Tech Tip: You can also change the position of a tab stop by placing your insertion point in the paragraph and then choosing <u>T</u>abs from the F<u>o</u>rmat menu. Enter a new position in the <u>T</u>ab Stop Position text box, click <u>S</u>et, and then choose OK to create the new tab stop.

How do I clear a tab stop?

To clear a tab stop:

1. Choose <u>T</u>abs from the F<u>o</u>rmat menu.

2. Select the tab stop you want to clear in the <u>T</u>ab Stop Position list box.

3. Click <u>C</u>lear and then choose OK.

Tech Tip: You can also drag the tab marker off of the ruler to clear a tab stop.

Is there any way to change the distance between the default tab stops?

You can easily adjust the spacing between the default tab stops in Word. By default, the distance between tab stops is 0.5 inches. To change this distance without individually resetting all of the tab stops:

1. Choose <u>T</u>abs from the F<u>o</u>rmat menu.

2. Enter the new distance between tab stops in the De<u>f</u>ault Tab Stops text box.

3. Click OK.

This modification only affects the current document. If you want to change the tab stops for all new documents, open the NORMAL.DOT template file located in your WINWORD\TEMPLATE directory and perform this same procedure.

Are there any shortcuts for setting tab stops in Word 6.0?

You can use the ruler to quickly set tab stops. To do so:

1. Display the ruler by choosing <u>R</u>uler from the <u>V</u>iew menu, if necessary.

2. Click the Tab Alignment button at the left end of the ruler until it displays the symbol for the type of tab stop you want to insert, as shown here:

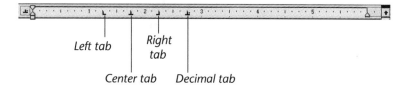

Left tab

Center tab

Right tab

Decimal tab

3. Click the position on the ruler at which you want to insert the tab.

Tech Tip: To apply a new tab setting to an entire document, first choose the Select A<u>l</u>l command from the <u>E</u>dit menu and then add the tab.

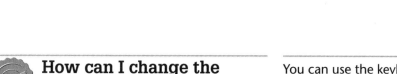

How can I change the alignment of paragraphs with the keyboard?

You can use the keyboard to quickly apply any of the four types of alignment that Word supports. Simply place the insertion point in the paragraph you want to align, or select all of the paragraphs you want to modify, and then press the appropriate key combination, as shown in Table 4-5.

Alignment	Key Combination
Left	CTRL+L
Right	CTRL+R
Centered	CTRL+E
Justified	CTRL+J

TABLE 4-5   You can use the keyboard to change the alignment of one or more paragraphs

You can also set paragraph alignment by clicking the Align Left, Center, Align Right, and Justify buttons on the Formatting toolbar, as shown here:

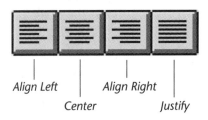

Align Left   Align Right

Center   Justify

 I want to change some of my character and paragraph formatting back to the default. What's the simplest way to do this?

You can easily reset your paragraph or character formatting either to the default defined by the style applied to it or to the default established by the Normal style in your document.
To revert to the applied style's paragraph formatting:

1. Move the insertion point to the paragraph whose formatting you want to reset. If desired, you can select multiple paragraphs to modify them all at once.

2. Press CTRL+Q.

To reset character formatting to that specified by the paragraph's style:

1. Select the text you want to reformat.

2. Press CTRL+SPACEBAR or CTRL+SHIFT+Z.

To change the formatting of a paragraph to the Normal style's default:

1. Move the insertion point to the appropriate paragraph or select multiple paragraphs.
2. Press CTRL+SHIFT+N or ALT+SHIFT+5 (from the numeric keypad).

My paragraphs seem to lose their alignment when I'm in outline view. What can I do?

You haven't actually lost your paragraph formatting—Word just doesn't show it in outline view. Simply switch to page layout or normal view to redisplay your line spacing, alignment, and indents.

How can I create a bulleted or numbered list?

Word provides a shortcut for creating bulleted or numbered lists, such as the ones shown in Figure 4-6. A list can consist of single words, single lines, or full paragraphs; whenever a paragraph mark occurs, Word creates a new list item. Word not only adds the bullets or numbers, but applies a hanging indent to each paragraph to which you apply these styles. This feature ensures consistent and appealing formatting; it also prevents accidental misnumbering.

To create a bulleted or a numbered list:

1. Type the list.
2. Select all of the paragraphs in the list.
3. Click either the Numbering button or the Bullets button on the Formatting toolbar, as shown here:

Numbering ——— *Bullets*

If you want to specify a particular bullet or numbering system when you format your list, perform these steps instead:

1. Select the list or paragraphs to format.

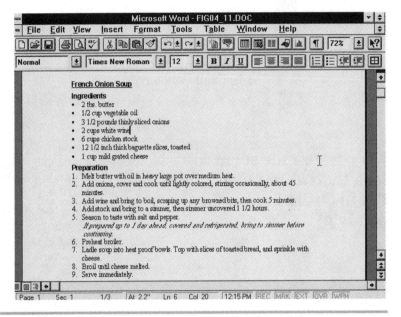

FIGURE 4-6   It's easy to create bulleted and numbered lists in Word 6.0

2. Choose Bullets and Numbering from the Format menu. Alternatively, click the right mouse button and select the command from the shortcut menu.

3. Click the Bulleted, Numbered, or Multilevel tab.

4. Select the desired format.

5. Click OK to display the new format.

If none of the existing formats meet your needs, select the one that's the most similar to what you want and click the Modify button to change the numbering system or the type of bullets used.

Tech Tip: To remove numbers or bullets from a list, reselect the paragraphs and then click either the Numbering or the Bullets button again. You can also choose Bullets and Numbering from the Format menu (or the shortcut menu) and then click Remove.

When I remove numbering from a paragraph in the middle of a list, Word renumbers the following paragraphs as 1 instead of continuing where it left off. How can I prevent this?

Word 6.0 offers a feature that is specifically designed to avoid this problem. To prevent the numbering from starting over again:

1. Select the paragraph(s) from which you want to remove numbering.

2. Right-click the selected text to display the shortcut menu.

3. Choose Skip Numbering.

Word automatically updates the numbering so that the unnumbered paragraphs do not upset the scheme of the surrounding paragraphs. The unnumbered paragraphs continue to have the same indentation of the text in the numbered steps.

Tech Tip: If, on the other hand, you have a series of numbered steps and want to restart the numbering at 1 in the middle of the list as you might do if you wanted to list four substeps under step 2, you must add a "blank" paragraph between the two lists by pressing ENTER twice after step 2. You may want to set the line spacing of this paragraph to a minimum so that the extra line break isn't apparent. When you attempt to restart the list with step 3 you need to choose Bullets and Numbering from the Format menu, select the Numbered tab, and choose Modify. Change the Start At number before selecting OK.

Can I tell Word to always use a diamond instead of a circle as the bullet symbol?

You can change the default bullet symbol by following these steps:

1. Choose Style from the Format menu.

2. Select All Styles in the List drop-down list box.

3. Select List Bullet in the Styles list box.

4. Click the Modify button.

5. Select the Add to Template check box to make this the default bullet symbol in any new documents you create using the current template.

6. Click the Format button.

7. Select Numbering.

8. If one of the predefined bullet styles suits your needs, simply select it.

9. If none of the existing bullets appeal to you, select the one that's most similar to what you want, and then click Modify to edit it. You can then click the Font button to display all the available fonts. You may want to choose another font, such as Wingdings, that offers additional symbols appropriate for use as bullets.

10. Click OK as many times as necessary to return to the Style dialog box.

11. Click Close.

Whenever you save your document, Word automatically updates the NORMAL.DOT template with any changes you made. However, it prompts you if you modified any other template. Click Yes to save the new bullet style.

How do I insert a column break in my document?

Column breaks mark the end of the current column and move the insertion point to the beginning of the next one. Any additional text you enter will appear in this new column.
To enter a column break:

1. Switch to page layout view, if necessary, by choosing Page Layout from the View menu or clicking the Page Layout View button to the left of the horizontal scroll bar.

2. Move the insertion point to where you want to insert the column break.

Tech Tip: You can also press CTRL+SHIFT+ENTER to insert a column break.

3. Choose Break from the Insert menu.

4. Select the Column Break option button then click OK.

Although you can insert a column break in other views, page layout lets you see how the columns will actually appear in the printed output. In the normal view, on the other hand, the break simply looks like a dashed line in the midst of the text so it's harder to get a sense of what the page will really look like.

All of a sudden, my columns disappeared on the screen, but they show up when I print the document. What's going on?

Your columns didn't actually disappear. When you are in page layout view, columns of text appear side-by-side, just as they do on a printed page, as shown in Figure 4-7. However, in normal view, the columns of text display one after another. If you suddenly see only one column on the screen, you probably just switched views somehow. For example, Figure 4-8 shows how the document in Figure 4-7 looks in normal view. To redisplay the columns side-by-side, simply select Page Layout from the View menu or click the Page Layout View button.

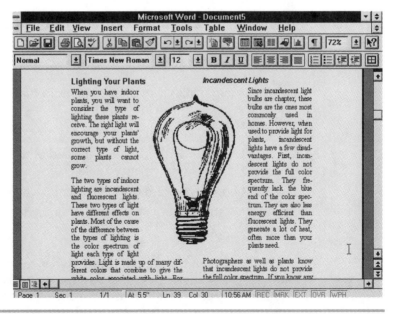

FIGURE 4-7   Page layout view displays the columns exactly the way they will look when printed

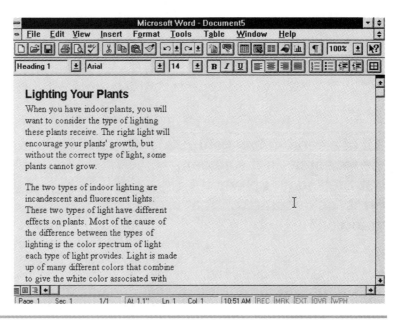

FIGURE 4-8 Columns appear one right after another in normal view

I want the newspaper style columns in my document to end at the same point on the page. Is there an easy way to produce this more professional look?

Word can automatically balance columns so that their bottom edges line up, as shown in Figure 4-9.
To balance the columns:

1. Move the insertion point to the end of the text you want to display in the balanced columns.

2. Choose Break from the Insert menu.

3. Click the Continuous option button under Section Breaks.

4. Choose OK.

Word evens out the bottom edges of your columns. You can now insert a next page, even, or odd section break after the continuous section break, if desired. Because Word only balances columns before a continuous section break, you must first add the continuous break before the noncontinuous one.

Newspaper columns   *Balanced newspaper columns*

FIGURE 4-9   You can create professional looking newspaper columns

How can I add a vertical line between my columns?

Adding a line between columns can make a multicolumn document much easier to read. Differentiating columns with lines is particularly useful when you have narrow margins or only a small distance between them. As Figure 4-10 illustrates, lines are an attractive way to help readers focus on one column at a time.

To add lines between columns:

1. Move the insertion point to the section of the document that contains the columns to which you want to add the vertical lines.

2. Choose Columns from the Format menu.

3. Select the Line Between check box and then click OK.

Tech Tip: The vertical line between two columns only appears on the screen in page layout view and print preview; even though you cannot see it in other views, it will show up in the printed output.

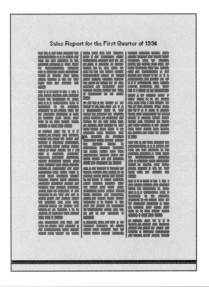

Sales Report for the First Quarter of 1994

FIGURE 4-10   You can add a line between columns to make them easier to read

What are sections?

You can use *sections* to apply different page formats to parts of your Word document. The options you can set for individual sections include:

- Paper size
- Orientation
- Margins
- Headers and footers
- Page numbering
- Line numbering
- Vertical alignment
- Newspaper columns

To take advantage of this capability, you must first break your document into sections and then apply formatting to each.

For example, suppose you are producing a long article or manuscript in Word. In this case, you might want to format the title page, main text, endnote pages, and index in different ways. To do so, you would make each of these components a separate section. You could then set the formatting for each section independent of the others. You might specify wider margins and vertical alignment on the title page, add a different header and footer to the endnote pages, and use multiple columns in the index section.

Just as pages end with page breaks, sections end with section breaks. Word offers four types of section breaks: next page, even page, odd page, and continuous. All three noncontinuous options start the text following the break at the top of either the next, the next even, or the next odd page, respectively. On the other hand, you use continuous section breaks to create several sections on the same page, as shown in Figure 4-11.

To insert a section break:

1. Choose Break from the Insert menu.

2. Select the option button for the type of section break you want to insert.

3. Click OK.

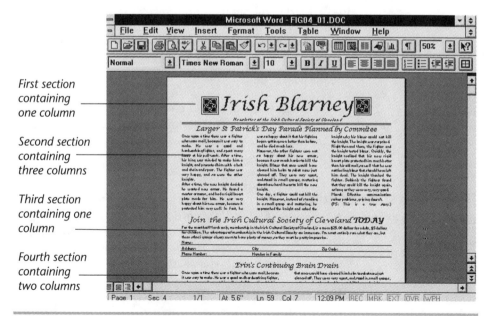

First section containing one column

Second section containing three columns

Third section containing one column

Fourth section containing two columns

FIGURE 4-11   Several sections on one page

How can I insert a manual page break in my document?

When you are working in a document, Word automatically starts a new page when the current page is full. These automatically inserted page breaks are called *soft page breaks.* As you edit your document, Word recalculates the amount of text on each page and adjusts the position of the soft page breaks, accordingly. When you insert a manual, or *hard*, page break, Word starts a new page at that particular point regardless of the amount of text on the page. Word doesn't rearrange these page breaks when you add, delete, or modify text in the document; if you want to change where they occur, you must manually delete or move them.

There are two ways to insert a manual page break. To do so from a menu:

1. Move your insertion point to the point at which you want the page break to appear.

2. Choose <u>B</u>reak from the <u>I</u>nsert menu.

3. Select the <u>P</u>age Break option button and then click OK.

To insert a hard page break using the keyboard:

1. Move your insertion point to the location at which you want to place the page break.

2. Press CTRL+ENTER.

To change the position of a hard page break, you can delete it and insert a new one in the desired location, or you can select the break and drag it to the new location.

How can I select a hard page break so that I can cut, copy, paste, or delete it?

To select a hard page break, first make sure your document is displayed in normal view. Normal view is the only view in which hard page breaks appear as a solid line across the screen, as shown here:

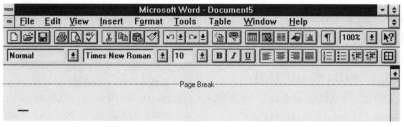

To select the break, simply double-click it and then use the appropriate commands or toolbar buttons to perform the desired action.

Can I control how often Word repaginates my document?

Word 6.0 readjusts the location of the soft page breaks when your computer is temporarily idle; that is, you aren't currently typing or otherwise modifying your document. In addition, Word automatically repaginates whenever you switch to page layout view or print preview.

You can turn off background repagination in all but page layout view and print preview. Then, pagination only occurs when you switch to one of these views or print the document.

To turn off background repagination:

1. Choose Options from the Tools menu.

2. Click the General tab.

3. Clear the Background Repagination check box and then click OK.

Tech Tip: In Word 2.0, you could choose the Repaginate Now command from the Options menu to force repagination. Because this menu command no longer exists, switch to either page layout view or print preview to perform this task on demand. A second option would be to choose Tools, Macro. In the Macros Available In field, select Word Commands, if it isn't already selected. Under Macro Name, select the ToolsRepaginate macro. Click Run.

Sometimes I end up with a heading at the bottom of a page with the text that belongs with it on the next one. Is there any way to keep them together?

You can mark a paragraph so that Word will keep it on the same page as the following one, even if it must override the standard pagination to do so. When you group each heading with at least one of the associated paragraphs on the same page, it's easier for your readers to follow your ideas. For example, if a heading falls at the end of a page, it makes it harder to understand the organization and flow of information; it also looks less professional.

To keep a heading and a paragraph or two paragraphs together on a page:

1. Move the insertion point to the heading or paragraph with which you want to keep with the following paragraph.

2. Choose Paragraph from the Format menu.

3. Click the Text Flow tab.

4. Select the Keep with Next check box and then click OK.

Tech Tip: You can add this format to a heading style so that the paragraph following a heading of this type always appears on the same page with it. The Heading 1, Heading 2, Heading 3, and Heading 4 styles available in the default NORMAL.DOT template are already set up in this way.

Can I prevent the first or last line of a paragraph from appearing all by itself at the bottom or top of a page?

Single lines such as these, called *widows* and *orphans*, can make it harder for your readers to follow your train of thought, as you can see in Figure 4-12. These "hanging" lines also give your documents a less professional appearance.

By default, Word 6.0 prevents widows and orphans in your document. You can double-check and reselect this setting, if necessary, by following these steps:

1. Choose Paragraph from the Format menu.

2. Click the Text Flow tab.

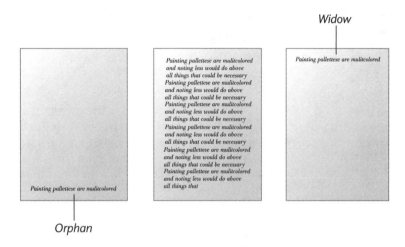

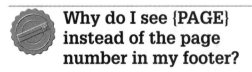

FIGURE 4-12   Widows and orphans make it harder for readers to understand
your document

3. Select <u>W</u>idow/Orphan Control.

4. Click OK to return to your document.

With this setting in effect, if an automatic page break would
leave a single line at the bottom of a page, Word moves it to the
top of the next page with the rest of a paragraph. If, on the
other hand, the last line of paragraph would end up all by itself
at the top of a page, Word moves the last line from the bottom
of the previous page to join it.

Why do I see {PAGE} instead of the page number in my footer?

When you tell Word to show field
codes instead of their results, {PAGE}
appears in place of the actual page
number. Although displaying field
codes is useful when you want to edit
the codes themselves, you probably want to turn this feature off
when you are proofing or formatting your document.

To show fields results instead of field codes:

1. Choose Options from the Tools menu.
2. Click the View tab.
3. Clear the Field Codes check box under Show Options.
4. Click OK.

Tech Tip: You can also move to an individual field and toggle between its code and the results by pressing SHIFT+F9.

Your footer should now display the correct page number. When you display field codes rather than the field results, Word inserts soft pages breaks based on the length of the codes themselves. If you then display or print the document with the field results, more than likely you'll find that the breaks occur in different locations.

Can I suppress the page number on the first page of my document?

By default, Word displays a page number on every page of a document when you use the Page Numbers command on the Insert menu. To change this setting so that no number appears on the first page:

1. Choose Page Numbers from the Insert menu.
2. Clear the Show Number on First Page check box and then click OK.

Tech Tip: This suppression feature will work even if you used the Page Numbers button on the Header and Footer toolbar to add your page numbers.

I am creating a booklet that consists of 8 1/2" by 11" pages folded in half. When I print the document, the first and last pages appear on the first sheet of paper, the second and second to last pages are on the second sheet, and so forth. How can I add page numbers to this document so they come out right in the finished booklet?

Your booklet is probably similar to the one shown in Figure 4-13. Numbering the pages in a booklet such as this can be very

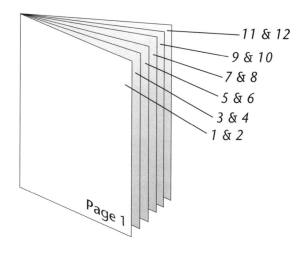

11 & 12

9 & 10

7 & 8

5 & 6

3 & 4

1 & 2

Page 1

FIGURE 4-13   It can be confusing to number pages in a booklet made by folding standard pages in half

confusing. However, in Word you can modify the Page field to insert the correct page numbers in a booklet of this type.

To start, insert a normal Page field on the right side of the first 8 1/2" by 11" page by using either of these methods:

- Place the insertion point where you want to locate the field. Choose Fi<u>e</u>ld from the <u>I</u>nsert menu, select Page in the Field <u>N</u>ames list box, and then click OK.

- Press CTRL+F9 and type **Page** between the field codes.

Next, you need to add this code to the left side of the first 8 1/2" by 11" page (which is actually the last page of the booklet) to display the correct page number:

{={Numpages}*2 – {Page} +1}

Note that Numpages and Page are both field codes, *not* text surrounded by curly brackets. To add the field, enter the field code for Page, select it, then press CTRL+F9 to place brackets around it. With the insertion point still in the Pages code, insert the Numpages field code. If you have other text entries such as the "*2" or "+1" in the example above, they are also typed within the field code. You have to reverse which side of the page these codes are on for the next page, then switch back again for the third, and so on.

For example, if you added these codes to a booklet made up of two 8 1/2" by 11" pages, you would see the page numbers indicated here:

	Left Side	Right Side
First sheet	4	1
Second sheet	2	3

I can see my header and footer in page layout view and in print preview, but they won't print. What's wrong?

Most likely, your header or footer extends into one of the page's nonprinting areas. In this case, the header or footer will not print.

The nonprinting areas of your document run along the top and bottom edges of the paper; your printer uses these borders to grab and feed the paper into itself. To determine the minimum margins you must set for your particular printer model, and thereby avoid this problem, check your printer manual.

Once you have this information, choose Page Setup from the File menu and then click the Margins tab. Modify the From Edge settings as necessary to ensure that the header and footer fall within the printing area of the page. Also, make sure that the values in the Header and Footer text boxes are smaller than the document's top and bottom margins, respectively.

How do I right-justify only some of the text in a header or footer?

You can selectively align all or part of a header or footer's text. To right-justify all of the text in a header or footer, display the header or footer and then either click the Align Right button on the Standard toolbar or choose Paragraph from the Format menu, select Right in the Alignment drop-down list box, and click OK.

Frequently, as in your case, you only want to right-align a portion of the header or footer text. For example, in Figure 4-14, Word left-aligns the paper's title, centers the page number, and right-aligns the date. You can use tab stops to create this effect.

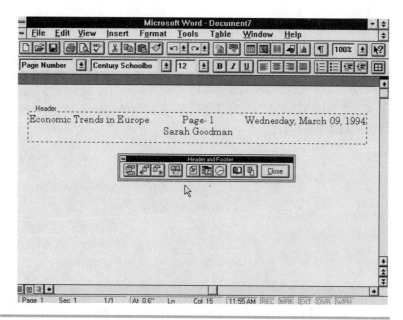

FIGURE 4-14   You can align the text in a single header in several different ways

To produce a header like the one shown in Figure 4-14:

1. Choose Header and Footer from the View menu to display a header.

2. Choose Tabs from the Format menu.

3. To set the center tab, click the Center option button under Alignment, enter the exact center of the page in the Tab Stop Position text box, and then click Set.

4. To set the right tab, click the Right option button under Alignment, enter the position of the right margin in the Tab Stop Position text box, and then click Set.

5. Click OK to insert the tab stops.

6. Enter the text to appear at the left margin and press TAB.

7. Enter the text to be centered and press TAB again.

8. Finally, enter the text to appear at the right margin.

9. Click Close on the Header and Footer toolbar.

I purposely created a wide margin at the top of my page but I want the header to appear directly above the document text. How do I do this?

To do this, you must change where the header text starts. By default, Word places headers one-half inch from the top edge of the page. In your case, you must change this setting to display the header right above the body of the document.

To specify exactly where you want the header to begin:

1. Choose Page Setup from the File menu.
2. Click the Margins tab.
3. In the Header text box, enter the amount of space Word should leave blank between the top edge of the paper and the beginning of the header.
4. Click OK to reposition the header.

Tech Tip: You can set a different distance for each section. For example, you might want the header on the first page to start lower than the one that appears in the rest of the document.

Similarly, you can enter a new value in the Footer text box on the Margins tab to reset the distance between your footer and the bottom edge of the page.

Is there some way to automatically insert the file name of a document in the header or footer?

You can use a field to automatically insert the file name in the header or footer (or the document itself) rather than typing this information. A field such as this may be helpful to use for identification purposes.

To insert the file name after displaying the header or footer:

1. Choose Field from the Insert menu.
2. Select Document Information in the Categories list box.
3. Select FileName in the Field Names list box.
4. Click OK to insert the field.

Is there any way to display a different header on the first page of my document?

Word lets you create a unique header that will appear on only the first page of a document. To specify this header, follow these steps:

1. Choose Page Set<u>u</u>p from the <u>F</u>ile menu.
2. Click the <u>L</u>ayout tab.
3. Select the Different <u>F</u>irst Page check box and then click OK.

To insert the header or footer for the first page of your document:

1. Move the insertion point to the first page.
2. Choose <u>H</u>eader and Footer from the <u>V</u>iew menu.
3. Create your header or footer as usual, and then click <u>C</u>lose on the Header and Footer toolbar, as shown here:

Tech Tip: Once you've added a unique header or footer on the first page, you can edit it from any page in the document. Simply display the Header and Footer toolbar and then click either the Show Next or Show Previous button until the First Page Header and First Page Footer buttons appear.

What happened to Word 2.0's Page Set<u>u</u>p command on the Forma<u>t</u> menu?

The Page Set<u>u</u>p command appears on the <u>F</u>ile menu in Word 6.0. As always, you can use this command to specify the page size, orientation, margins, and paper source. You can also use the <u>L</u>ayout tab in the Page Setup dialog box to set section formatting, such as the placement of headers and footers, vertical alignment, and line numbering. (In Word 2.0, you accessed these options with the <u>S</u>ection command on the Forma<u>t</u> menu.)

Is there any way to quickly place a border around every page in my document?

Yes, you can quickly place a border around each page of your document by adding a rectangle to a header or footer with Word's Draw feature. Follow these steps to add a border to every page:

1. Choose <u>H</u>eader and Footer from the <u>V</u>iew menu.

2. Click the Drawing button on the Standard toolbar to display the Drawing toolbar. Alternatively, you can choose <u>T</u>oolbars from the <u>V</u>iew menu, select the Drawing check box, and then click OK.

3. Click the Rectangle button on the Drawing toolbar and drag the mouse diagonally across the entire page.

4. Double-click the rectangular border to modify its appearance, if desired.

5. Click <u>C</u>lose on the Header and Footer toolbar.

Switch to print preview to see the border.

Tech Tip: You can also set the rectangle's size in step 4 by selecting it and then choosing Drawing <u>O</u>bject from the <u>F</u>ormat menu. Click the Si<u>z</u>e and Position tab to specify the height and width. You can also change the line style and color by selecting options on the <u>L</u>ine tab; similarly, use the <u>F</u>ill tab to indicate a fill color and style. When you are finished making your selections, click OK.

Can I insert text in my document's margins?

There are two ways in which you can position text outside the body of the document. You can either place the text in a frame and then position the frame in the margin, or you can create a text box and then move it into the margin, as shown in Figure 4-15.

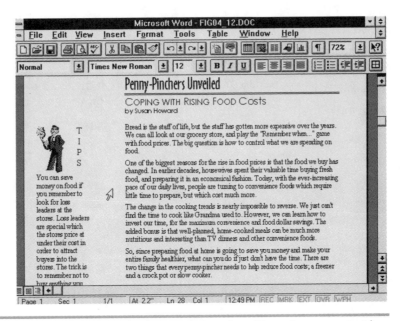

FIGURE 4-15   You can position text in the margin by using either a frame or a text box

To place text in the margins by using a frame:

1. Enter the text you want to appear in the margin.

2. Select this text.

3. Choose Frame from the Insert menu.

4. Reposition the frame by dragging it with the mouse, or by choosing Frame from the Format menu and then specifying the new location.

Tech Tip: You can use the same techniques for placing graphics in the margin of a document.

Follow these steps to create a text box and move it into the margin:

1. Display the Drawing toolbar by clicking the Drawing button on the Standard toolbar. Alternatively, you can choose Toolbars from the View menu, select the Drawing check box, and then click OK.

2. Click the Text Box button.

3. Drag the mouse pointer in the document to create the text box.

4. Click the text box, so that the insertion point appears in the box

5. Type the text.

6. Use the mouse to reposition the text box, or choose Drawing Object from the Format menu to indicate the new location.

Printing and Fonts

In the past, most printing problems revolved around getting output that looked significantly different than what you saw on the screen. Today, word processors such as Word 6.0 can display a document exactly the way it will appear when printed. With Word for Windows' WYSIWYG (what-you-see-is-what-you-get) feature, you actually see boldface, underline, and other formatting as you create and edit your document.

Today's print problems often relate to printer definitions, hardware, or the use of special features such as fonts and unusual paper sizes. The problems discussed in this chapter range from simple tasks, such as creating a rush document, to more sophisticated options, such as printing double-sided documents and collating multiple copies. For a list of "easy fixes" to common printing problems, first take a look at the Frustration Busters.

FRUSTRATION BUSTERS!

Before you start looking for a complicated solution to a printing problem you encounter in Word for Windows, check the following simple fixes. You'll be amazed how often these minor oversights cause major headaches!

- *Is the printer turned on?* It may sound simple, but it's often the culprit.

- *Does the printer have paper?* This solution also seems obvious--that is, until you've spent 15 minutes trying to solve a problem caused by an empty paper tray.

- *Is the printer on-line?* Most printers have a button that takes the printer on- and off-line. Usually, this button has a light or some other indicator that lets you know the printer is on-line. When the printer is off-line, it cannot receive information from the computer.

- *Can another application print?* You can use the Notepad accessory to quickly test whether the problem rests with Word itself or with the Windows printer settings. In other words, you need to find out whether the problem is exclusive to the Word application. Open or create a text file in the Notepad accessory, then choose Print from the File menu. If the file prints, Windows' settings for the printer are correct. You can also check the printer configuration by double-clicking the Printers icon in the Control Panel.

- *Are you printing on a network?* If so, the problem may relate to the network itself. In this case, you should contact your network administrator, who should be able to resolve the difficulty. If the printer is assigned exclusively to you, you might also try connecting it directly to your computer and printing without the network.

Is there a shortcut for printing?

A Print button appears on the Standard toolbar in Word 6.0. When you click this button, Word prints your document immediately using the default print options. You can also press CTRL+P to display the Print dialog box without using the menu.

Can I see what my finished document will look like before I print it?

Print preview lets you see your document as if it were printed. To switch to this view, you can either choose Print Preview from the File menu or click the Print Preview button on the Standard toolbar, shown here:

Figure 5-1 shows a preview of a document. From this view, you can see the entire page, which makes it easier to find layout

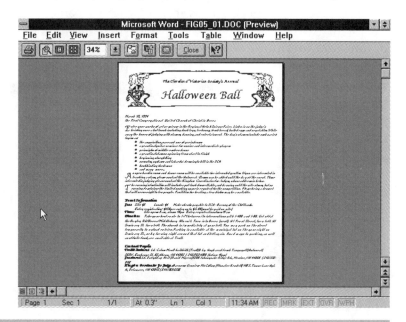

FIGURE 5-1   You can preview a document before you print it

errors that you might not notice in another view. To return to your previous view, press ESC or click <u>C</u>lose on the Print Preview toolbar.

Can I print more than one file at once in Word?

Instead of opening and printing files one a time, you can select several files to print all at once. To print multiple files:

1. Choose <u>F</u>ind File from the <u>F</u>ile menu.

You will either see the Find File or the Search dialog box. If you haven't searched for files before you will see the Search dialog box, and need to create a search then select OK before the Find Files dialog box is displayed. Make sure your search path points to the directories where the files you want to print are stored. You can click <u>S</u>earch in the Find File dialog box to change the search path so that it includes all of these files.

2. When all the files you want to print appear in the Find File dialog box, select them by clicking the first file name and then holding down SHIFT while you click the last one. If you want to print files that are not listed consecutively, press CTRL as you click each file name. The files you want to print should be highlighted in the <u>L</u>isted Files list box, as shown in Figure 5-2.

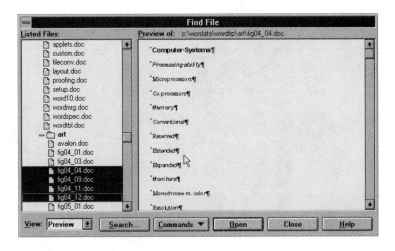

FIGURE 5-2   You can select multiple files to print at one time

3. Click <u>C</u>ommands and choose <u>P</u>rint.

4. Click OK to print all of the selected documents.

 How do I install my new printer so that Word can print to it?

There are two stages involved in setting up a printer: attaching it to your computer, and installing the printer driver.

Attaching the printer consists of physically running a cable from the printer to the correct port on your computer. Your printer's documentation should explain how to do this.

The *printer driver* is a file that contains all of the information needed to let your applications communicate with the particular printer. Once you install the printer driver in Windows, all of your Windows applications are able to print to the printer.

To install the Windows printer driver:

1. Make sure you have your Windows Setup disks handy.

2. Open the Windows Control Panel by double-clicking its program item in the Program Manager's Main program group.

3. Double-click the Printers icon or choose <u>P</u>rinters from the <u>S</u>ettings menu.

4. Click <u>A</u>dd.

5. Select your printer in the <u>L</u>ist of Printers list box.

If your particular printer does not appear in this list box, check your printer's documentation. You need to find out whether there is another printer that yours can emulate, then select that printer in the list box, or see if an updated Windows printer driver file comes with the printer. If you have the printer files on a disk, choose Install Unlisted on Updated Printer option from the top of the printer list.

6. Click <u>I</u>nstall.

7. If Windows prompts you for one of the Windows Setup disks, insert it in the appropriate drive and click OK to install the printer driver. (If no prompt displays, Windows created the printer driver using files already stored on your computer's hard disk.)

8. Select the new printer's name in the Installed Printers list box.

9. Click the Set as Default Printer button, if you want Word (and all other Windows applications) to automatically print to this printer.

10. Click Close then choose Exit from the Settings menu.

The new printer is now installed and ready to print.

Tech Tip: If you have installed more than one printer, you can change which printer is the default for all the Windows applications right from within Word. To do so, choose Print from the File menu, click Printer, select a printer in the Printers list box, click Set as Default Printer, choose the Close button, and click OK.

How do I set up Word to print envelopes or mailing labels?

Printing a single envelope or mailing label is as easy as printing a regular document in Word 6.0. You simply let Word define the size of the paper to match the envelope or mailing label's dimensions.

Tech Note: See Chapter 13, "Envelopes and Labels," for more detailed information about generating and printing envelopes and labels.

Follow these steps to quickly print an envelope or label:

1. Choose Envelopes and Labels from the Tools menu.

2. Click either the Envelopes tab or the Labels tab.

3. Enter the address(es) you'd like to appear in the output.

4. Click the Options button to verify or change the envelope or label size.

5. Click Print.

I turned off background repagination. Will Word still repaginate my document before printing it?

Even if you turn off background repagination, Word automatically repaginates your document when:

- You print the document.
- You switch to print preview or page layout view.
- You compile an index or a table of contents.

To turn background repagination on or off:

1. Choose <u>O</u>ptions from the <u>T</u>ools menu.
2. Click the General tab.
3. Select or clear the <u>B</u>ackground Repagination check box, accordingly, then click OK.

How can I cancel a print job that I've already sent to the printer?

The method you use to cancel a print job depends on how far along it is in the printing process. When you print your document, a series of steps occur:

1. As Word prepares the document for printing, it displays its progress in the status bar.

   If background printing is turned off, you can cancel printing by pressing ESC. If background printing is activated, you cannot cancel printing at this point.

2. Word prints the document to a temporary file, displaying a small printer icon in the status bar to indicate the page that it's currently printing.

   If background printing is turned off, you can cancel printing at this point by pressing ESC. If background printing is turned on, you can cancel printing by double-clicking the printer icon in the status bar, or by choosing <u>P</u>rint from the <u>F</u>ile menu then clicking <u>S</u>top Print.

3. The Windows Print Manager sends the temporary file to the printer. To cancel printing at this stage you must do so from the Print Manager.

4. If the Print Manager has already finished sending the print job to the printer, you can only cancel the job by resetting the printer itself.

Tech Tip: If you are printing on a network, you must use network commands to cancel a print job from the queue.

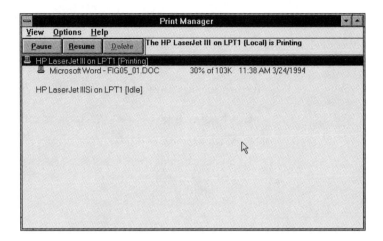

FIGURE 5-3 The Print Manager window displays the current print job

To cancel printing from the Print Manager:

1. Open the Print Manager, as shown in Figure 5-3, by double-clicking its program item in the Program Manager's Main program group.

2. Select the print job you want to cancel, then click Delete.

3. Click OK at the prompt.

4. Close the Print Manager by choosing Exit from the View menu or double-clicking the Control menu box.

Tech Note: The Print Manager is actually a lot more complicated than this answer implies. Many different temporary printing files may exist. The Print Manager prints each one, in turn, in the background, so that you can continue working in Windows without waiting for your document to print. Windows even lets you control the order in which the Print Manager sends the temporary files to the printer by setting each job's priority level. In this case, the Print Manager prints high-priority files before ones of lower priority.

How do I change the priority of a print request?

You can change the order in which your documents print by using Windows' Print Manager. The Print Manager manages all the printing you do from your Windows applications.

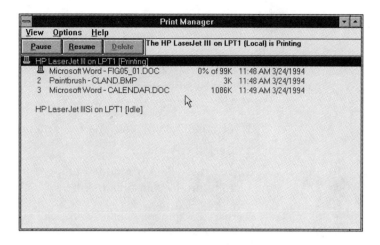

FIGURE 5-4   The Print Manager can print several documents in succession

To reprioritize your print job:

1. Press ALT+TAB until you see "Print Manager." Windows displays the Print Manager window, which should look like the one shown in Figure 5-4.

2. Select the document you want to print sooner.

3. Press CTRL+UP ARROW to move the document to the desired position in the list.

Tech Tip: You cannot move the "rush" print job ahead of the job that Windows is currently printing, which displays a miniature printer icon next to it.

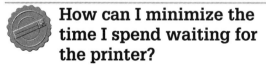

How can I minimize the time I spend waiting for the printer?

Like most Windows applications, Word 6.0 automatically minimizes the amount of time you spend waiting for a document to print by using background printing. With background printing, Word only briefly occupies the editing area while it prepares the document for printing. You can then continue working as Word prints the document.

You can tell whether Word is printing in the background by looking at the status bar. If a small printer icon with a changing number appears instead of the time, Word is currently printing that page of the document to a temporary file.

To make sure the background printing option is selected in Word 6.0:

1. Choose <u>O</u>ptions from the <u>T</u>ools menu.

2. Click the Print tab.

3. Select the <u>B</u>ackground Printing check box, then click OK to return to your document.

Tech Terror: Background printing works with most, but not all, printers. For example, the Hewlett-Packard Deskjet 500c cannot print in the background.

Why do I see the error message "Margins set outside printable area of the page" when I try to print?

Word displays this message if your margins are so small that your printer cannot print the document. Your printer uses a portion of the paper's top edge to feed in the paper; therefore, it can't print in this area. Word offers you the option of fixing this error. If you click <u>F</u>ix, Word automatically sets the margins so that the document falls entirely within your particular printer's printing area.

To determine the minimum margins your document must have, follow these steps:

1. Double-click the Write program item in the Program Manager. This Windows accessory usually appears in the Accessories program group.

2. Choose <u>P</u>age Layout from the <u>D</u>ocument menu.

3. Type **0** in the <u>L</u>eft, <u>R</u>ight, <u>T</u>op, and <u>B</u>ottom text boxes to set the margins to zero.

4. Click OK.

5. A message box displays the minimum margins for the current printer.

6. Click OK to return to the Page Layout dialog box.

7. Click Cancel then choose Exit from the File menu to close the Write accessory.

To change the printer margins to zero for a Postscript printer:

1. Return to the Word document.
2. Choose Print from the File menu.
3. Click the Printer button.
4. Click Options.
5. Click None under Margins.
6. Click OK, click Close, then click OK again to return to your document.

Is there some way to speed up printing when I just want to proof a document?

You can print a draft of your document more quickly than a fully formatted version. Draft output is particularly useful when you just want to look over the text, not review the format of the document.

To print draft output:

1. Choose Print from the File menu.
2. Click Options.
3. Select the Draft Output check box in the Printing Options section.
4. Choose OK twice to print the document as a draft.

To revert to high-quality output, perform these steps again to clear the Draft Output check box.

Exactly what appears in draft output depends entirely on the type of printer you are using. If you are using a dot-matrix printer, probably none of your character formatting will display. Most laser printers, however, print the character formatting, but not any graphics. Postscript printers, on the other hand, print both formatted text and graphics.

I used the Insert menu to add some symbols to my document. I can see these symbols on the screen in every view but when I print the document a space appears in the output instead of the symbol itself. What's the problem?

More than likely, you are printing your document as draft output. Certain printers skip graphical characters, including the symbols that Word creates, when you print a draft copy.

To print your document with the symbols:

1. Choose Options from the Tools menu.
2. Click the Print tab.
3. Clear the Draft Output check box.
4. Click OK.

How can I print annotations?

Annotations allow reviewers to insert comments into a document without actually changing its contents.

Annotations are like electronic "sticky notes." Because annotations are not part of the regular text, they normally do not appear when you print a document.

To print annotations along with the document:

1. Choose Print from the File menu.
2. Click Options.
3. Select the Annotations check box under Include with Document.
4. Click OK twice to print the document along with its annotations, as shown in Figure 5-5.

Document

Fun With Computers This seminar is for handling computer phobia. You will work with a computer to develop basic computer skills. You will start a computer, start a few applications, and develop an awareness for the features a computer can provide. This course is not for learning a specific package. The computers you will use in this course have many different packages that may not necessarily match what you have at home. The skills you will develop in this course will help you feel comfortable using the computer.[MC1] **What is a Computer** You work with so many gadgets that you can easily assume everything is computerized—especially if it isn't working **What Are All Those Buttons For** Your TV has buttons that let you set the TV to show the programs you want to watch. A computer has several different parts **Starting The Computer** Starting a computer is just like starting a TV since you must turn it on. Once you turn it on, the equipment needs to know what to do next[MC2]	Page: 1 [MC1]Sue, let's try stressing what the course is good for, rather than what it won't do for them Page: 1 [MC2]Missing period here.

Annotations

FIGURE 5-5   You can print a document with annotations

Tech Tip: This setting change remains in effect for all documents you print until you change the setting back.

Alternatively, you can print only a document's annotations by following these steps:

1. Choose <u>P</u>rint from the <u>F</u>ile menu.

2. Select Annotations in the <u>P</u>rint What drop-down list box.

3. Click OK to print the annotations without the document.

Can I print the summary information with my document?

You can print any or all of the following with the document: summary information, field codes, drawings, annotations, and hidden text.

To tell Word which of these items to print along with the document:

1. Choose Print from the File menu.

2. Click Options.

3. Select or clear the appropriate check boxes under Include with Document.

4. Click OK twice to print the selected items as well as the document.

You can also print the summary information, annotations, styles, AutoText entries, or key assignments without printing the document itself. To do so:

1. Choose Print from the File menu.

2. Select the desired item in the Print What drop-down list box.

3. Click OK to print the selected item.

How can I print selected pages, rather than printing the entire document?

Often, you may want to print only a single page or a subset of your document. For example, you might want to print only those pages on which you've made changes (presuming the edits didn't affect the document's pagination), or the one page to which you added a graphic, or just those pages whose printed originals you misplaced. Whatever the reason, printing specific pages is a straightforward process in Word.

To print only selected pages:

1. Choose Print from the File menu.

2. If you just want to print the current page, select the Current option button. Similarly, you can select one or more pages before choosing Print, then select the Selection option button.

3. To print any other set of pages, enter the pages to print in the Pages text box. You can specify pages by their page numbers in the document or as pages of a specific section, as Table 5-1 indicates.

4. Click OK to print the selected pages.

To print...	Enter...	Example
A single page	The page number	5
A range of nonconsecutive pages	The page numbers, separated by commas	5, 9
A range of consecutive pages	The page numbers, separated by a hyphen	5-9
A single section	The section reference, which you create by typing **s** followed by the section's number	s4
A range of contiguous sections	The first and last section references, separated by a hyphen	s1-s3
A range of noncontiguous sections	The section references, separated by a comma	s1, s3
A range of pages within a section that starts with a continuous section break	The page references, which you create by typing **p** followed by the page number (counting from the beginning of the section), then **s** and the section number, separated by a hyphen	p2s4-p5s4
A range of contiguous pages from more than one section	The page references, separated by a hyphen	p2s2-p3s4
A range of noncontiguous pages from more than one section	The page references, separated by commas	p2s2,p1s4,p8s3

TABLE 5-1   You can print selected pages from a document

Tech Note: When you type the page numbers you want to print, they do not have to be in numerical order. For example, Word interprets 1, 5, 10 and 10, 5, 1 as the same specification.

My underlined text appears correctly on screen but it doesn't print. What's wrong?

You may have a corrupt WINWORD.OPT file. This file stores the settings you specify with the Options command on the Tools menu.

To create a new copy of this file:

1. Exit Word.

2. Open the Windows File Manager.

3. Move to and open the WINWORD directory (or whatever directory contains the Word for Windows program files).

4. Select WINWORD.OPT.

5. Choose Rename from the File Manager's File menu.

6. Type a new name, such as **WINWORD.OLD**, in the To text box.

7. Click OK to rename the WINWORD.OPT file.

8. Restart Word for Windows.

When Word cannot rename the WINWORD.OPT file, it creates a new one. This should solve the problem. If so, delete the old one to avoid leaving an unnecessary file on your disk.

Tech Tip: If you have customized your copy of Word, you may want to make backups of WINWORD.OPT and NORMAL.DOT (in the WINWORD\TEMPLATE subdirectory); these two files contain many of your customized settings. If they become corrupt at some point, you can simply replace them instead of having to reset all of your options.

If the problem persists, you need to replace your printer driver. Make sure you have the disk that contains the printer driver on hand; this will be either a Windows Setup disk or a disk that came with your printer.

To remove your existing printer driver and install a new one:

1. Open the Windows File Manager.

2. Move to and open the WINDOWS\SYSTEM directory.

3. Select your printer driver file. Printer driver file names refer to the printer model and have a .DRV extension.

4. Choose Re_name from the _File menu.

5. Enter a new name with a different extension in the _To text box.

6. Click OK to rename the file.

7. Open the Windows Control Panel.

8. Double-click the Printers icon or choose _Printers from the _Settings menu.

9. Select your printer then click _Remove. Windows displays an error message that says it cannot find the file, which you can disregard.

10. Click _Add.

11. Select your printer in the _List of Printers list box, then click _Install.

If your printer is not included on this list, select Install Unlisted or Updated Printer in the _List of Printers list box, then click _Install.

12. Word prompts you to insert the appropriate disk in drive A. (You can specify a different drive, if necessary.) Insert your disk, then click OK.

13. When the installation is complete, select your printer in the Installed _Printers list box.

14. Click the S_et as Default Printer button, if desired, to make this printer the default for all Windows applications.

15. Choose E_xit from the _Settings menu, press ALT-F4, or double-click the Control menu box to close the Control Panel.

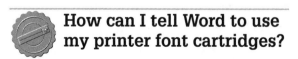

How can I tell Word to use my printer font cartridges?

Windows applications, including Word, can use the font cartridges installed on your printer as long as the printer driver knows they are there. Once the printer driver knows which font cartridges you have, you can select any of these fonts whenever you format text in your document.

To install a font cartridge for a Windows printer driver, follow these steps:

1. Open the Control Panel by double-clicking its icon in the Main program group of the Program Manager.

2. Double-click the Printers icon or choose Printers from the Settings menu to open the Printers dialog box.

3. Select the name of the printer with the cartridges in the Installed Printers list box.

4. Click Setup.

5. Select the installed cartridge in the Cartridges list box. If you have more than one cartridge, click the first one and then hold down CTRL as you click the others.

6. Click OK.

7. If desired, click Set As Default Printer so that Word and other Windows applications automatically print to this particular printer.

8. Choose Close.

9. Press ALT+F4, choose Exit from the Settings menu, or double-click the Control-menu box to close the Control Panel.

As long as the printer is selected as the default, all the fonts provided by the cartridges appear in the list of available fonts whenever you format text in Word.

I don't like the size of my superscript and subscript text. Is there any way to change it?

In Word 6.0, the size of superscript or subscript text and its distance from the baseline depends on the particular font you are using. However, you can change how far above or below the baseline the text appears if you format it as raised or lowered text.

To change the text's format and appearance:

1. Select the text.
2. Open the Font dialog box by either right-clicking the text, then choosing Font on the shortcut menu, or choosing Font from the Format menu.
3. Select the size you want to use for the text in the Size list box on the Font tab.
4. Click the Character Spacing tab.
5. Select Normal, Raised, or Lowered in the Position drop-down list box to determine the text's placement in relation to the baseline.
6. Enter the number of points you want to appear between the baseline and the raised or lower text in the By text box. You can either type the value or use the up and down arrows to select one.
7. Click OK.

By reformatting the text as raised or lowered, you not only achieve a superscript or subscript effect, but can determine the exact size of the text itself.

Why is the top of my superscript text cut off when I print?

If the tops of superscript characters are not printing properly, your line spacing is too narrow. You can fix this problem by either increasing the line spacing or decreasing the size of the superscript text:

To increase the line spacing:

1. Choose Paragraph from the Format menu.
2. Click the Indent and Spacing tab.
3. You can select a wider line spacing in the Line Spacing drop-down list box. Alternatively, you can enter a new value in the At text box by either typing it or using the up and down arrows to select one.
4. Click OK to return to your document.

To decrease the point size of the superscript characters:

1. Select the text you want to format.

2. Choose <u>F</u>ont from the F<u>o</u>rmat menu.

3. Click the Fo<u>n</u>t tab.

4. Select a smaller font size in the <u>S</u>ize list box or enter it in the text box.

5. Click OK to return to your document.

 ## When I try to print from Word 6.0 over a PC NFS network, either the document doesn't print completely or I get an error message. Why can't I print?

Word 6.0 comes with OLE 2.0, which requires Mandatory Record Locking. This feature locks all the records in use so that only one application can use them at any given time. PC NFS, on the other hand, supports Advisory Record Locking, which does not lock the records. When you try to use Word 6.0 with PC NFS, the different record locking settings conflict.

If you are running Windows 3.1, you can work around this conflict by following these steps:

1. Open the Control Panel by double-clicking its program item in the Program Manager's Main program group.

2. Double-click the Printers icon, or choose <u>P</u>rinters from the <u>S</u>ettings menu.

3. Select the <u>U</u>se Print Manager check box, then click Close.

4. Choose E<u>x</u>it from the <u>S</u>ettings menu, press ALT-F4, or double-click the Control menu box to exit the Control Panel.

5. Open the Print Manager by double-clicking its icon in the Program Manager's Main program group.

6. Choose <u>N</u>etwork Settings from the <u>O</u>ptions menu.

7. Clear the <u>U</u>pdate Network Display and <u>P</u>rint Net Jobs Direct check boxes.

8. Click OK and then choose E<u>x</u>it from the <u>V</u>iew menu to close the Print Manager.

9. Reopen the Control Panel by double-clicking its icon.

10. Double-click the Printers icon or choose <u>P</u>rinters from the <u>S</u>ettings menu.

11. Click <u>C</u>onnect.

12. Clear the <u>F</u>ast Printing Direct to Port check box.

13. Click OK, then click Close.

14. Choose E<u>x</u>it from the <u>S</u>ettings menu.

If you are running Windows for Workgroups 3.1 or 3.11, use this procedure instead:

1. Open the Print Manager by double-clicking its icon in the Program Manager's Main program group.

2. Choose <u>B</u>ackground Printing from the <u>O</u>ptions menu.

3. Choose <u>N</u>etwork Settings from the <u>O</u>ptions menu.

4. Clear the <u>S</u>end Documents Directly to Network check box.

5. Click OK.

6. Click <u>C</u>onnect.

7. Clear the <u>F</u>ast Printing Direct to Port check box.

8. Click OK and then choose E<u>x</u>it from the <u>V</u>iew menu.

You should now be able to successfully print your documents from Word 6.0.

Is there anything I can do to make it easier to read highly stylized fonts on the screen?

When you are using with a highly stylized font, such as script, the letters are often difficult to read on the screen. This difficulty reflects the limitations of the screen drivers for these fonts. Other fonts may be hard to read because they are so ornate.

To minimize this problem while you are creating and editing your document, you may want to use an easier-to-read font, such as Times New Roman or Courier New. Once you have finalized the document's contents, you can format the text with the desired font.

Is there any way to print only the odd pages in my document?

You can tell Word to print only the odd or the even pages of a document by following these steps:

1. Choose Print from the File menu.
2. Select either Odd Pages or Even Pages in the Print drop-down list box at the bottom of the dialog box.
3. Click OK to print the selected pages of the document.

I'd like to print my document on both sides of the page. How do I do this?

You can only print on both sides of a page if your printer is equipped to do so; many printers are not. To find out if your printer supports double-sided, or duplex, printing, check your printer's documentation.

If your printer supports duplex printing, you must tell your printer driver to use this feature in Windows. To set up your Windows printer driver for duplex printing:

1. Choose Print from the File menu.
2. Click Printer.
3. Click Options twice.
4. Select either the Long Edge or the Short Edge option button to determine how the double-sided output prints, as shown in Figure 5-6. (The specific name of the option you use to enable or disable double-sided printing may be different if you are using a printer other than a Hewlett-Packard LaserJet.)
5. Click OK twice, then choose Close to return to the Print dialog box.
6. Click OK to print your double-sided document.
7. Unless you want all of your printed output from Windows to be double-sided, reset this option by choosing Print from the File menu and clicking Printer again.
8. Click Options twice.

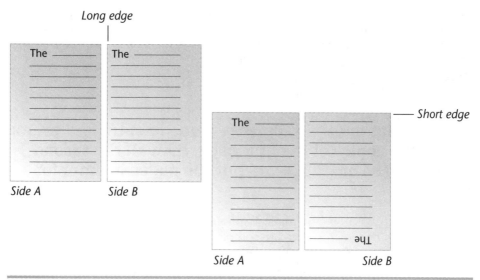

FIGURE 5-6 You can perform double-sided printing along the long or short edge of a page

9. Select the <u>N</u>one option button, and then click OK twice.

10. Choose Close and click Cancel.

Tech Tip: Not all HP LaserJet IIIsi printers have the duplex print option installed. You can run the 05 Self Test to see if it's installed on your printer. Press and hold the Print Fonts/Test key on the printer's control panel until 05 SELF TEST appears on the display. After it prints the report, check whether the Installed Options line lists Duplex Unit. If not, you must install it before you can perform double-sided printing.

If your printer does not support duplex or double-sided printing, you can still print on both sides of the page—it just takes a little more effort and patience. To do so:

1. Print the odd pages of your document by selecting Odd Pages in the P<u>r</u>int drop-down list box at the bottom of the Print dialog box.

2. Feed the output back into the printer so that it will now print on the back of those sheets.

3. Print the even pages of the document on the back of the odd pages by selecting Even Pages in the P<u>r</u>int drop-down list box.

Tech Tip: If you use the second method, make sure that your pages are in the correct order before you print the even sides. You want the first even page to print on the back of page 1, not on the back of the last odd page in your document.

 When I print multiple copies of a document, Word prints out all the copies of the first page, then all the second pages, and so on. Can Word put the pages in order for me?

Word can automatically arrange your multipage, multicopy documents to create complete copies as it prints, as shown in Figure 5-7.

To have Word perform this process, called *collating*, follow these steps:

1. Choose Print from the File menu.

2. Enter the number of copies you want in the Copies text box.

3. Select the Collate Copies check box.

4. Click OK to print the document.

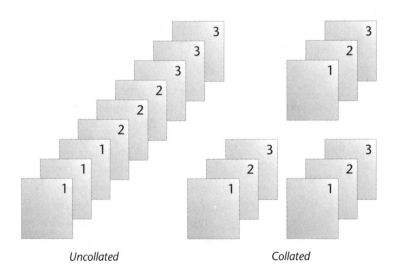

Uncollated   *Collated*

FIGURE 5-7   Word can collate pages to keep multiple copies of a document in order

Why are my bullets printing differently than they appear on the screen?

If your printed output uses a different character than you see on the screen for a single bullet, you probably didn't use a TrueType font when you inserted the bullet. TrueType fonts print exactly the way they appear on the screen; ones that aren't, may or may not.

Solving this problem is quite easy:

1. Select a bullet in the document.

2. Choose Fo_n_t from the F_o_rmat menu.

3. Select a TrueType font in the _F_ont list box. A TrueType font displays a double-T next to its name.

4. Click OK to return to the document and check your bullet.

Tech Note: You won't have this problem if you add bullets as part of a Word 6 bulleted list since a TrueType font is automatically selected. The problem only applies when you insert a bullet or other special character on your own.

Tech Tip: If you originally inserted the bullet using the _S_ymbol command on the _I_nsert menu, you must first delete it. You can then reinsert it using a different font.

Why can't I get a color graph to print correctly?

If you try to print a Word document that contains a chart with color dithered patterns created with Microsoft Graph on a Hewlett-Packard DeskJet 500C, 550C, or ColorPro series printer, the result appears in black-and-white. The monochrome output results because Graph does not correctly process the dithered information. Before you can print the color chart from Word, you need to edit the chart to change the dithered patterns to solid ones.

Whenever I try to print a Word document on my HP DeskJet printer, I get a "Printer is Busy" message. How do I print my documents?

Earlier versions of the HP DeskJet printer drivers may conflict with Word 6.0. You can turn off the Print Manager to resolve this problem so you can print your documents.

To disable the Print Manager:

1. Double-click the Control Panel icon, which usually appears in the Program Manager's Main program group.

2. Double-click the Printers icon or select Printers from the Settings menu to display the Printers dialog box.

3. Clear the Use Print Manager check box and then click Close.

4. Close the Control Panel by choosing Exit from the Settings menu, pressing ALT+F4, or double-clicking the window's Control menu box.

Tech Tip: You can repeat this process by selecting the Use Print Manager check box to use the Print Manager from other applications.

Why does the list of available fonts seem to change whenever I use a different printer driver?

Word mostly depends on the current printer driver to determine the available fonts, because some printers can only print certain fonts. For example, a Generic/Text Only printer driver can print relatively few fonts; a Hewlett-Packard LaserJet III printer driver, on the other hand, supports a wide variety of typefaces. When you switch to another printer, Word looks at the appropriate driver to find out which fonts it can print. Word, therefore, displays many more fonts in the Font list box when you select the Hewlett-Packard LaserJet III printer than when you specify Generic/Text Only.

My friend has a better printer, but she doesn't have Word. Can I still print my Word documents on her printer?

Yes, you can print your Word documents on her printer, even though she has neither Word nor a compatible word-processor. Before you can use her printer, you need to print your Word document to a file, then copy this file to a disk. When you print to a file, Word not only stores the text, but all of the commands the printer needs to properly format and insert graphics in the document. You can then take your disk to your friend's computer and simply copy the file to her printer to print your Word document.

To print a Word document to a file and then print it directly from the operating system:

Tech Terror: Before printing to file, you must select the correct printer driver for the printer on which you will print the document; otherwise, the final output will be gibberish.

1. Choose Print from the File menu.

2. Click Printer.

3. Select the appropriate printer driver in the Printers list box for the printer on which you will ultimately print the document.

4. Click the Set as Default Printer button, then choose Close.

5. Select the Print to File check box.

6. Click OK.

7. If you want, you can choose a different directory in which to store this file.

8. Enter the name of the file in the File Name text box. Notice that the file has a .PRN extension.

9. Copy the .PRN file to a floppy disk.

10. Remove the floppy disk, take it to the other computer, and insert it.

11. Copy the .PRN file to the port to which the printer is attached (usually, the printer is connected to LPT1). For example, you might enter:

```
COPY A:\MYDOC.PRN >LPT1
```

at the DOS prompt, then press ENTER, assuming the floppy disk is in drive A.

The letters that appear on my screen are different from the ones I type. Help!

The most likely cause of this problem is that you are using Bitstream FaceLift fonts, and the Bitstream cache has become corrupt. To remedy this situation:

1. Close Word and any other open applications.

2. Exit Windows.

3. Switch to the directory in which the Bitstream fonts are stored.

4. Delete the CACHEDMP.CCH file from the directory.

5. Type **WIN** at the prompt to restart Windows.

The CACHEDMP.CCH file automatically rebuilds itself, producing a "clean" copy of the file. What appears on the screen should match what you type from now on.

Westside Deliveries

524 W. Exchange St. Ste. E
Akron, OH 44302

Sam Jenkinson
4320 Castle Drive
Fairlawn, OH 44333

FIGURE 5-8   You can print a document with different orientations

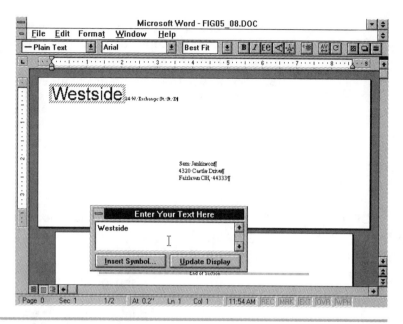

FIGURE 5-9   WordArt displays its own menu bar and toolbar

Can I print both normally and sideways on the same page?

Yes, you can print text with different orientations on the same page. For example, Figure 5-8 depicts an envelope with text printed both vertically and horizontally. To achieve this effect, you must create the text that uses the other orientation using Word's WordArt applet.

To create text that has a different orientation:

1. Choose <u>O</u>bject from the <u>I</u>nsert menu.

2. Select Microsoft WordArt 2.0 in the <u>O</u>bject Type list box and then click OK.

WordArt displays its menu bar and toolbar, as shown in Figure 5-9.

3. Enter your text in the Enter Your Text Here dialog box then click <u>U</u>pdate Display.

4. Select one of the two up and down effects, which are indicated by the up and down arrows in the first drop-down list box in the toolbar.

5. Click outside the WordArt object to return to your document.

You can now move and manipulate the WordArt object the same way you would any other inserted graphic, except that you cannot rotate it.

 When I print, my pages appear in reverse order. What can I do to prevent this?

Various printer models feed paper differently. By default, Word prints the first page first, and so on. However, some printers stack the pages with the first page at the bottom, so that you need to re-sort them after they're printed. If you're having this problem, you can print your documents in reverse order so that they stack correctly.

To print your document in reverse order:

1. Choose Options from the Tools menu.

2. Click the Print tab. (You can also display the Print tab by clicking the Options button in the Print dialog box.)

3. Select the Reverse Print Order check box then click OK.

This printing option becomes the default until you change it back.

 **Tech Tip:** You may want to print your documents in reverse order on a regular basis if you use a laser printer, or any other type that offers more than one way to eject paper.

When I want to use a different printer to print a single document, why do I have to make it the default in Word 6.0? It wasn't like that in Word 2.0.

Actually, Word 2.0 and Word 6.0 work the same way: When you select a new printer in Word, you are defining that printer as the default Windows printer. Word 2.0 simply didn't let the user know that it was doing so, whereas Word 6.0 does.

To change to another printer in Word 6.0:

1. Choose <u>P</u>rint from the <u>F</u>ile menu.

2. Click Prin<u>t</u>er.

3. Select the printer you want to use in the <u>P</u>rinters list box.

4. Click the Set as <u>D</u>efault Printer button, and then choose OK to return to the Print dialog box.

In Word 2.0, the steps were quite different and didn't make it clear that you were selecting a new default printer. To change printers in Word 2.0, you simply chose P<u>r</u>int Setup from the <u>F</u>ile menu, selected a new printer, and clicked OK. If you then double-clicked the Printers icon in the Control Panel, however, you would see that the printer you selected became the default Windows printer.

Tech Tip: Unless you are planning to print to the new printer consistently, switch back to your default printer as soon as you print the document. Otherwise, all of your Windows application will print to this printer.

Special Features

This chapter covers an array of Word features that can help you manage and streamline the production of your documents. They include document summaries, document statistics, AutoCorrect, AutoText, revisions, annotations, bookmarks, hyphenation, dropped capitals, sorting, and formulas. If you haven't already used these features, give them a try—you may find they not only enhance your work but save you time.

FRUSTRATION BUSTERS!

Here's a brief description of the timesaving, easy-to-use features discussed in this chapter:

A *document summary* stores a document's title, author, subject, and keywords. It provides a brief description of a document's contents to help you correctly locate and identify it.

Word can report summary data for a document, called *document statistics*, such as when it was last saved, its size, and the number of words, pages, lines, and paragraphs that it contains.

Word's *AutoCorrect* feature can automatically change a word to either another word, a phrase, or a picture. You can use AutoCorrect to fix your most common typos, to spell out abbreviations, and to replace text automatically.

The *AutoText* feature is similar to AutoCorrect, except that Word only makes a replacement when you tell it to do so.

Revision marks indicate any changes made to a document during editing. Word marks all added and deleted text. You can then review and selectively accept or reject these changes.

You and your readers can use *annotations* to add comments to a document without actually inserting them in the text. You can even add recorded sound annotations!

Bookmarks are placeholders within a document. You can use a bookmark to make it easy to return to a certain passage in a document, to mark cross-references and index entries, or to flag text that you plan to repeat in another location. (Chapter 14, "Working with Large Documents," describes how to use bookmarks to identify cross-references and indexes.)

Hyphenation splits long words so that your text lines up more evenly along the right margin. You can let Word automatically use hyphens in the appropriate locations or you can suppress hyphenation altogether.

You can use an oversized capital letter, or *dropped capital*, to give your document a polished, attention-getting look.

Word's *sorting* feature lets you order lines and paragraphs according to text, numbers, or dates.

When you need to perform a quick calculation, you can use Word to compute the results of a simple *formula*.

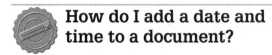

How do I add a date and time to a document?

You can add the current date and time to your document by following these steps:

1. Move the insertion point to the location where you want the date and/or time to appear.

2. Choose the Date and Time command from the Insert menu.

3. Select the desired format in the Available Formats list box.

4. Click OK to add the date and/or time to your document in the selected format.

One special feature of this command is the Insert as Field check box option, which determines how Word adds the date and time to the document. When you insert a date or time with this check box cleared, only the actual text for the date or time is inserted. This date or time does not change as you edit the document. On the other hand, if you insert a date or time with the Insert as Field check box selected, Word adds a field that displays the current date or time. Word updates this field whenever you reopen your document.

For example, if you want the date on which the document was created to always appear in the document, as you might with an invoice, you would clear the check box; on the other hand, you would select this check box if you want the field to change to indicate the current date every time the document is read or printed, as you might with a standard overdue payment notification.

Tech Tip: You can insert the current date or time by pressing ALT+SHIFT+D or ALT+SHIFT+T, respectively. In either case, it will have the same format as the last date and time you added. Similarly, Word will insert either text or a field, depending on whether the Insert as Field check box was selected the last time you added a date or time.

How do I change the document's summary information?

You can change a document's summary information at any time by simply choosing the Summary Info command from the File menu. You can then edit the title, subject, author, keywords, or comments in the Summary Info dialog box, shown here:

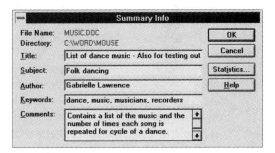

Tech Tip: You can display document summaries when you are looking at files in the Find File dialog box by selecting Summary from the View drop-down list box. This dialog box appears when you choose Find File from the File menu or click the Find File button in a dialog box that lets you select files.

How do I get Word to prompt me for summary information when I first save a document?

If you follow these steps, Word will prompt you for summary information whenever you save a file with a new file name:

1. Choose Options from the Tools menu.
2. Click the Save tab.
3. Select the Prompt for Summary Info check box.
4. Click OK.

The next time you save a document with a new file name, Word will display the Summary Info dialog box. After you enter the appropriate information, click OK to save the summary along with the document.

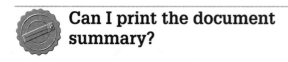

Can I print the document summary?

Yes, you can print a document summary. How you do so depends on whether the document whose summary you want to print is currently open:

- If the document is open, you print the summary by choosing Print from the File menu, selecting Summary Info in the Print What drop-down list box, and clicking OK.

- If the document is not open, choose Find File from the File menu to list the file or files whose summaries you want to print. After you select the files, choose Print from the Commands drop-down menu, select Summary Info in the Print What drop-down list box, and then click OK.

Tech Tip: If you want to print the document summary when you print the document, click the Options button in the Print dialog box, select the Summary Info check box under Include with Document, and select OK. All of the documents you print include the summary information until you change this option back

Can I open all the documents at one time that have certain summary information in common?

You can search for documents that meet particular criteria—in this case, which have certain entries in their summaries—and then open only those that satisfy the search.

To find and open files based on their summary information entries:

1. Choose Find File from the File menu, or click the Find File button in any dialog box in which you can make a file selection.

2. Click Search and then Advanced Search. If you have not specified a search before, the Search dialog box opens instead of the Find File dialog box. If the Search dialog box appears, you can simply select Advanced Search.

3. Click the Summary tab.

4. Type the document summary entries you want to find in the appropriate text boxes.

5. Click OK twice to find all of the documents with the specified entries in their summary information.

6. Select the documents that Word finds, then click <u>O</u>pen to open all of these documents at once.

I am looking at the statistical information Word collected for one of my documents. Why isn't it correct?

The statistical information that Word displays reflects the condition of the file at the time that it was last saved. To update this, you must resave the file. Then, when you choose Summary <u>I</u>nfo from the <u>F</u>ile menu and click the Stati<u>s</u>tics button, the information should be current.

Is there any way to see more detailed statistical information about my document?

Word includes a SuperDocStatistics macro in the MACRO60.DOT template found in the WINWORD\MACROS directory that you can run to display a dialog box like the one shown in Figure 6-1. You can then click any of the buttons on the left to see more detailed information about that particular topic or item.

Tech Tip: To run this macro, you may need to copy it to NORMAL.DOT. Chapter 7, "Customization, Styles, and Templates," and Chapter 16, "Fields and Macros," include questions about transferring a macro between templates.

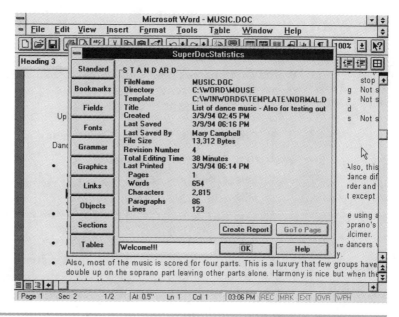

FIGURE 6-1   A document summary created with the SuperDocStatistics macro

How can I find out how many words I have in my document?

Word has a feature called Word Count that displays the number of words, characters, pages, paragraphs, and lines in a document. Word Count also shows the number of footnotes and endnotes, if the Include Footnotes and Endnotes check box in the Word Count dialog box is selected. When you choose Word Count from the Tools menu, Word displays a dialog box like the one shown here:

Tech Tip: You can perform a count on just a portion of a document by selecting the text before you choose Word Count from the Tools menu.

Can Word 6.0 help me create a document that is written at an appropriate level for my readers?

Word's Grammar feature can generate a readability statistics report after it analyzes the text's grammar. To turn this option on, follow these steps:

1. Choose Options from the Tools menu.

2. Click the Grammar tab.

3. Select the Show Readability Statistics check box and then click OK.

4. Choose Grammar from the Tools menu to perform the check.

When Word finishes examining your document, it displays a readability statistics report similar to the one shown in Figure 6-2.

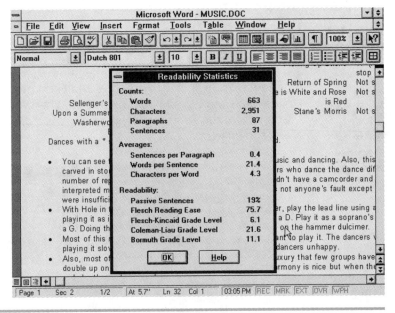

FIGURE 6-2   Readability statistics for a document

Option	Effect
Replace <u>T</u>ext as You Type	Changes one entry into another. You can use this option to fix common spelling mistakes, such as typing **teh** for **the**. You can also use this option to spell out abbreviations or replace text with a graphic, such as a company logo.
Change 'Straight Quotes' to 'Smart Quotes'	Changes the inch and foot marks normally used for apostrophes and quotes to "curly" ones that enclose the text.
Correct TWo INitial <u>C</u>Apitals	Changes the second letter in a word to lowercase when you accidentally enter both the first and second letters of a word in uppercase and subsequent letters in lowercase.
Capitalize First Letter of <u>S</u>entences	Capitalizes the first letter of a word following a period, exclamation point, or question mark.
Capitalize <u>N</u>ames of Days	Automatically capitalizes the days of the week.

TABLE 6-1   You can use AutoCorrect to fix common mistakes

What does AutoCorrect do?

AutoCorrect is a powerful, new Word 6.0 feature that intelligently modifies your document, fixes common mistakes, and makes certain other changes you specify. You can choose which types of corrections it makes by choosing <u>A</u>utoCorrect from the <u>T</u>ools menu. Table 6-1 summarizes the effects of available options.

Tech Tip: Word does not make AutoCorrect changes until you type a space or enter a tab after the word.

Is there a way to improve the look of quotes and apostrophes in Word for Windows 6.0?

Yes, there is a new feature in Word 6.0 that replaces the SmartQuotes macro in 2.0. AutoCorrect can replace straight apostrophes and quotes with curly ones so that your document has a more finished look.

To activate this feature:

1. Choose AutoCorrect from the Tools menu.
2. Select the Change 'Straight Quotes' to 'Smart Quotes' check box.
3. Click OK.

   Now, whenever you type quotes or apostrophes, Word replaces them with curly ones that match the direction of the nearby text.

How do I add my own AutoCorrect entries?

You can add AutoCorrect entries while you are checking the spelling of a document or by choosing the AutoCorrect command from the Tools menu.

To add an AutoCorrect entry while when you are spell checking a document:

1. Check the spelling of a document that includes the word that you want AutoCorrect to replace.
2. When Word finds the misspelled word that you want to use as the AutoCorrect entry, type the desired replacement in the Change To text box in the Spelling dialog box.
3. Click AutoCorrect.

To add an AutoCorrect entry using the menu:

1. Select the text, graphics, or combination of the two that you want to use as the replacement entry. (If you do not preselect an entry, you can type it in step 4.)
2. Choose AutoCorrect from the Tools menu.
3. Type the text that you want Word to replace in the Replace text box. For example, you might type **teh.**

4. Make any changes to the replacement entry in the <u>W</u>ith text box, which contains the entry you selected in step 1. If you didn't preselect an entry, you can type one now.

5. If you preselected an entry, you can select the <u>F</u>ormatted Text option button to format the replacement text exactly as it appeared in the current document. Alternatively, you can select the <u>P</u>lain Text option button to have the replacement text inherit the formatting of whatever it replaces. (If you typed the entry in the <u>W</u>ith text box, these option buttons are not available.)

6. Click <u>A</u>dd.

7. Repeat steps 3, 4, and 5 for each AutoCorrect entry you want to add.

8. Click OK.

Tech Tip: You can delete an AutoCorrect entry when you no longer want Word to make a particular correction for you. Choose <u>A</u>utoCorrect from the <u>T</u>ools menu, select the replacement entry you want to remove in the list box or type it in the <u>R</u>eplace text box, and then click <u>D</u>elete.

I added entries to the AutoCorrect feature but Word isn't making the corrections as I type. Why?

In order for the AutoCorrect feature to replace text while you type, the Replace <u>T</u>ext As You Type feature must be turned on. To turn on this feature:

1. Choose <u>A</u>utoCorrect from the <u>T</u>ools menu.

2. Select the Replace <u>T</u>ext as You Type check box.

3. Click OK.

I like to add my company's logo to my documents. Is there a way to expedite this process?

Word's AutoCorrect feature can easily insert your logo in any document. In order to use this feature for your logo, you must first add the logo to AutoCorrect. Then, Word can place the logo in your document whenever you type the keyword associated with it.

To add your logo to Auto Correct:

1. Add your logo to a new document.

2. Select the logo.

3. Choose AutoCorrect from the Tools menu. A portion of your logo appears in the With text box.

4. Type a keyword in the Replace box. This should be a unique word that will not be used for any other reason when typing a document.

5. Click Add then click OK.

Now that you've added your logo as an AutoCorrect entry, follow these steps to insert it in your document:

1. Move the insertion point to where you want the logo to appear.

2. Type the unique keyword and press SPACEBAR.

Your logo replaces the keyword in the document.

For example, suppose you have added the logo shown in the top half of Figure 6-3 as the AutoCorrect entry for the keyword Complogo. When you type **Complogo,** as shown in the bottom half of Figure 6-3, then enter a space, Word replaces the word "Complogo" with the logo itself. You can make this substitution in any document.

If this process doesn't work when you first try it, make sure that the Replace Text as You Type check box is selected in the AutoCorrect dialog box, which you display by choosing AutoCorrect from the Tools menu.

Tech Tip: If you want to selectively replace the keyword with the logo, make it an AutoText entry instead of an AutoCorrect entry.

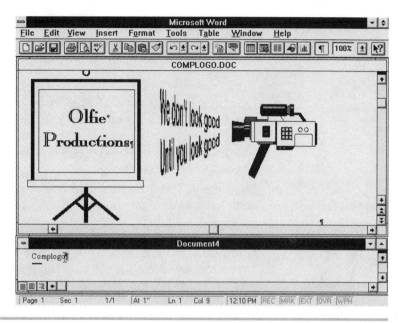

FIGURE 6-3   You can use AutoCorrect to replace text with a logo

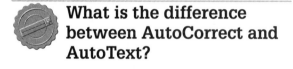

What is the difference between AutoCorrect and AutoText?

Both AutoCorrect and AutoText can replace document text with another entry. AutoCorrect replaces text automatically; AutoText only replaces text when you direct Word to do so. Therefore, you should use AutoCorrect for text replacements you want to occur every time the incorrect entry appears, such as spelling out abbreviations and fixing your most frequent spelling mistakes. On the other hand, use AutoText for text you only want to replace some of the time or don't replace as often.

In addition, AutoCorrect is available to all documents, regardless of the template used, whereas AutoText entries only apply to documents that use the same template in which they were created. To make one or more AutoText entries available to all your documents, you must copy the AutoText entries to the NORMAL.DOT global template.

How do I use an AutoText entry?

There are two ways in which you can access an existing AutoText entry:

- Type the name of the AutoText entry in your document and then press F3. For example, if you have an AutoText entry named Letter Open that enters your usual opening paragraph for letters, you can simply type **Letter Open** and press F3 to insert it.

- Choose AutoText from the Edit menu, select the AutoText entry to add to the document in the Name list box, and click Insert. If desired, before you click Insert, you can select either the Plain Text or Formatted Text option button to determine whether the AutoText entry adopts the current formatting at the insertion point's location or uses the character and paragraph formatting of the AutoText entry itself.

Tech Tip: The Spike is an AutoText entry that comes with Word. You can use the Spike to collect text and graphics from several locations and insert them in another location. The Spike is described in Chapter 3, "Working with Your Word Document."

How do I create my own AutoText entries?

You can create custom AutoText entries that you use to replace portions of text in your documents when desired. An AutoText entry may consist of text, graphics, or a combination of these.

To add an AutoText entry, follow these steps:

1. Select the text and/or graphics that you want to use as the replacement entry. (Unlike AutoCorrect, you must select an entry from a document.)

2. Choose AutoText from the Edit menu.

3. Type the word or phrase in the <u>N</u>ame text box that you want Word to replace when you apply AutoText.

4. Select the template in which you want to store the AutoText entry in the <u>M</u>ake AutoText Entry Available To drop-down list box. If you leave the default of All Documents (Normal.dot) selected, you can access the AutoText entry from any document.

5. Click <u>A</u>dd to add the entry.

Tech Tip: To delete an AutoText entry, choose AutoTe<u>x</u>t from the <u>E</u>dit menu, select the AutoText entry in the <u>N</u>ame list box, click <u>D</u>elete, and then choose Close.

How can I copy an AutoText entry from one template to another?

AutoText entries are stored as part of a template. You can copy an AutoText entry from one template to another so that you can access it from other documents. If you store an AutoText entry in the NORMAL.DOT template, Word makes it available in all your documents.

To copy an AutoText entry between templates:

1. Display Word's Organizer by choosing <u>M</u>acro from the <u>T</u>ools menu, <u>T</u>emplates from the <u>F</u>ile menu, or <u>S</u>tyle from the F<u>o</u>rmat menu, then clicking the Organizer button.

2. Click the <u>A</u>utoText tab.

3. Click Close <u>F</u>ile on the left-hand side of the dialog box.

4. Click Open <u>F</u>ile (which replaces the Close <u>F</u>ile button) and select the template from or to which you want to copy the AutoText entry.

5. Select the AutoText entry in either list box.

6. Click <u>C</u>opy and then Close.

Several of my colleagues are reviewing a document for me. How can I identify all of the changes that each person makes?

Word's revision marking feature can keep track of the changes each user makes by marking his or her additions and deletions in a particular color. Revision marks not only show you where others have—and haven't—made modifications, they also let you identify *who* made *what* edits.

You can protect your document during the review process to ensure that everyone else's changes are marked as revision marks, not incorporated into the document itself. When you set protection, you create a password that prevents anyone else from turning off revision marks. Then, after the reviewers have added their comments to the document, you can selectively accept and reject their suggestions.

To protect the document for revisions, follow these steps:

1. Choose Protect Document from the Tools menu.

2. Select Revisions.

3. Type the password to protect this document in the Password text box.

4. Click OK.

5. Word asks you to confirm the password by entering it twice. Type the password again and click OK.

Tech Tip: You will need this password later to modify the document based on the comments you receive, so be sure to keep a record of it.

Your document is now protected for revisions. If you choose Revisions from the Tools menu, you will see that the Mark Revisions While Editing check box is dimmed, which means that you cannot select it. Word automatically turns this feature on when you protect a document for revisions.

With revision marking enabled, Word keeps track of all the changes made whenever the document is edited and marks them accordingly. Unless you change the settings, Word underlines additions and strikes through deletions, as shown in Figure 6-4. When there are multiple reviewers the marks, by default, appear in a different color for each user.

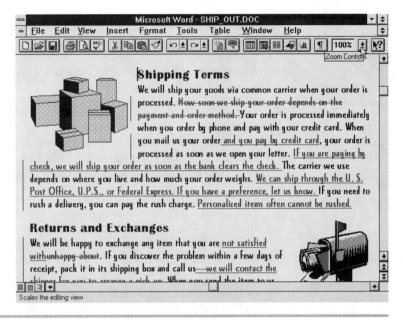

FIGURE 6-4   Revision marks show which text was added and deleted

You display revision marks in a document by choosing Re_visions from the _Tools menu, selecting the Show Revisions on _Screen check box, and then clicking OK. If you select the Show Revisions in _Printed Document check box in this same dialog box, Word also prints the revisions when you print the document.

Once the reviewers have finished making their revisions, you can review them to determine which ones you want to permanently incorporate in the document.

To accept and reject revisions:

1. Choose Un_protect Document from the _Tools menu.

2. Type the password you created to protect the document in the _Password text box and then click OK.
    At this point, the document is no longer protected and any changes you make to the document will not appear as revisions.

3. Choose Re_visions from the _Tools menu or double-click the MRK indicator in the status bar.

4. You can apply or reject the revision marks in three ways:

Tech Tip: If you select part of a document before you choose Re<u>v</u>isions from the <u>T</u>ools menu, you can click the <u>A</u>ccept All or Reject All button to retain or remove all of the revisions in the highlighted text at once.

- You can apply all of the revisions by clicking <u>A</u>ccept All and then choosing <u>Y</u>es when Word prompts for confirmation. Word deletes all of the text marked as such and retains the inserted text. All revision marks are removed from the text.

- You can reject all of the revisions by clicking Reject All and then choosing <u>Y</u>es when Word prompts for confirmation. Word restores all of the text marked as deleted and deletes all of the inserted text; in other words, it returns the document to its pre-revision state. The revision marks no longer appear.

- You can selectively accept and reject revisions by clicking <u>R</u>eview. In the Review Revisions dialog box that Word displays, you click the Find buttons to move from one revision mark to another. For each edit, Word displays the user who made it and the date and time of entry. Simply click <u>A</u>ccept or <u>R</u>eject to retain or remove the currently highlighted revision. When you are finished, choose Close.

Can I change how Word marks revisions?

By default, Word underlines insertions and strikes through deletions. It also places a line in the margin to highlight paragraphs in which revisions occur. You can modify these settings, if you wish. Word offers the options of formatting inserted text with boldface, double underline, italics, or no character formatting at all instead of the single underline option. It can also hide deleted text instead of striking through it. You can choose to display the revised lines in the left, right, or outside margin, or not at all. You can also specify different colors for each of these markings.

To change how Word marks revisions:

1. Choose <u>O</u>ptions from the <u>T</u>ools menu and click the Revisions tab, or choose Re<u>v</u>isions from the <u>T</u>ools menu and click <u>O</u>ptions. Either command displays the options for revision marks.

2. Select how revised text is marked.

For inserted and deleted text, you can select the desired formatting in the Mark drop-down list boxes. You can also pick colors for these marks in the Color drop-down list boxes. The default color is By Author, which uses a different color for each author so you can easily identify each person's revisions as you review the document. Similarly, you can specify the placement and color of revised lines in the associated Mark and Color drop-down list boxes.

3. Click OK to close the Options dialog box.

Tech Tip: You can include revision marks in your printed output by choosing Revisions from the Tools menu, selecting the Show Revisions in Printed Document check box, and then clicking OK. When you print the document, either all text prints as black, or the text that is marked with colors may appear in various shades of gray, depending on your printer. If you want to print revision marks, it is a good idea to change how they are indicated to a feature such as strikethrough or underlining to make sure the revision marks appear clearly.

Several coworkers will be reviewing my document. I want them to add their comments but not in the document itself. How can I do this?

In a situation such as this, you can protect your document for annotations and then distribute the protected version. The reviewers only are able to add comments as annotations. Unlike revisions, annotations are totally separate from the main text of a document. They let the people reviewing the document add comments and suggest changes without actually modifying the document's text. Once they finish, you can easily examine their notes and address them accordingly.

When you protect a document, you are protecting it for only a specific feature: revision marks, annotations, or forms. In this case, if you don't protect the document before you distribute it, your reviewers will be able to alter the document itself as well as add annotations.

To protect the document, follow these steps:

1. Choose Protect Document from the Tools menu.

2. Select Annotations.

3. Type the password to protect this document in the Password text box.

Tech Tip: You will need this password to modify the document later based on the comments you receive, so be sure to keep a record of it. Don't forget, passwords are case sensitive.

4. Click OK.

5. Word asks you to enter the password again to confirm it. Type the password again and click OK.

At this point, the document is protected so your readers can only add annotations to the document. If you look through the menus, you can see that many of the commands are dimmed, which indicates that they are unavailable. The status bar also displays a message that the document is locked.

To add an annotation to a protected document, follow these steps:

1. Move the insertion point to where you want to insert an annotation. If the note relates to a particular sentence or paragraph, you can make it easy to identify by selecting the text before you create the annotation. Then, when someone opens the annotation, the text will appear shaded.

2. Choose <u>A</u>nnotation from the <u>I</u>nsert menu, or press ALT+CTRL+A.

Word opens an annotation pane, like the one shown in Figure 6-5, and adds an annotation mark at the insertion point's location. Note that the annotation mark indicates the initials of the reviewer as well as a number. If you selected text before adding the annotation mark, it remains shaded, just like field codes.

3. Type the annotation.

4. Add any additional annotations by switching to the document pane and repeating steps 1, 2, and 3. You can switch between panes by either clicking the other pane or pressing F6.

5. Click <u>C</u>lose in the annotation pane when you are finished.

Tech Tip: If the annotation marks don't appear in your document, you can display them by choosing <u>O</u>ptions from the <u>T</u>ools menu, clicking the View tab, selecting Hi<u>d</u>den Text, and then clicking OK. You can also click the Show/Hide button on the Standard toolbar to reveal all non-printing characters. Annotation marks automatically display when the annotation pane is open.

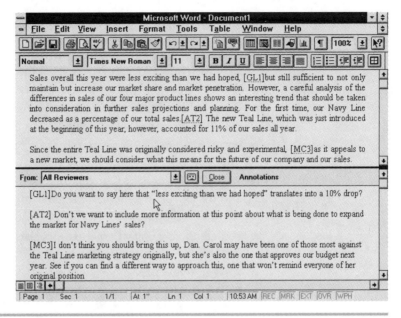

FIGURE 6-5   Word displays an annotation pane when you insert or review
annotations in a document

To review the annotations:

1. Choose Unprotect Document from the Tools menu.

2. Type the password that protects the document in the
   Password text box and click OK.

At this point, the document is no longer protected so you can
make the changes to it.

3. Open the annotations pane by choosing Annotations
   from the View menu or by double-clicking one of the
   annotation marks in the document.

4. Review the annotations, keeping the following features
   in mind:

- You can control which reviewer's comments appear in the annotation pane by selecting a specific name in the annotation pane's From drop-down list box. To redisplay all of the annotations, simply reselect the default, All Reviewers.

- Word automatically opens the annotation pane when you double-click an annotation mark.

- You can delete an annotation by selecting its mark in the document and then pressing DEL.

- You can transfer text between the annotation pane and the document by dragging and dropping it or by using the Clipboard.

- You can quickly select any text associated with an annotation by pressing ALT+F11.

- You can move to another annotation by choosing Go To from the Edit menu and then selecting Annotations in the Go To What list box. You can pick a particular reviewer's name, if desired, in the Enter Reviewer's Name drop-down list box. Alternatively, you can enter the relative number of the annotation to which you want to move. For example, you could type **+3** to move to the third annotation forward from the insertion point's location.

5. Click Close in the annotation pane's toolbar when you are finished reviewing the annotation marks.

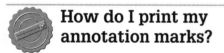

How do I print my annotation marks?

Word can print annotation marks either as part of a document or separately. When you print annotations with the document, the annotation marks appear in the document and the actual text of the annotations prints on a separate page at the end. When you print annotations separately, Word includes the page number, the reviewer's initials, and the actual comments.

To print the annotation marks with the document, follow these steps:

1. Choose Print from the File menu.

2. Click Options.

3. Click the Print tab.

4. Select the Annotations check box.

5. Click OK twice to print your document with the annotations.

To print just the annotations:

1. Choose Print from the File menu.

2. Select Annotations in the Print What drop-down list box.

3. Click OK.

How can I add voice annotations and sounds to my Word documents?

There are two ways to add sounds to your Word documents: as voice annotations or as sound objects. Either way, you can play the sound when you double-click the icon that represents it within the document.

Tech Tip: You can only add voice annotations if you have a sound board and a microphone with which to record what you say. You can add a prerecorded sound object as long as you have the file.

Adding a sound object inserts an embedded object in your document. In this case, the icon appears within the document itself; sound annotations, on the other hand, display in the annotation pane.

To add a sound object to your document, follow these steps:

1. Move the insertion point to where you want the sound object icon to appear.

2. Choose Object from the Insert menu.

3. Select Sound in the Object Type list box and click OK.

4. Record a sound and then indicate you are finished in whatever way your sound board requires. Alternatively, you can insert an existing sound file as a sound object by selecting the Create from File tab and then selecting the file to insert. If Word prompts you to confirm that you want to update the sound object, click Yes.

Word displays an icon, like the one shown here, in your document:

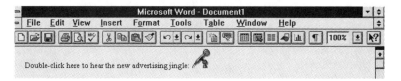

Voice annotations are just like other annotations, except that the icon appears in the annotation pane not the document. To add a voice annotation, follow these steps:

1. Move the insertion point to the text in the document to which the annotation relates.

2. Choose <u>A</u>nnotation from the <u>I</u>nsert menu, or press ALT+CTRL+A, to add an annotation mark to the document and open the annotation pane, if necessary.

3. Click the Insert Sound Object button in the annotation pane's toolbar, shown here:

4. Record the annotation and then indicate that you are finished in whatever way your sound board requires. If Word prompts you to confirm that you want to update the sound object, click <u>Y</u>es.

The annotation pane now includes a sound icon.

 I rearranged my document and now my bookmarks are in the wrong places. Do I need to add them all over again?

Reassigning a bookmark is very easy in Word:

1. Select the new location to which you want to move an existing bookmark.

2. Choose <u>B</u>ookmark from the <u>E</u>dit menu.

3. Select the name of the bookmark that you want to reassign.

4. Click <u>A</u>dd.

Word moves the bookmark to the new location.

Is there any way to view bookmarks in a document?

A new feature in Word 6.0 is the ability to display bookmarks in your documents. If you highlighted text before creating the bookmark, Word encloses the selection in a pair of gray square brackets, such as [this is the text]; otherwise, it simply displays a gray I-beam to indicate the bookmark's location, as shown here:

To turn this feature on:

1. Choose <u>O</u>ptions from the <u>T</u>ools menu.

2. Click the View tab.

3. Select the <u>B</u>ookmarks check box.

4. Click OK.

This feature only indicates the placement of bookmarks in a document; it does not display their names.

I have an I-beam in my document and I can't get rid of it. What do I do?

This I-beam indicates that a bookmark exists at that location. You can suppress the display of bookmarks by choosing <u>O</u>ptions from the <u>T</u>ools menu, clicking the View tab, clearing the <u>B</u>ookmarks check box, and then clicking OK.

You can also remove the bookmark if and when you no longer need it. To permanently delete the bookmark, place the insertion point at the I-beam, choose <u>B</u>ookmark from the <u>E</u>dit menu, click <u>D</u>elete, and then choose Close.

How can I repeat the contents of a bookmark?

If you assign a bookmark to text in your document, you can easily insert the same text at another location, using a field.

To create the bookmark and insert the bookmark field:

1. Select the text that you want to repeat elsewhere.

2. Assign the text to a bookmark by:

   a. Choosing <u>B</u>ookmark from the <u>E</u>dit menu.

   b. Entering the bookmark's name in the <u>B</u>ookmark Name text box.

   c. Selecting <u>A</u>dd.

3. Move the insertion point to where you want to repeat the text assigned to the bookmark.

4. Enter a bookmark field which displays the bookmark's contents as its results by:

   a. Pressing CTRL+F9 to insert the field characters, which look like curly brackets.

   b. Typing the bookmark's name inside the field characters.

   c. Pressing F9 to update the field and show the bookmark's contents.

Can I create buttons to move quickly to a bookmark?

Word includes buttons like the ones shown in the following to let you quickly move to another location, such as a bookmark. To activate buttons such as these, you can either double-click them or move to them and press ALT+SHIFT+F9.

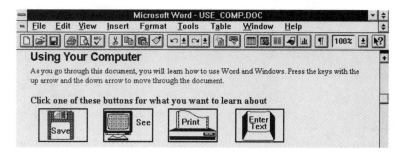

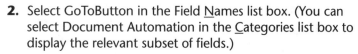

To add buttons like the ones shown above, follow these steps:

Tech Tip: The GoToButton field does not automatically display a button. Instead, you must copy a button style graphic to the field code while creating it (step 4), or format the text which displays as a result of this field as a button.

1. Choose Fi**e**ld from the **I**nsert menu.

2. Select GoToButton in the Field **N**ames list box. (You can select Document Automation in the **C**ategories list box to display the relevant subset of fields.)

3. Type the name of the bookmark to move to at the end of the entry in the **F**ield Codes text box followed by a comma. You can also select the bookmark by clicking the **O**ptions button, selecting the bookmark's name in the Bookmark **N**ame list box, clicking **A**dd to Field, and then choosing OK.

4. Type the text to display on the button itself at the end of the entry in the Field **C**odes text box.

If you want to display a .BMP graphic on the button instead of text, you can press CTRL+INS at this point to paste it from the Clipboard. You need to have copied it to the Clipboard before starting this process. Alternatively, you can use the IncludePicture field to add a picture.

5. Click OK.

To move to the bookmark, either double-click the newly added button or select the button and press ALT+SHIFT+F9.

Can I prevent Word from hyphenating part of my document?

You can stop Word from hyphenating specific paragraphs. To do so:

1. Select the text in which you do not want hyphenation.

2. Choose <u>P</u>aragraph from the F<u>o</u>rmat menu.

3. Click the Text <u>F</u>low Tab.

4. Select the <u>D</u>on't Hyphenate check box, then click OK.

This turns off hyphenation for the entire paragraph(s). When you turn the hyphenation feature on, Word simply skips over these paragraphs and doesn't attempt to hyphenate them.

Tech Tip: By default, hyphenation is turned off in Word documents. You can turn it on using the steps given for the next question.

How can I make sure hyphenation is always turned on in my documents?

To ensure that Word automatically and properly performs hyphenation in your document, you not only must turn it on but make sure that no paragraphs are locked against it.

To turn hyphenation on:

1. Choose <u>H</u>yphenation from the <u>T</u>ools menu.

2. Select the <u>A</u>utomatically Hyphenate Document option, and then click OK.

To ensure that no paragraphs are locked against hyphenation:

1. Choose Select A<u>l</u>l from the sdit menu.

2. Choose <u>P</u>aragraph from the F<u>o</u>rmat menu.

3. Click the Text <u>F</u>low tab.

4. Clear the <u>D</u>on't Hyphenate check box, then click OK.

You only need to check the paragraph setting if Word is not hyphenating correctly. If you find that Word hasn't hyphenated several paragraphs, you may also want to check that the style they use has the hyphenation option enabled.

How can I create dropped capitals in my documents?

In Word 6.0, you can create a dropped capital right from the menu. Figure 6-6 shows a dropped capital produced using this feature.

To create a dropped capital:

1. Place your insertion point in the paragraph whose first character you want to format as a dropped capital letter.

2. Choose <u>D</u>rop Cap from the F<u>o</u>rmat menu.

3. Select <u>D</u>ropped or In <u>M</u>argin to determine how the text wraps around the dropped capital.

4. Select a font in the <u>F</u>ont drop-down list box.

5. Specify the size of the dropped capital by entering the number of lines (up to 10) it should use in the <u>L</u>ines to Drop drop-down list box.

6. Set the amount of space you want to appear between the dropped capital and the text by entering a measurement in inches in the Distance from Te<u>x</u>t text box.

7. Click OK to create a dropped capital for the current paragraph.

Tech Tip: To create a dropped graphic, simply insert it at the beginning of the paragraph before you choose <u>D</u>rop Cap from the F<u>o</u>rmat menu. Word resizes the graphic automatically. You can also drop more than one character, as shown in Figure 6-5, by selecting them before you choose <u>D</u>rop Cap from the F<u>o</u>rmat menu.

FIGURE 6-6   Dropped capitals in a document

How do I sort text by words other than the first word in a paragraph?

A *delimiter* is a character that Word uses to determine the units of text during sorting. When you designate a space as the delimiter, Word recognizes each word as a single unit. You can then use Word's sorting options to reorder by the individual words.

To sort according to a word, follow these steps:

1. Select the text you wish to sort. If no text is selected, Word automatically selects all of it.

2. Choose Sort Text from the Table menu.

3. Select Options.

4. Select the Other option button, then press SPACEBAR in the text box to enter a space. This defines the delimiter as a space.

5. Select OK.

6. Select the word you want to sort by in the Sort By drop-down list box, such as Word 2.

7. Select any other desired sorting options.

8. Click OK to sort the text.

How do I calculate formulas?

In Word for Windows 2.0, you could highlight an equation and tell Word to calculate it. You could then move to another location in your document and paste the result of the equation from the Clipboard. For example, if you selected 1+ 2 and then chose Calculate from the Tools menu, Word 2.0 computed the result and stored it on the Clipboard. If you moved to another location and chose Paste from the Edit menu, the number 3 appeared in your document.

Although, this calculation feature no longer appears on the default menus in Word 6.0, it is still available. To add the Calculate command to your Tools menu:

1. Choose Customize from the Tools menu.

2. Click the Menus tab.

3. Select All Commands in the Categories drop-down list box.

4. Select ToolsCalculate in the Commands list box.

5. Select &Tools in the Change What Menu drop-down list box.

6. Click the Add button, then choose Close.

7. Open the Tools menu to see the new Calculate command.

If you want Word to display the results of a formula at a specific location in your document, place the formula in an field. To create such a field:

1. Move the insertion point to the location at which you want Word to display the formula's result.

2. Press CTRL+F9 to create a field.

3. Type = followed by the formula to evaluate.

4. Press ALT+F9 to display the result of the equation.

Tech Tip: For more detailed information about using fields and adding formulas to them, see Chapter 16, "Fields and Macros."

Can I fax a document directly from Word?

You can fax any document from Word as long as you have a Windows fax program and a fax modem installed on your computer.

Tech Terror: Faxing from Word for Windows only works if the fax program is a genuine Windows application, not a DOS application running under Windows.

To fax a document using an installed Windows fax program and a fax modem:

1. Choose Print from the File menu.

2. Click Printer.

3. Select your fax driver in the Printers list box.

4. Click Set as Default Printer.

5. Click Close to return to the Print dialog box.

6. Click OK to fax your document.

The steps from this point on vary depending on your fax program. Consult your fax software's documentation for instructions about how to set up the phone call and send the document.

Customization, Styles, and Templates

7

Customization features let you modify Word to match your individual work style and projects. You access most of Word's customization features by choosing either Customize or Options from the Tools menu. Customize allows you to change your toolbars, menus, and keyboard assignments to suit your needs. Options offers a wide range of choices with which you determine how you want to view, edit, and print your documents. In fact, there are so many items you can control in the Options dialog box that it contains 12 different tabs!

You can also customize your documents by using and modifying the templates that come with Word. *Templates* are special files that serve as models when you create documents. They contain styles, default formats, AutoText entries, macros, toolbars, menus, and keyboard assignments. Your selection of the template to use as the basis for your document determines exactly which of these items are available. With their built-in features, templates not only ensure a consistent appearance among similar documents, but make it easier to create them.

FRUSTRATION BUSTERS!

When you choose <u>O</u>ptions from the <u>T</u>ools menu, Word displays a dialog box that uses 12 tabs to organize all of its settings. You can switch to another tab by clicking it or by typing the first letter of its name. The following table lists the different tabs and describes the types of settings available on each one.

Tabs	Customization Settings
AutoFormat	Determine how and what AutoFormat changes when you use it to format a document
Compatibility	Specify how Word converts data files created in other applications into Word documents
Edit	Selectively enable Word's editing features
File Locations	Specify the paths where Word looks for various types of files
General	Determine certain overall options, such as whether background repagination and help for WordPerfect users are enabled
Grammar	Indicate the desired type and style of grammar for which Word checks your documents
Print	Designate how Word prints your documents and what it prints with them
Revisions	Determine the marks and colors Word uses to indicate different types of revisions
Save	Set how, with what, and how often Word saves your documents
Spelling	Specify what Word does and doesn't check for spelling and which custom dictionaries it uses
User Info	Store the user information used by other Word features
View	Determine which window elements display on the screen and what items appear in your documents

How can I use the status bar?

The status bar appears at the very bottom of the application window. It not only displays a lot of useful information about your document but also provides shortcuts to some common tasks. By default, the status bar displays the current page number; the section number; the total number of pages; the position of the insertion point in inches, lines, and columns; and the current time. It also displays the status of some key features, such as WordPerfect Help and revisions.

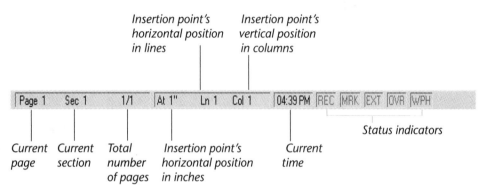

Insertion point's horizontal position in lines

Insertion point's vertical position in columns

Page 1   Sec 1   1/1   At 1"   Ln 1   Col 1   04:39 PM   REC   MRK   EXT   OVR   WPH

Status indicators

Current page   *Current section*   *Total number of pages*   *Insertion point's horizontal position in inches*   *Current time*

You can double-click the various items in the status bar to access certain Word commands and features, as listed in the following table:

Item to Double-Click	Effect
Position statistics	Opens the Go To dialog box
REC	Opens the Record Macro dialog box, or toggles between recording and not recording a macro
MRK	Opens the Revisions dialog box
EXT	Turns extend mode, for selecting text, on and off
OVR	Toggles between insert and overtype mode
WPH	Turns WordPerfect Help on or off
WPN	Turns the WordPerfect Navigation keys on and off

Can I change the directory in which Word saves my files?

To change the default location of saved documents:

1. Choose Options from the Tools menu.
2. Click the File Locations tab.
3. Select Documents in the File Types list box
4. Click Modify.
5. Use the Directories and Drives list boxes to specify a different path, or type it in the Location of Files text box.
6. Click OK.
7. Click Close to store the new settings.

Word now saves all of your documents in the new default directory. Of course, you can still enter a different path when saving an individual document to store it in a different location.

When I highlight text and press DEL, Word prompts me to confirm the deletion. Is there a way to get rid of this prompt?

You can turn this prompt off altogether. In fact, the only reason it appears is that WordPerfect Help and/or the Word Perfect Navigation Keys are turned on, which cause Word to act like WordPerfect.

To turn off this feature:

1. Choose Options from the Tools menu.
2. Click the General tab.
3. Clear the Help for WordPerfect Users check box.
4. Clear the Navigation Keys for Word Perfect Users, then click OK.

You can also turn this feature off by using the WordPerfect Help itself:

1. Choose WordPerfect Help from the Help menu.
2. Click Options.

3. Clear the Help For <u>W</u>ordPerfect Users and <u>N</u>avigation Keys for Word Perfect Users check boxes.

4. Click OK then click <u>C</u>lose.

My toolbar buttons are very small. Can I make them larger?

You can enlarge your toolbar buttons so they look like the ones shown here, which is particularly helpful if you are using an SVGA video display:

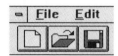

To change the size of the toolbar buttons:

1. Choose <u>T</u>oolbars from the <u>V</u>iew menu.

2. Select the <u>L</u>arge Buttons check box and then click OK.

Tech Tip: After you increase the size of the buttons, you may need to rearrange your toolbars so that all of the buttons fit on the screen.

Can I change the default font?

You can select the font you want Word to use automatically in every new document. This font is specified by the Normal style in your Normal template.

To select a different default font:

1. Choose <u>F</u>ont from the F<u>o</u>rmat menu.

2. Use the <u>F</u>ont, F<u>o</u>nt Style, and <u>S</u>ize list boxes to indicate the font you want to use as the default.

3. Click the <u>D</u>efault button.

4. When Word asks if you want to make the change permanent, click <u>Y</u>es.

Word saves the new font specification in the Normal template file. By default, Word bases all new documents on this template. However, if you select another template when you create a document, it uses the default font specified by that template instead.

Tech Tip: When you save a new default font, it becomes part of the template that was used to create the current document (only if you check the Add to Template option when modifying the style). For example, if you change the default when you are working in a document based on the Letter template, then only the documents created with this particular template automatically use the newly selected font. Documents created with other templates, including NORMAL.DOT, won't reflect the changed setting. To reset the default font for only the text in the current document, choose Style from the Format menu and select a different font for the Normal style.

Can I remove the toolbars and menu bar to see more of my document without changing the Zoom percentage?

You can hide all of the elements of the Word application and document windows by choosing Full Screen from the View menu. The current document expands to fill the entire screen as shown in Figure 7-1. To restore the hidden elements, just press ESC, press ALT V, U, or click the Full Screen toolbar button that appears on your screen.

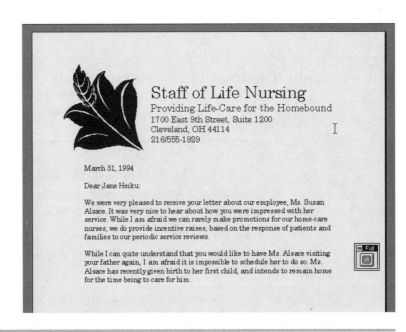

FIGURE 7-1   You can display a document in full screen view

Is there any way to remove some but not all screen elements to display more of my document?

You can selectively remove the status bar and each of the scroll bars to devote more space to your document. To do so:

1. Choose <u>O</u>ptions from the <u>T</u>ools.

2. Click the View tab.

3. Clear one or more of the Status <u>B</u>ar, Hori<u>z</u>ontal Scroll Bar, and <u>V</u>ertical Scroll Bar check boxes.

4. Click OK.

If you remove the status and scroll bars, your Word window will look like the one shown in Figure 7-2.

Tech Tip: To remove a toolbar from the window, right-click it to display the shortcut menu. Then select the toolbar's name. If the name doesn't appear in the shortcut menu, select More Toolbars to open the Toolbars dialog box then clear its check box in the <u>T</u>oolbars list box and select OK.

FIGURE 7-2   A Word window without the status and scroll bars

Is there any way to avoid losing all of my work if my computer crashes?

You can tell Word to automatically save files at a specific interval while you work. However, these files, which have a .ASD extension, are only temporary—Word deletes them when you save or close the associated documents. .ASD files are designed to help you recover data if your system stops functioning for whatever reason without giving you time to save your documents. In the event of a system crash, these files are invaluable. When you restart Word, it automatically searches for any .ASD files and updates your documents with their contents, thereby restoring the work you would have otherwise lost. However, because .ASD files are not permanent, this automatic feature is not a substitute for regularly saving your files.

To have Word automatically save documents as you work:

1. Choose Options from the Tools menu.

2. Click the Save tab.

3. Select the Automatic Save check box.

4. Enter a value between 1 and 120 in the Minutes text box to specify the interval between saves. This number equals the maximum amount of work that you could lose in the event of a system crash.

Tech Tip: For additional information about .ASD files, see Chapter 2, "Setup."

5. Click OK.

Can I change the colors in the Word window?

You change the colors in the Word window by modifying those used by all Windows applications in the Windows' Control Panel. You can set the colors of most window elements, including buttons, title bars, borders, the background, scroll bars, commands, buttons, and highlighted text. In fact, the only visual elements you can't choose a color for are the insertion point and the mouse pointer. The insertion point's color depends on the background colors you select; your mouse pointer's color is set by your mouse driver.

To change the colors in the Word window:

1. Open the Control Panel by double-clicking its program item in Windows' Main program group.

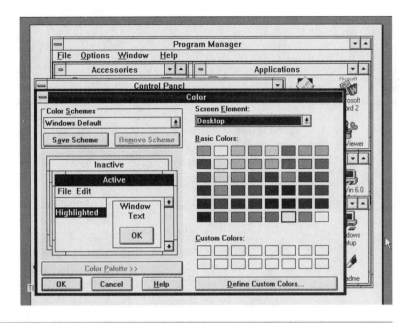

FIGURE 7-3   You can create a custom color scheme

Tech Tip: To display white text on a blue background, similar to WordPerfect, select Options from the Tools menu, then click the Blue Background, White Text option on the General Tab.

2. Double-click the Color icon, or choose Color from the Settings menu.

3. Preview the existing Windows' color schemes by selecting each one, in turn, in the Color Schemes drop-down list box. If one appeals to you, skip directly to step 9.

4. If you want to create a new, custom color scheme, click Color Palette to expand the Color dialog box, as shown in Figure 7-3.

5. Select an element whose color you want to change in the Screen Element drop-down list box. Alternatively, you can simply click the element in the sample window on the left-hand side.

6. Click one of the colors shown in the Basic Colors section.

7. Repeat steps 5 and 6 for each element you want to modify.

8. Save the new color scheme by clicking Save Scheme, typing a name for it, and then clicking OK.

9. After selecting or constructing a color scheme, click OK.

10. Choose E**x**it from the **S**ettings menu.

Can I change how Word displays my name and initials?

Word references the name you entered during the installation in document summaries, annotations, the return address on envelopes, and when marking revisions.
To change this user information:

1. Choose **O**ptions from the **T**ools menu.

2. Click the User Info tab.

3. Enter your name as you wish it to appear in the **N**ame text box, your initials in the **I**nitials text box, and your mailing address in the **M**ailing Address text box.

4. Click OK.

Can I tell Word to use centimeters instead of inches?

You can specify which unit of measure Word uses by following these steps:

1. Choose **O**ptions from the **T**ools menu.

2. Click the General tab.

3. Select either Inches, Centimeters, Points, or Picas in the **M**easurement Units drop-down list box.

4. Click OK to implement the change.

All of your measurements now appear using the new measurement unit, including the positions displayed in the status bar; on the ruler; and the entries for margins, tabs, and frame positions in dialog boxes. For example, your ruler looks like this:

L · I · 1 · I · 2 · I · 3 · I · 4 · I · 5 · I · 6 · I · 7 · I · 8 · I · 9 · I · 10 · I · 11 · I · 12 · I · 13 · I · 14 · I · 15

Can I stop Word from beeping when errors occur?

You can turn off the feature that causes Word to beep when an error occurs. To do so:

1. Choose <u>O</u>ptions from the <u>T</u>ools menu.

2. Click the General tab.

3. Clear the Beep on Error <u>A</u>ctions check box.

4. Click OK to return to your document

I don't see the "progress meter" in the status bar when I save a document, but it appears on my coworkers' systems. How can I display it on my computer?

Word does not have a specific option that turns this feature on or off. In your case, it probably doesn't appear because of the color scheme you've chosen. If your buttons are set to display in white, this indicator may not appear.

To change the color so that you can see this feature:

1. Double-click the Control Panel's program item in Windows' Main program group.

2. Double-click the Color icon, or choose <u>C</u>olor from the <u>S</u>ettings menu.

3. Click Color <u>P</u>alette.

4. Select Button Face in the Screen <u>E</u>lement drop-down list box.

5. Select a color other than white in the <u>B</u>asic Color section.

6. Click OK and then choose E<u>x</u>it from the <u>S</u>ettings menu to close the Control Panel.

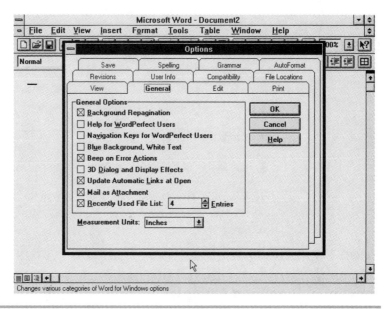

FIGURE 7-4   A dialog box and the status bar without 3D

Word suddenly lost its three-dimensional appearance. What did I do?

If your dialog boxes look like the one shown in Figure 7-4, you simply changed one of your General option settings.
   To restore the 3D effect in the status bar and dialog boxes:

1. Choose Options from the Tools menu.
2. Click the General tab.
3. Select the 3D Dialog and Display Effects check box.
4. Click OK.

Can I change the shortcut keys that execute macros or commands in Word 6.0?

Word lets you change the assignment of any of your shortcut keys. For example, you can designate a different key combination to run a macro or to apply a specific format. Word's key assignments are completely flexible; you can change these designations at any time.

Word stores these key assignments in templates. If you only want the shortcuts to be available in a particular type of document, you can assign them in the appropriate template. If you want key assignments to be consistent throughout your documents, you can save them in the Normal template.

To change a key assignment in Word:

1. Choose Customize from Tools menu.

2. Click the Keyboard tab.

3. Select a category of commands or Word features in the Categories list box. The category you select determines the commands or items that appear in the right-hand list box.

4. Select the command or other item in the second list box to which you want to assign a key or whose shortcut you want to change.

5. To assign a new key combination or modify an existing one, move the insertion point to the Press New Shortcut Key text box. Press the actual key combination you want to assign and then click Assign. For example, to assign CTRL+SHIFT+X to a command, press CTRL+SHIFT+X.

6. To remove a key assignment from the command or item, select the key assignment in the Current Keys list box and click Remove.

7. Select the template in which you want to save the modified key assignment in the Save Changes In drop-down list box. You can save the changes in any of the templates used by the current document, which, in most cases, includes the global Normal template.

8. Click Close when you are finished editing the key assignments.

There are four files listed at the bottom of the File menu. Why?

These files, like the ones shown below, are the four that you have most recently used. To retrieve one of these files, you simply choose it, just as you would choose any other command from the File menu. This feature makes it easy to retrieve files you work with often.

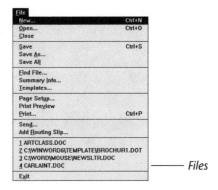

Files

Word 6.0 offers you an easy way to either remove this list entirely or change how many filenames are displayed. To change these settings:

1. Choose Options from the Tools menu.

2. Click the General tab.

3. Select or clear the Recently Used File List check box to turn this feature on or off.

4. Enter the number of files you want displayed, if any, in the Entries text box. You can display up to nine filenames on the menu.

5. Click OK.

6. Open the File menu to see the effect of your changes.

Is there a shortcut for editing menus?

Word offers a shortcut for removing items from your menus. To quickly remove a menu command:

1. Press ALT+CTRL+HYPHEN. Your mouse pointer becomes a black horizontal bar.

2. Choose the menu option you want to remove.

If the current document was created using the Normal template, Word saves the change to the menu when you save the file or exit Word. Otherwise, it prompts you to confirm that you want to save the menu modifications to the current template.

Are there any shortcuts for working with the toolbars?

You can use the toolbars' shortcut menu to simplify and expedite your work with them. Just right-click anywhere on a toolbar to open a shortcut menu. Select the toolbar you want to display, or choose Customize to modify your toolbar, toolbar buttons, menus, and key assignments.

 Is there an easy way to pick which toolbars I want to display?

Word provides a shortcut for hiding or showing toolbars. Simply position your pointer over any toolbar and click the right mouse button. Word displays a shortcut menu such as this one:

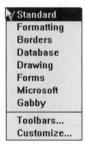

Choose the name of the toolbar you want to display from the shortcut menu. Check marks indicate the toolbars that already appear on the screen; you can click any name to hide the associated toolbar. An alternative way to select toolbars is to choose Toolbars from the View menu.

 My toolbar list boxes are too narrow to display long font and style names. What can I do?

Follow these steps to modify the width of these boxes so they can accommodate the longer names:

1. Choose Customize from the Tools menu.
2. Click the Toolbars tab.

3. Click the list box you want to modify; a dotted line appears around it.

4. Drag the right edge of the list box until the dotted line reflects the size you want the list box to be. When you release the mouse button, Word resizes the list box accordingly, as shown here:

 Tech Terror: This method may not work if you are running Windows for Workgroups.

5. Click Close.

I don't like the new toolbar. Can I use the old Word 2.0 toolbar?

If you prefer the Word 2.0 toolbar rather than the Word 6.0 ones, you can display this toolbar instead. To do so:

1. Choose Toolbars from the View menu.

2. Select the Word for Windows 2.0 check box in the Toolbars list box.

3. Click OK.

 **Tech Tip:** You can remove the Word 6.0 toolbars from the window by right-clicking them, then selecting their name from the shortcut menu.

Can I rearrange the toolbars on my screen ?

You can easily change the position of any or all of your toolbars. Word can display toolbars along each of the four edges of the application window as well as float them in the middle of it, as shown in Figure 7-5.

To move a toolbar, simply click any empty space above, below, or between the buttons, and then drag the toolbar to the desired location. (If you click a button by mistake, you will activate the button instead.) As you move the toolbar through

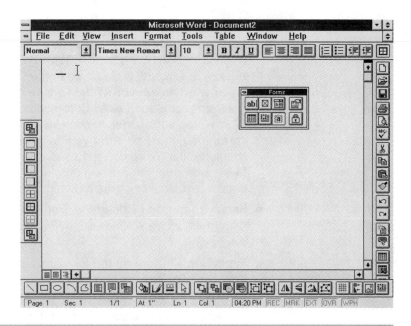

FIGURE 7-5   You can display toolbars on all four sides and floating in the Word window

the middle of the window, it appears in the floating position. When you move it close to one of the edges, it *snaps* to the edge. Release the mouse button when the toolbar appears in the desired location.

Tech Tip: You can quickly hide a floating toolbar by clicking the Close box in its upper-left corner.

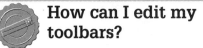

How can I edit my toolbars?

Editing toolbars is easy in Word 6.0. To do so:

1. Display the toolbar you want to edit.

2. Choose <u>C</u>ustomize from the <u>T</u>ools menu.

3. Click the <u>T</u>oolbars tab.

4. Add, remove, or rearrange the toolbar buttons.

- Add a button by selecting a category of actions in the Categories list box, then dragging a button from the Buttons section to the toolbar. When you select the button, its function is displayed in the Description area. If you select an item other than a type of action in the Categories box, such as All Commands, Fonts, or Macros, the Button area becomes a list box with a corresponding name. After you drag the list box item to the toolbar, Word designates an appropriate button face by choosing an existing one, or allowing you to enter a text label or create a picture of your own.

- Remove a button by dragging it off the toolbar to the document; when you release the mouse, the button disappears.

- Reposition a button on the toolbar by dragging it to a new position. You can also move a button from one toolbar to another using this technique.

5. Click Close to return to your document with the modified toolbars displayed.

Can I edit the face of a toolbar button that I already created?

To edit the face of a button that you previously created:

1. Choose Toolbars from the View menu.

2. Click Customize.

Tech Tip: You can also perform steps 1 and 2 by pointing to a toolbar, clicking the right mouse button to display the shortcut menu, and choosing Customize.

3. Right-click the toolbar button you want to modify to display a shortcut menu. Table 7-1 lists the commands you can choose and their functions.

Command	Action
Copy Button Image	Copies the image on the current button to the Clipboard
Paste Button Image	Pastes the image from the Clipboard to the button
Reset Button Image	Restores the original button image
Choose Button Image	Displays the custom button images that come with Word
Edit Button Image	Displays the Button Editor dialog box in which you can modify the button image

TABLE 7-1   You can use the shortcut menu commands to edit a button face

Can I use clip art files to create custom toolbar buttons?

You can use bitmap (.BMP) files, such as images created in Paintbrush, as custom button faces. After you create or select the file, you simply copy the image to the Clipboard and then paste it to the button by performing these steps:

1. Open the image in the Windows Paintbrush accessory.
2. Select the image and then choose <u>C</u>opy or Cu<u>t</u> from the Paintbrush <u>E</u>dit menu.
3. Switch to Word.
4. Choose <u>T</u>oolbars from the <u>V</u>iew menu.
5. If necessary, select the check box for the toolbar that contains the button you want to edit in the <u>T</u>oolbars list box.
6. Click <u>C</u>ustomize.
7. Right-click the button you want to modify.
8. Choose Paste Button Image from the shortcut menu to replace the existing button face with the .BMP image on the Clipboard.
9. Click Close to return to your document.

All of my toolbars and menus just disappeared. How do I get them back?

You've probably switched to full screen view accidentally. Full screen view displays your document using the entire screen; it hides the toolbars, menu bar, and other Word window elements, such as the status bar, scroll bars, and title bar, as shown in Figure 7-1. There are three methods of returning to your previous view:

- Click the Full Screen button on the small floating toolbar that appears, which is usually located in the lower-right corner.

- Press ESC.

- Press ALT+V to open the <u>V</u>iew menu and then choose F<u>u</u>ll Screen. Even though you can't see the menu bar, the pull-down menus are still available.

Tech Tip: If Word displays a dialog box for a repeat value when you press ESC, WordPerfect Help is turned on. In this case, use one of the other two methods to leave full screen view.

What is the difference between paragraph and character styles?

Styles consist of a set of formatting features. When you apply a style to text, all of the formatting associated with that style is applied to that text. You can easily reformat text by changing its style.

Paragraph and character styles differ in terms of how much text they affect and the types of formatting they apply.

- *Paragraph styles* affect entire paragraphs, not just portions of text. You use paragraph styles to apply such formatting as line spacing, alignment, indents, widow and orphan control, frames, borders and shading, and bullets and numbering. You can also apply character formatting, such as font size and boldfacing, with paragraph styles. For example, this paragraph's style creates a bulleted list with a particular indentation.

■ *Character styles* affect individual characters or selected text and apply formatting such as small caps, font size, and italics. For example, you might use a character style called Defined to italicize terms when you first mention them in an article. If you then wanted to change the formatting of these terms, you could simply edit the Defined style instead of each term individually. When you edit a style, all the text to which it's applied appears with the new formatting.

I like the way I formatted the text in one of my documents. Can I save the formatting as a style?

You can create a paragraph style by extracting the formatting applied to your text. In this way, you avoid having to recreate the formatting from scratch every time you want to use it.

Tech Tip: You only create paragraph styles from formatted text, not character styles.

To create a paragraph style based on existing text:

1. Display the Formatting toolbar, if necessary, by right-clicking any toolbar and choosing Formatting from the shortcut menu.

2. Select the paragraph whose formatting you want to use as the basis for the style.

3. Click the Style list box on the Formatting toolbar, or press ALT+SHIFT+S.

4. Type a name for the new style in the box, then press ENTER.

Word creates the new style based on the formatting of the selected paragraph. The style's character formatting is determined by the first character in the paragraph. If you only select a portion of text in the paragraph, the first character of the selected text sets the character formatting for the style.

There are a lot of styles in the Style dialog box that I don't recognize. What are they and where did they come from?

You have probably selected All Styles in the Lists drop-down list box. In this case, Word displays all of the styles available in the document. In addition to the styles actually used and any that you created, this list may display a number of others that you've never noticed before.

Word has many *system styles* that it uses to format different types of text in your document. For example, Word applies styles when you use the Bullets & Numbering feature to create numbered or bulleted lists, when you format headers and footers, and when you create envelopes and mailing labels. Word applies these styles automatically when you choose these features. You can modify a system style just as you would any other in Word.

Is there an easy way to tell which styles are applied to different paragraphs?

You can create a *style area* to the left of your document to display the associated style names. To create a style area:

1. Choose Options from the Tools menu.
2. Click the View tab.
3. Enter a measurement in the Style Area Width text box.
4. Click OK to return to your document.

Your document now displays the style applied to each paragraph along the left edge of the document, as shown in Figure 7-6. You can enlarge or reduce the size of the style area by changing the measurement in the Style Area Width text box.

Tech Tip: You can also resize the style area by dragging the dividing line that separates the style area from the document.

If your style names are too long to display alongside your document, you can assign style *aliases* that appear instead in both the style area and the Style list box on the Formatting toolbar. To create an alias for an existing style:

1. Choose Style from the Format menu.

2. Select the style to which you want to apply an alias in the Styles list box.

3. Click Modify.

4. At the end of the style's name in the Name text box, type a comma then the alias you want to use.

5. Click OK then click Close.

The alias you entered after the comma in the Name text box now appears in the style area to the left of the document and in the Style list box on the toolbar.

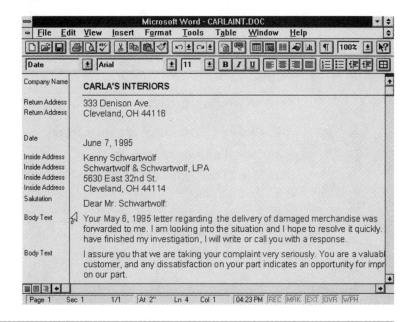

FIGURE 7-6   You can display the paragraph styles used in your document

When I choose <u>N</u>ew from the <u>F</u>ile menu, I see a <u>T</u>emplate list box with just one entry. What are templates and why do I have only the one called Normal?

You probably have only the Normal template because you performed a Minimal installation. Alternatively, you may have done a Custom installation but elected not to install the templates. It is also possible that the path to your template directory is set incorrectly.

Templates are a special type of document used to create other documents. Templates contain settings for menus, toolbars, keyboard assignments, AutoText entries, macros, styles, graphics, and text. When you create a document using a specific template, it uses the entries and settings of the template as its default settings.

Word comes with many templates for creating a variety of documents, from papers to press releases. In your case, you can add these templates to your system by double-clicking the Word Setup icon and performing a Maintenance installation.

How do I change the default directory in which Word stores and looks for templates?

To set the template default directory:

1. Choose <u>O</u>ptions from the <u>T</u>ools menu.
2. Click the File Locations tab.
3. Select User Templates in the <u>F</u>ile Types list box.
4. Click <u>M</u>odify.
5. Select the directory you want instead in the <u>D</u>irectories list box or enter it in the <u>L</u>ocation of Files text box.
6. Click OK then click Close.

I add my letterhead to nearly every document I create. Is there a shortcut I can use to make this easy?

You can create a template to automatically display your letterhead in any document you create with it.

To create a personalized letterhead template:

1. Choose <u>N</u>ew from the <u>F</u>ile menu.
2. Select the T<u>e</u>mplate option button in the New section of the dialog box.
3. Create your letterhead as usual and make any other formatting changes that you'd like to include in all the documents you create with the new template.
4. Choose <u>S</u>ave from the <u>F</u>ile menu.
5. Enter a name for the template in the File <u>N</u>ame text box and click OK.

By default, Word saves the template with a .DOT extension in the WINWORD\TEMPLATE subdirectory.

To create a document using the new letterhead template:

1. Choose <u>N</u>ew from the <u>F</u>ile menu.
2. Select the letterhead template in the <u>T</u>emplate list box and click OK.

Be certain that <u>D</u>ocument remains selected in the New box. Your letterhead automatically appears in the new document.

Why does Word tell me that it cannot open the existing NORMAL.DOT file?

The NORMAL.DOT template is the file in which Word stores many of the settings and customization features that you use with all of your documents. Word displays this error message when you have either insufficient resources or a corrupt Normal template file.

To check your system resources:

1. Switch to the Program Manger.

2. Choose <u>A</u>bout Program Manager from the <u>H</u>elp menu.

Check your system resources percentage; if it is 50% or less, this may well be your problem.

3. Click OK.

If low system resources are the cause of this error, try closing all of your applications, restarting Windows, and opening Word again.

If insufficient resources are not the cause, your NORMAL.DOT file may be corrupted. You can test this by renaming your current NORMAL.DOT file, then restarting Word. If Word can't locate an existing NORMAL.DOT file, it automatically creates a new one that restores the original default settings.

To create a new NORMAL.DOT file:

1. Start the File Manager by double-clicking its program item in the Main program group.

2. Open the WINWORD\TEMPLATE subdirectory. (If Word for Windows 6.0 is installed in a directory other than WINWORD, substitute its path instead.)

3. Select the NORMAL.DOT file. (Be careful not to double-click it; doing so will start Word.)

4. Choose Re<u>n</u>ame from the <u>F</u>ile menu.

5. Type a new filename for this file in the <u>T</u>o text box, such as **NORMAL.OLD**.

6. Click OK to rename the file.

7. Exit the File Manager and restart Word. If the error message doesn't appear, your NORMAL.DOT file was damaged.

What are global templates and how do I use them?

Global templates are available to all documents. For example, the Normal template is a global template. You can also make other templates global for the current session of Word so that you can access their macros, toolbars, and AutoText entries from any open documents. However, the templates revert to their non-global state when you exit Word; you must make them global again each time you restart Word.

To make a template global:

1. Choose Templates from the File menu.

2. If necessary, add the template to the Global Templates and Add-ins list box by clicking Add, selecting the template in the File Name list box, and then clicking OK.

3. Select the check box for the template in the Global Templates and Add-ins list box.

4. Click OK.

Can I copy data between templates?

You can use Word's Organizer to copy styles, AutoText entries (formerly called glossary entries in Word 2.0), macros, and toolbars from one template to another. From a document, there are three ways to display the Organizer:

- Choose Templates from the File menu and then click Organizer.

- Choose Macro from the Tools menu and then click Organizer.

- Choose Style from the Format menu and then click Organizer.

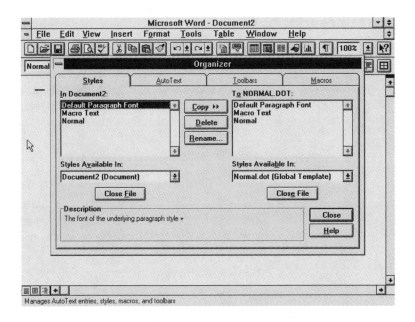

=== Organizer dialog box ===

Microsoft Word - Document2

File   Edit   View   Insert   Format   Tools   Table   Window   Help

100%

Normal

Organizer

Styles | AutoText | Toolbars | Macros

In Document2:

Default Paragraph Font
Macro Text
Normal

Copy ▸▸
Delete
Rename...

To NORMAL.DOT:

Default Paragraph Font
Macro Text
Normal

Styles Available In:

Document2 (Document)

Close File

Styles Available In:

Normal.dot (Global Template)

Close File

Description

The font of the underlying paragraph style +

Close
Help

Manages AutoText entries, styles, macros, and toolbars

FIGURE 7-7   You can use the Organizer to manage and copy template entries

Clicking the Organizer button opens a dialog box like the one shown in Figure 7-7. The tab that appears in front depends on which command you used to access the Organizer. You can then click any tab to copy, delete, and rename template entries.

For example, you can copy a macro from one template to another by following these steps:

1. Click the Macros tab.

2. The Organizer dialog box features two list boxes that display the macros in the current and the global templates. If only one of these displayed templates will be involved in the copy, click the Close File button under its text box to remove its list of macros. If the two templates are the ones you want to use, skip to step 4.

3. Click the Open File button under the empty list box and open the template from or to which you want to copy the macros. At this point, one list box should include the macros you want to copy, and the other should show the macros that already exist in the template to which you want to add the macro.

Tech Tip: You can also rename and delete macros by using the Organizer.

4. Highlight the macro you want to copy and click <u>C</u>opy. Repeat this step until you have copied all of the macros you want.

5. Click Close.

Word 6.0 doesn't ask me to confirm before it saves changes to my Normal template. Can I tell it to prompt me first?

By default, Word 6.0 saves changes to the Normal template without asking for confirmation. If you are accustomed to Word 2.0, which included such a prompt, you may not realize that Word 6.0 has been saving these modifications to your Normal template all along.

You can change this setting, however, so that Word prompts you for confirmation before it saves such changes in the Normal template. To do so:

1. Choose <u>O</u>ptions from the <u>T</u>ools menu.

2. Click the Save tab.

3. Select the Pr<u>o</u>mpt to Save Normal.dot check box.

4. Click OK.

Can I preview the styles in different templates without printing them?

Tech Tip: In many cases, you can also select <u>E</u>xample in the Preview section to see a sample document based on

The Style Gallery lets you see the styles in each template on the screen. To use the Style Gallery:

1. Choose Style <u>G</u>allery from the F<u>o</u>rmat menu.

2. Select the template that contains the styles you want to see in the <u>T</u>emplate list box.

3. Select the <u>S</u>tyle Samples option button in the Preview section.

The <u>P</u>review of list box displays the name of each style in the template, formatted according to that particular style's specifications, as shown in Figure 7-8.

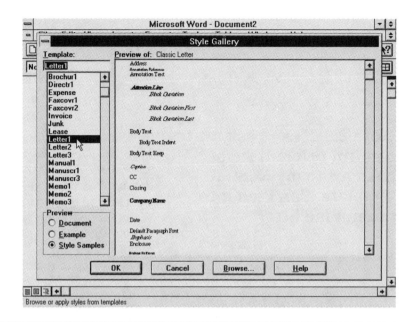

FIGURE 7-8   The Style Gallery lets you preview the styles in different templates

Can I use macros and AutoText entries from another template in my current document?

Yes, you can simply attach another template to the current document to use its macros and AutoText entries. When you attach a template, only the features become available; no text is added to your document. In addition, you can specify whether Word retains the styles in the current document or updates them to match those in the template you attach.

To attach a template:

1. Choose Templates from the File menu.

2. Click Attach.

3. Select the name of the template you want to attach in the File Name list box, then click OK.

4. Select the Automatically Update Document Styles check box if you want to change the styles in the document to correspond to those in the new template; Word only updates styles if they have the same name.

Tech Tip: You can create several interlocking templates in which all of the styles have the same names. For example, you might have a Draft template and a Final template that contain styles with identical names but different formatting. When you attach the Final template to a document that was originally based on the Draft template and update the styles, all of the formatting would change accordingly.

5. Click OK.

The attached template's macros and AutoText entries are now available in the current document.

Can I see how my document will look formatted with the styles in a particular template before I actually attach it?

Word 6.0 includes a Style Gallery that lets you preview how a different template would format the current document. To use the Style Gallery:

1. Choose Style Gallery from the Format menu.

2. Select a template in the Template list box.

Tech Tip: You can select the Example option button in the Preview section to view the styles applied to a sample document.

3. Select the Document option button in the Preview section to preview how the document would look if you attached the template and applied its styles.

4. Click OK to return to your document.

When I use a wizard, I get the message "Cannot open Document error 1025." How do I run the wizard?

A *wizard* is a special Word feature that leads you through the process of creating certain types of documents and prompts you for appropriate information. If you receive this message when you try to use a wizard, your AUTOEXEC.BAT file doesn't load the SHARE.EXE program properly. Follow these steps to check and modify your AUTOEXEC.BAT file:

1. Choose <u>R</u>un from the <u>F</u>ile menu in the Program Manager.

2. Type **SYSEDIT** in the <u>C</u>ommand Line text box and then click OK.

3. Switch to the window in the System Configuration Editor that contains the AUTOEXEC.BAT file, if necessary.

4. Check that the line loading SHARE.EXE reads as follows:

```
C:\DOS\SHARE.EXE /L:500 /F:5100
```

5. Edit this line, if necessary. Also, remove any parameters such as @LOADHIGH from the beginning of this line to eliminate memory conflict, and make certain that the SHARE line is located at the top of the AUTOEXEC.BAT.

6. Choose <u>S</u>ave from the System Configuration Editor's <u>F</u>ile menu.

7. Close any open applications then exit Windows.

8. Reboot your computer so that the changes take effect.

Can the Calendar Wizard place each date in its own square, like a wall calendar?

The Calendar wizard uses tabs, not a table format, to create a calendar. It therefore has no mechanism for automatically producing a calendar with squares. However, once you produce a calendar with the wizard, you can convert its dates into a table and add borders to create a calendar such as the one shown in Figure 7-9:

To create such a calendar:

1. Choose <u>N</u>ew from the <u>F</u>ile menu.

2. Select Calendar Wizard in the <u>T</u>emplate list box and click OK.

May						
Sun	Mon	Tues	Wed	Thu	Fri	Sat
	1	2	3	4	5	6
7	8	9	10	11	12	13
14	15	16	17	18	19	20
21	22	23	24	25	26	27
28	29	30	31			1995

FIGURE 7-9 A calendar with grid lines

3. Respond to the wizard's prompts to create the calendar.

4. Once the calendar appears, select all of it, including the names of the days and the dates.

5. Choose Convert Text to Table from the Table menu. Word automatically enters the number of tabular columns in the Number of Columns text box and selects the Tabs option button. Sometimes Word enters 8 in the Number of Columns text box because the Calendar Wizard includes a tab before the first date in the weeks. Accept this setting, then delete this extra column after creating the table.

6. Click AutoFormat.

7. Select Grid2 in the Formats list box, clear the First Column check box, and then click OK twice to convert the calendar to a table.

8. Choose Borders and Shading from the Format menu to add the lines between dates.

9. To provide the maximum writing space, select the squares that contain the dates, choose Paragraph from the Format menu, and remove any spaces that appear before the numbers.

Tech Tip: You can add spaces after the numbers to make the rows taller. You can also set the row height by choosing the Cell Height and Width command from the Table menu.

10. If your table has an empty column, place the cursor in the column or highlight the column, choose Delete Cells from the Table menu, select the Delete Entire Column option button, and then click OK.

11. Readjust the column widths, as necessary, so that they are all the same.

File Management

When you stop to think about what you create with Word, your printed documents probably come to mind first. However, all of your documents also exist as files stored on disks. Managing these files is very important to your success with Word. Before you can work with your documents, you need to be able to find, open, move, and convert them, as necessary. These skills can help you avoid the frustration of not being able to locate the right file or discovering that it's no longer working the way it did before.

FRUSTRATION BUSTERS!

Here are some quick and easy steps you can take to prevent file problems in Word:

- Make sure you have enough disk space. If you run out of disk space, Word displays one of several error messages, depending on what you are doing at the time. Word needs enough disk space to store not only the documents you create but the temporary files it uses when you are editing or printing.

- Handle your disks with care and store them in a safe location when you are not using them. Exposure to heat, smoke, and magnetic fields can damage disks.

- Back up your important documents.

- Don't delete your old word processor from your hard disk until you have converted all of the documents you want to use in Word.

When I save files to a network drive, I get the error "Word cannot save or create this file. Make sure the disk is not full or write protected. *path filename*." How do I save my files?

You may see this message when you save the document for the first time. On the other hand, you may be able to save it the first time but get this error when you try to save the document again. This error occurs if Word can't find SHARE.EXE on the network drive where you wish to save the file. Sometimes, even if SHARE.EXE is loaded on you local hard drive, Word cannot save to the network unless it's there as well.

You may also encounter this problem if you're working with Word on a network and SHARE.EXE is not properly loaded. Alternatively, you may see "Cannot open document" or "File is in use by another user" when you try to open the file on a network drive. To avoid these problems, make sure SHARE.EXE is loaded properly on the network drive.

If you encounter these errors and are not using a network, double-check that your AUTOEXEC.BAT includes a statement that loads SHARE.EXE. If so, you may need to increase the parameters that SHARE.EXE uses for file locking capabilities. (The defaults are /L:500 /F:5100.) Remember, after you modify your AUTOEXEC, you must close your applications, exit Windows, and reboot your computer for the changes to take effect.

Why do I see the message "Cannot open *Filename*?"

This message, as well as "Word cannot open the document *filename*," may appear for any of the following reasons:

- The document may be corrupt. If so, open the file in Microsoft Windows Write and then cut and paste the text into a Word for Windows document.

- The document may have been created in a beta version of Word and cannot be opened in a later version. You can try using the method described above for recovering the data.

- The file format is not recognized. You need to open the last application in which you worked with the file and save the data in a different format.

What guidelines does Word use for naming documents?

Word documents can have any valid DOS filename. Valid DOS filenames consist of one to eight characters, followed by a period and an optional extension of one to three characters. By default, Word assigns the .DOC extension to all document files. You can use any character in a filename, except a space or the following: * ? , ; [ ] + = /\ : | > <. You can only use a period to separate the filename from the extension. Although you can use other characters, you are more likely to avoid filename problems if you restrict yourself to letters, numbers, and the underscore character (_).

Tech Tip: To open Word documents that you saved with a file extension other than .DOC, you must either select the appropriate file type in the List Files Of Type drop-down list box or enter the proper extension in the File Name text box. Usually, it is easier to just let Word specify the file extensions for you.

 I'm trying to save a document to another directory, but all the settings are dimmed in the Save As dialog box so I can't change them. What is going on?

The document that you are trying to save is a template, which Word can only save to a specific location. If you want to save the template as a document, you need to open a new document and paste the contents of the template into it. To do so:

1. Click the Show/Hide button on the Standard toolbar to display paragraph marks and other hidden characters.

2. Select the entire template, except the last paragraph mark in the document.

Tech Tip: The last paragraph mark contains the template information. If you copy it, the new file will still be defined as a template.

3. Choose Copy from the Edit menu.

4. Choose New from the File menu.

5. Make sure that the Document option button, not Template, is selected, then click OK to open a new document based on the Normal template.

6. With the insertion point in the new document, choose Paste from the Edit menu.

You can save the new document, which now contains the information from the template, wherever you like. Note, however, that Word didn't copy any of your styles, AutoText entries, macros, or toolbars to the new document.

I opened a document from my floppy drive and now I want to save it to another disk. I keep getting an error message that my disk drive is invalid. What is wrong?

By design, Word for Windows does not allow you to open a file from a floppy drive, insert another disk in that drive, and then save the file to the other floppy. This is a limitation due to the way Word for Windows uses temporary files. When you open a document, Word creates a temporary file in the same location as your document file. When you attempt to save it to a different floppy disk, Word cannot access the temporary file it created. To save a document from one floppy disk to another, first save the file to the hard disk, switch disks, and then resave the file to the other floppy disk.

 Why do I get the message "File is in use. Do you wish to make a copy?" when I start Word?

When you run Microsoft Word for Windows from a network, such as Microsoft LAN Manager and Novell NetWare, the program files and the main directory in which they are located must be marked as read-only. Otherwise, the "*File* is being used by *user*. Do you want to make a copy?" message appears when more than one user tries to access the program.

You should also check to make certain that share is loaded properly. Multiple share references and/or improper parameter settings will also return this error.

Tech Tip: The SET TEMP statement in the AUTOEXEC.BAT file must point to a directory to which the user has at least Read, Write, Delete, and Create rights. Word requires these rights when it creates temporary files.

Why does Word display the message "Error finding doc####.tmp file?"

This error appears when you try to edit a document and Word cannot find the associated temporary file. Word needs this temporary file to complete the edits before it can save them.

If you were working from a file on a floppy disk, reinsert the disk. If the error persists, the disk may have limited space or be damaged. If the file is stored on your hard disk, the drive may be out of space or contain bad sectors. Finally, if the file is located on a network drive, you may have insufficient rights to the directory in which it is stored.

Word stores temporary files separately from those controlled by the SET TEMP statement in the AUTOEXEC.BAT file. To specify where Word stores its temporary files:

1. Choose Options from the Tools menu.
2. Click the File Locations tab.
3. Select AutoSave Files in the File Types list box.
4. Click Modify.
5. Select the directory in which you want Word to store its temporary files.
6. Click OK then click Close.

Why do I get the message "Unrecoverable Disk Error on File~DOC####.TMP?"

Word displays this message when it cannot open a .TMP file in the current directory. This situation occurs when you open a file from a floppy disk and then switch disks, or when you have insufficient rights to a directory on a network drive. In the first case, you can avoid switching disks by first saving the file to the hard drive and then copying it back to another floppy. If the problem involves your network rights, contact your network administrator to gain Read, Write, Delete, and Create rights to the directory in which Word stores the temporary files.

My document contains a lot of pictures and is very large. Is there anything I can do to reduce the size of the file?

You can reduce the file's size by inserting links in your document instead of the graphics themselves. When you use links, the graphics are still stored in their original locations, not in the document. Word automatically finds these linked graphics files and updates the images whenever you display or print the document.

To insert pictures as links:

1. Delete the original graphic by selecting it and pressing DEL.

2. Move the insertion point to where you want the graphic to appear.

3. Choose Picture from the Insert menu.

4. Select the file you want to insert in the File Name list box.

5. Select the Link to File check box.

6. Clear the Save Picture in Document check box.

7. Click OK.

8. Repeat this procedure for each graphic you want to link to your document.

This technique dramatically reduces your file size because only the link, not the picture, is saved in the Word document, as shown in Figure 8-1.

Do not edit linked graphics in Word if you still want to keep the file small. Word uses the Word Draw feature to edit graphics. Because Draw cannot save graphics files, it converts any linked graphic you edit with it to an embedded object, which is then saved as part of the document. Therefore, even though you originally inserted one or more graphics as linked objects, once you edit them with Draw, the size of the file increases.

Tech Terror: If you clear the Save Picture in Document check box when you create a link, you cannot edit the graphic using Word Draw, because there is no data stored in the file that it can access nor can it open the graphic file. In this case, you must use the application in which the graphic was originally created to edit it.

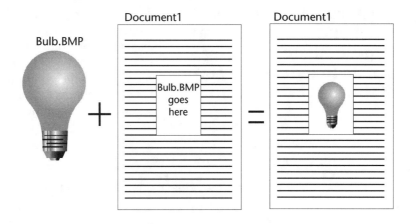

FIGURE 8-1   You can insert a link to a graphic in your Word document

You can decrease the size of documents without graphics by turning off Word's fast save feature. When Word *fast saves* a document, it appends any changes to the file instead of actually incorporating them into it. Word codes the edits so that it can correctly integrate them into the file when you next retrieve it. Therefore, while a fast save is quicker than a normal, full save, the resulting file is not as compact.

To turn off the fast save feature:

Tech Terror: If you delete or move graphics files to which there are links in one of your documents, Word won't be able to find them and therefore won't be able to update the images. In this case, Word doesn't display the graphics in your document at all.

1. Choose <u>O</u>ptions from the <u>T</u>ools menu.

2. Click the Save tab.

3. Clear the Allow <u>F</u>ast Saves check box.

4. Click OK.

I saved my Word for Windows document, then gave it to a friend who works on a Macintosh. He could read the document, but when he printed it out, it wasn't the same as the one I gave him. Why?

By default, Word saves documents by using a special fast save feature. Fast saving is quick because it doesn't actually resave the entire document; instead, it only saves the changes you've made since you opened the document. Word stores the edits with special coding at the end of the file, then integrates them when you next open the file.

When you open a Word for Windows document in Word for the Macintosh, Word for the Macintosh cannot reassemble all the pieces that Word for Windows saved. Therefore, when your friend opened and printed the document in Word for the Macintosh, the document printed contained only the text that you saved the second to last time. The last set of changes you made, which were still in the special format, were lost.

To correct this problem, you need to disable the fast save feature in Word 6.0 and then resave the document before giving it to your friend. To turn the fast save feature off:

1. Choose <u>O</u>ptions from the <u>T</u>ools menu.
2. Click the Save tab.
3. Clear the Allow <u>F</u>ast Saves check box.
4. Click OK.

Save the document by choosing the <u>S</u>ave command from the <u>F</u>ile menu and then give a copy to your friend. The version he sees should now match yours.

What is a search and how do I use one with the Find File feature?

The search aspect of the Find File feature lets you define exactly which files Word displays in the Find File dialog box. To create a search, you need to open the Search dialog box, shown here:

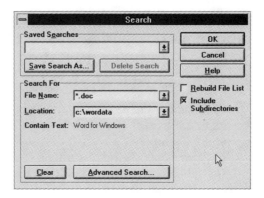

The Search dialog box appears the first time you choose Find File from the File menu, or when you click Search in the Find File dialog box.

To create a search:

1. Enter the filename specification you want to search for in the File Name text box.

You can use two wildcard characters in your search: ? and *. The ? takes the place of one character, while * stands for any number of characters. For example, SALE???.DOC matches SALEJAN.DOC, SALEFEB.DOC, and SALEMAR.DOC, whereas SAL*.DOC matches SALEJAN.DOC, SALE.DOC, and SALESREP.DOC.

2. Enter the directory you want to search in the Location text box. This can be a root directory or a specific directory on any drive, including a network drive. If you want to search all the subdirectories of the directory you specify, select the Include Subdirectories check box.

3. Enter a name in the Saved Searches text box. (Optional)

4. Click Save Search As to save the search for later use, or click OK to use this search only once.

Word can also look for files in several different directories. In addition, you can create complex searches that find files based on their summary info, particular text entries in the document, or the date on which they were created or last edited.

To perform an advanced search:

1. In the Search dialog box, click Advanced Search.

2. Click the appropriate tab and select your settings:

   ■ The Location tab lets you select multiple directories to search in the Directories box and click Add to display them in the Search In list box.

   ■ The Summary lets you specify summary information entries or document text entries for Word to find in files. Input the entry or text you want to find in the appropriate text box.

   ■ The Timestamp tab lets you select files based on when they were created or most recently saved by entering a date or range of dates.

3. Click OK twice to return to the Search dialog box and display the selected files.

4. If desired, save the advanced search settings by entering a name in the Saved Searches text box and then clicking Save Search As.

Figure 8-2 depicts the results of a search for files in the WORDATA directory and its subdirectories that contain the words "Word for Windows."

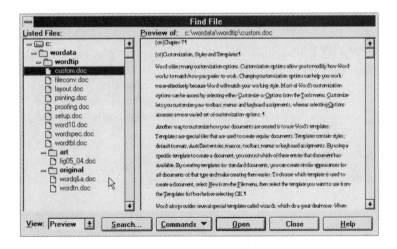

FIGURE 8-2   The Find File dialog box lists the results of the search

I want to delete some document files. Can I do this without leaving Word?

You can use the Find File feature to delete files from within Word. To do so:

1. Choose <u>F</u>ind File from the <u>F</u>ile menu.

2. If you have used this feature before, Word displays the last group of files you selected. You need to click the <u>S</u>earch button to display the Search dialog box. If you have not used the Find File feature before, the Search dialog box appears automatically.

   In the Search dialog box, enter your criteria in the File <u>N</u>ame and <u>L</u>ocation text boxes to find a group of files that includes the ones you want to delete, then click OK.

3. Select the files you want to delete in the <u>L</u>isted Files list box.

4. Select <u>C</u>ommands then <u>D</u>elete; alternatively, you can press the DEL key.

5. Select <u>Y</u>es to confirm that you want to delete the selected file or files.

6. Click Close to exit the Find File dialog box.

How do I select multiple files in the Find File dialog box?

You can delete, copy, open, or print multiple files at once in Word by selecting them in the Find File dialog box. To select more than one nonconsecutive file:

Tech Tip: If you accidentally select a file, you can unselect it by pressing CTRL and clicking the filename. This procedure keeps the other files selected.

1. Click the first filename in the <u>L</u>isted File text box.

2. Press CTRL and click each additional filename you want to select.

To select consecutive files:

1. Click the first file you want to select in the Listed Files list box.

2. Press SHIFT and click the last file you want to select. Word selects all of the files in between, including the two you selected.

   At this point, any file operation you perform affects all of the selected files.

Can I create new directories for my documents without leaving Word?

You can use Word's Find File feature to create new directories in which to store your documents. To create a directory:

1. Choose Find File from the File menu.

2. If the Search dialog box appears, select Word Documents (*.doc) in the File Name drop-down list box, enter the WINWORD directory (or the name of whatever other directory you want to contain the subdirectory) in the Location text box, and then click OK.

3. Select a file you want to move to the new directory, if desired.

4. In the Find File dialog box, choose Copy from the Commands drop-down menu.

5. Click New in the Copy dialog box.

6. Enter the complete path of the new directory in the Name text box, then click OK to create the directory.

7. Click OK to copy the selected file to the new directory, or click Cancel to leave it empty.

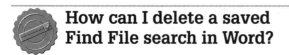

How can I delete a saved Find File search in Word?

To delete a saved search:

1. Choose Find File from the File menu.

2. Click Search.

3. Select the search that you want to delete in the Saved Searches list box.

4. Click Delete Search and then click Yes when prompted.

5. Click OK to return to the Find File dialog box.

6. Click Close.

What are the different types of file passwords?

Word 6.0 provides two types of passwords that you can apply when saving a file: protection passwords and write reservation passwords.

- A *protection password* prevents anyone who does not have the password from opening the document. Without the protection password, a user can't even use the Find File feature to view the document.

- A *write reservation password* lets other users open the document, but prevents them from saving any edits to it. In other words, users without the password can read and modify the document, but they must save the new version with a different name. This feature is often used on networks to distribute a document to users who can then edit and save it to their own drives.

Tech Tip: There are other passwords that you can use to protect a document for annotations, revisions, or forms. These passwords do not prevent a user from opening or saving a document. Instead, they allow users to make only one type of change to the document.

I forgot my password. Is there some way to remove it so that I can use the file?

No, you cannot remove a password unless you can first enter it. Word has no provision for opening a password-protected document without the password. Even Microsoft can't help you on this one. Therefore, pick passwords that you will remember—no matter what! Better yet, record them in a safe, logical place.

Tech Terror: Passwords are case-sensitive; you must enter them exactly as you did the first time. For example, if you accidentally pressed CAPS LOCK before you entered the password "Jane," you must type **jANE** to access your file.

I want to enter a password for my document. How many and which characters can I use?

A password can be up to 15 characters long. It can include numbers, letters, spaces, and symbols. For security purposes, Word does not display the password itself, but an asterisk (*) for each character as you type it.

How do I change a password in a document?

You can enter a new password by following these steps:

1. Open the document (whose password you want to change) using the existing password. If you don't have this password, you can't change it.
2. Choose Save As from the File menu.
3. Click Options.
4. Delete the asterisks that represent the existing password in either the Protection Password or Write Reservation Password text box.
5. Enter the new password, then click OK.
6. Re-enter the new password when Word prompts you to confirm it and then click OK.
7. Click OK in the Save As dialog box to save the document with the new password.

How can I delete a password?

To delete a document's password:

1. Open the document (whose password you want to delete) using the existing password. If you don't have this password, you cannot open or work with the file.

2. Choose Save <u>A</u>s from the <u>F</u>ile menu.

3. Click <u>O</u>ptions.

4. Delete the asterisks that represent the existing password in either the <u>P</u>rotection Password or <u>W</u>rite Reservation Password text box.

5. Click OK twice.

Word isn't accepting my password when I try to open my document. What am I doing wrong?

The most likely problem is that you are simply typing the password incorrectly. Try opening the file again and retyping the password carefully. Also, because passwords are case-sensitive, press CAPS LOCK and re-enter the password; it's possible this feature was on when you originally saved the document. Also, double-check your records to ensure that you are using the correct password for your document.

What's the difference between embedding and linking?

Object Linking and Embedding (OLE) lets you share data between applications. With OLE, you can create a file, such as a graphic or spreadsheet, in one Windows application and then either link or embed it to another file created in with the same or a different application. Linking and embedding objects differ in terms of what you can do with the data and where it is stored.

With *linking*, the data remains in its own file. Your Word document simply contains a connection, or *link*, that tells it where to find that object. For example, suppose you design your company logo with the Windows Paintbrush accessory and save it in a file called LOGO.BMP. If you add a link to this logo to your Word document, the logo itself is still stored in LOGO.BMP; Word simply displays and updates the image in the document by referring to that file. When you edit the logo in Word, Paintbrush, or another application, all the links to the file are automatically updated. In this case, if you choose a different background color for the logo in Paintbrush, this change appears in your Word document when you next open it.

Embedding stores the data for an object in its original format in the Word file itself. For example, if you embed the company logo you created with Paintbrush in a Word document, the graphic actually becomes a part of your Word file. You do not actually have to save the logo in its own .BMP file, but can just create it in Paintbrush, copy it to Word using the Clipboard and then discard the copy in the Paintbrush. Because the logo is contained in your Word document, you cannot use it in other documents or applications. Also, you can only edit the image from within Word, since there is no .BMP file for Paintbrush to open.

The advantage of linking and embedding objects over just copying data is that you can edit them in the application in which they were created without leaving Word. For example, assuming you want to edit the company logo that you embedded or linked in your Word document, all you have to do is double-click the object to open Paintbrush and make your modifications.

In this way, OLE lets you combine the features of several types of applications all in one document. Figure 8-3 depicts the basic differences between linking and embedding data in a Word document.

Linking

Embedding

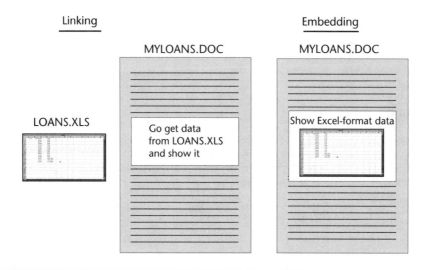

MYLOANS.DOC

MYLOANS.DOC

LOANS.XLS

Go get data
from LOANS.XLS
and show it

Show Excel-format data

FIGURE 8-3   Linking versus embedding data in your Word document

Is there a way to link text between documents?

Yes, you can create a link between two Word documents the same way you create links between documents in two different applications. To create the link:

1. Select the text you want to link.
2. Choose <u>C</u>opy from the <u>E</u>dit menu.
3. Switch to the second document.
4. Choose Paste <u>S</u>pecial from the <u>E</u>dit menu.
5. Click Paste <u>L</u>ink then click OK.

If you are displaying field codes, the code indicates the text that is linked to the document, as shown below. (To toggle between displaying field codes and field results, move to the field and press SHIFT+F9.)

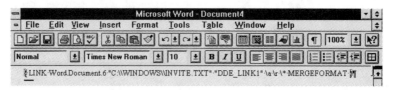

Tech Tip: You can also link data between documents by using the Field command on the Insert menu to add an IncludeText field. This field displays the text and graphics that appear in another document as its results. When you add an IncludeText field, you need to supply the document's filename and a bookmark to display only a portion of the document.

Can I force Word to update a link?

Word 6.0 makes it easy for you to edit OLE links in your document. You can specify how the link updates, force it to update, or change the file to which the link is connected.

To edit a link:

1. Choose Lin<u>k</u>s from the <u>E</u>dit menu to display the Links dialog box, shown here:

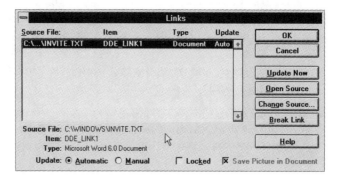

2. Select the link you want to change or update in the <u>S</u>ource File list box.

3. Specify the link settings:

■ Select the <u>A</u>utomatic or <u>M</u>anual option buttons to determine how Word updates the linked data. With <u>A</u>utomatic, Word updates the data whenever the linked file changes; <u>M</u>anual updates the file only when you choose to do so. To prevent inadvertent updating of the link, select the Loc<u>k</u>ed check box; the linked data cannot be updated until this check box is cleared.

- To break the link, and simply display the data in Word, click Break Link, then click Yes. Once broken, a link cannot be restored.

- To edit the linked data, click Open Source.

- To change the file to which the link connects or to make the link refer to a different section of the same source file, click Change Source and then select another file.

- Update the linked data by clicking Update Now.

4. Click OK after you have specified your changes.

I inserted a Word document as an OLE object in another Word document. Now my headers and footers are missing. What's going on?

If you insert one Word document as an OLE object in another, the inserted document's header and footer override the other document's. For example, if you insert DOC1 into DOC2, the modified DOC2 now has DOC1's header and footer. To retain DOC2's original header and footer, copy and paste the text from DOC1 to DOC2 instead of inserting it as an OLE object.

Tech Terror: If you copy and paste the text instead of linking it, do not include the last paragraph mark. Similarly, do not use Select All from the Edit menu to select the text. If you do, the headers and footers will still be overridden.

When I tried to edit an embedded object, I got the message "Word cannot edit the object." What's up?

You need to make sure that Word can find the application's file. To do so, open your WIN.INI file in Word and review the section called [Embedding]. The application used to create the embedded object, including its complete path, must appear in this section for you to perform your edit. If that application is not listed, simply add a line, similar to those already there, referencing its program file, then save WIN.INI. Remember to save WIN.INI as a text file, not a Word document.

What's the difference between using the Clipboard to paste an Excel worksheet to my Word document and inserting it?

You can embed an Excel spreadsheet into a Word document, as shown in Figure 8-4, using either of the methods mentioned. You can copy an Excel worksheet range to the Clipboard and choose Paste Special from the Edit menu to paste it to your Word document. Alternatively, you can choose Object from Word's Insert menu to add the worksheet. In either case, the worksheet is embedded in your document. When you use the Clipboard, Word displays only the contents of the specified range. Inserting the worksheet, on the other hand, provides the flexibility to change worksheet columns and rows that appear in the Word document.

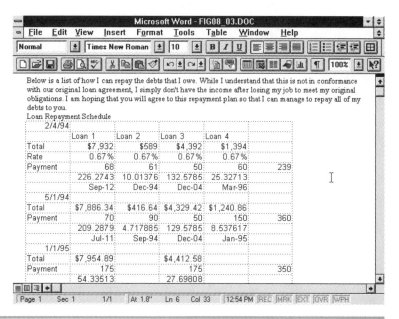

FIGURE 8-4   An Excel spreadsheet embedded in a Word document

When I try to update my Excel links, Word says "The action cannot be completed because Excel is busy." What happened?

This error occurs if you link an Excel version 4.0 object, such as a workbook, worksheet, or chart, to a Word 6.0 document. You can either open Excel so that it's running when you update the links or "unlink" the object. If you unlink the object, it cannot be relinked; you must reinsert it to recreate the link.

How do I save a file in ASCII format?

You can save a file in ASCII format to make it easy to transfer it to another program or platform. Almost all programs accept ASCII files, so converting your Word document allows you to use it in other Windows and non-Windows applications. Files saved in ASCII format contain only those characters described by the ASCII code. All formatting, such as boldface or italics, is stripped out, leaving plain text.

To save a file in ASCII format:

1. Create the document.

2. Choose <u>S</u>ave <u>A</u>s from the <u>F</u>ile menu.

3. Select MS-DOS Text or Text Only in the Save File as <u>T</u>ype drop-down list box.

4. Click OK.

What word processing formats can Word 6.0 open?

Word 6.0 can convert files from the following word processing formats:

- Microsoft Word for Windows 2.0
- Microsoft Word for DOS versions 3.0-6.0
- Microsoft Word for Macintosh versions 4.x-5.x
- WordPerfect for DOS/Windows versions 5.x
- RFT-DCA
- Microsoft Write for Windows
- Rich Text Format

You can obtain additional conversion filters by:

- Contacting Microsoft's Product Support Service at (206)462-9673 to find out the name of the files you need and then accessing the Microsoft BBS (Bulletin Board Service) by calling (206)936-6735.

- Sending the upgrade card that came with Word to Microsoft to receive more conversion filters.

Can I open a Lotus Ami Pro document in Word 6.0?

Word 6.0 does not include an Ami Pro text converter, and therefore cannot directly open an Ami Pro file. However, Ami Pro 3.0 can open and save files in both the Word for Windows 2.0 format and the Rich Text Format (.RTF). To open an Ami Pro document in Word, open the file in Ami Pro, save it in either the Word for Windows 2.0 or RTF format, and then open the file in Word 6.0.

I recently switched from Professional Write to Word for Windows 6.0. Can I open my Professional Write files in Word 6.0?

No, Word does not provide a conversion filter for Professional Write files. You must use Professional Write to save your documents in the Microsoft Word for DOS format, then open them in Word 6.0 to convert them to the new format. You may want to contact the manufacturer of Professional Written Software Publishing Corporation, at (608) 274-9715. They may have information regarding a third-party conversion utility that you might use.

Can I save a Word document using a different format?

You can use Word to create documents and then save them in a different format. To do so:

1. Choose Save As from the File menu.

2. Select a file format in the Save File as <u>T</u>ype drop-down list box.

3. Enter a filename in the File <u>N</u>ame text box.

4. Click OK twice.

Tech Tip: Although the Microsoft Excel Worksheet format appears in the Save File as <u>T</u>ype drop-down list box, you can't actually save a Word file as a spreadsheet. This converter is only used to open spreadsheet files in Word.

What database formats can Word read?

You can use the <u>D</u>atabase command on the <u>I</u>nsert menu to bring data into your Word documents from most popular database applications, as shown in Figure 8-5. This feature lets you add large amounts of data that you have already entered in a database to a Word document without re-entering it. This feature is particularly helpful when you want to create a merge file, a directory, or a product catalog.

DENOM	TYPE	DATE	MEMO
Half	Liberty Cap	1793	United States Regular Issue Coin Diameter - 22mm Weight - 6.74 grams Designer - Adam Eckfeldt
Half	Liberty Cap	1796	United States Regular Issue Coin Diameter - 23.5mm Weight - 5.44 grams 1796 With Pole
Half	Classic Head	1810	United States Regular Issue Coin Diameter - 23.5mm Weight - 5.44 grams Designer - John Reich
Five	Shield Type	1867	Nickel Five Cent Piece Diameter - 20.5mm Weight - 5 grams Designer - James B. Longacre 1867 With Rays Plain Edge
Five	Liberty Head	1912D	Nickel Five Cent Pieces

Product List

FIGURE 8-5   You can insert data from a database into a Word document

Word 6.0 can read data from the applications listed in Table 8-1.

Can I convert all of my WordPerfect files into the Word 6.0 format at the same time?

Yes, Word 6.0 comes with a macro that can convert multiple files into the new format all at once. To use this macro:

1. Choose <u>T</u>emplate from the <u>F</u>ile menu.

2. Click A<u>d</u>d.

3. Use the <u>D</u>irectories box to display the contents of the WINWORD\MACROS directory.

4. Select CONVERT.DOT in the File <u>N</u>ame list box, then click OK twice.

5. Choose <u>M</u>acro from the <u>T</u>ools menu.

6. Select BatchConversion in the <u>M</u>acro Name list box, then click <u>R</u>un.

This procedure starts the BatchConversion Wizard, which walks you through the steps necessary to convert multiple files to or from the 6.0 format. Simply respond to the prompts to convert all of your WordPerfect files to the new format.

Tech Tip: If you can't find the MACROS subdirectory, you probably didn't install the macros when you originally set up Word. Before you can convert your file, you need to perform a maintenance installation to add the macro files.

Extension	Format
.DBF	Microsoft FoxPro
.QRY	Microsoft Query
.XLS	Microsoft Excel
.MDB	Microsoft Access
.DBF	dBASE
.DB	Paradox

TABLE 8-1   Word can read files created in a variety of database applications

Can I create Help files using Word 6.0?

You can create help files for your macros, just like the ones you use in Word and other Windows applications. To create a Help file, first produce the document in Word and save it in the .RTF format. Then, use the Microsoft Help Compiler to generate the Help file. The latest version of the Microsoft Help Compiler works with the new Word for Windows .RTF format.

To get the most recent Microsoft Help Compiler program, you can download it from Microsoft Download Library by calling (206) 936-6735. As of this writing, the file is called HC505.EXE.

I run Word 2.0 on my home computer but I use Word 6.0 at work. Why can't my home computer read the files I bring home from work?

Word 6.0 uses a different file format than Word 2.0. For compatibility, Word 6.0 comes with a special converter that lets it open files saved in Word 2.0. Because Word 2.0 preceded Word 6.0, it obviously doesn't have such a built-in converter to read files created in this new release. You can, however, save your Word 6.0 documents in the Word 2.0 format by following these steps:

1. Display the document in Word 6.0 that you want to use on your home computer.

2. Choose Save As from the File menu.

3. Select Word for Windows 2.0 from the Save File as Type drop-down list box.

4. Enter a name for the file in the File Name text box.

5. Specify the directory in which you want to save the file in the Directories list box and then choose OK.

Microsoft has also made available a converter that lets Word 2.0 open Word 6.0 documents. To request a copy, contact Microsoft Product Support at (206) 462-9673.

I don't like the way my files look when I convert them to the Word format. Can I modify these settings?

Word 6.0 lets you control certain formatting options when you convert a file created in another application. To set these options:

1. Choose Options from the Tools menu.
2. Click the Compatibility tab.
3. Select the original format of the files you are converting in the Recommended Options For drop-down list box.
4. The Options list box lists the compatibility options you may want to use while working with converted documents. Your selection in the Recommended Options For drop-down list box determines which of the options are turned on or off. You can modify these settings by selecting or clearing the appropriate check boxes.
5. Click OK.

Why can't I see any underlining after I convert my WordPerfect file into Word?

When you convert a WordPerfect file to a Word 6.0 format, the paragraph spacing is automatically set to the exact point size of the text. Therefore, the reason you cannot see the underlining is that there simply isn't room to see the line under the text. You can redisplay the underlining by adjusting the line spacing.

To change the line spacing in the converted file:

1. Choose Select All from the Edit menu, or press CTRL+A.
2. Choose Paragraph from the Format menu.
3. Click the Indents and Spacing tab.
4. Select Single in the Line Spacing drop-down list box, then click OK.

After converting my WordPerfect file to Word 6.0, it contains a lot of {PRIVATE} fields. What are they and where did they come from?

Private fields are new in Word 6.0. Word uses them to retain the data needed to convert the file back to its original format. Private fields do not affect the layout of the document in Word and, by default, are formatted as hidden text; they only appear on the screen if you are displaying hidden text. If you prefer not to see the fields, simply click the Show/Hide button on the Standard toolbar.

When I convert files to Word 6.0 format, I always have to make the same formatting changes. Can I automate this process?

You can create a macro to perform these repetitive formatting tasks for you when you convert files to the Word 6.0 format. To create such a macro, you open a document to convert, then record the formatting changes you make to it. You can then use this macro to apply these same changes automatically to other files that you convert.

To create the formatting macro:

1. Open a document you want to convert.

2. Choose Macro from the Tools menu.

3. Enter **REFORMAT** in the Macro Name text box.

4. Click Record.
   To add the macro to a menu, click Menus, then Add to add the macro at the end of the Tools menu. (Alternatively, you can assign the macro to a toolbar button or a key combination.)

5. Click Close.

Word displays the Record Macro toolbar, shown here, to indicate that you are recording a macro:

6. Choose Select All from the Edit menu.

7. Make all of the formatting changes you want to make throughout each converted document.

   For example, you might choose Font from the Format menu to change the typeface or size, Page Setup from the File menu to change your margins, Styles from the Format menu to change the formatting applied to styles, Paragraph from the Format menu to change line and paragraph spacing, and Replace from the Edit menu to replace one type of formatting or a text entry with another.

8. When you are satisfied with the appearance of your document, click the Stop button on the Record Macro toolbar.

To use the new macro:

1. Open a converted document.

2. Choose Reformat from the Tools menu to automatically make the formatting changes.

How do I import files created in the Windows Cardfile accessory?

To import a Cardfile list into Word 6.0:

1. Start the Windows Control Panel by double-clicking its program item in the Program Manager's Main program group.

2. Double-click the Printers icon or choose Printers from the Settings menu.

3. Select the Generic/Text Only printer driver in the Installed Printers list box. If the printer driver is not listed, you need to install it.

4. Click Set as Default Printer.

5. Click Connect.

6. Select FILE: in the Ports List box and click OK.

7. Click Close, then choose Exit from the Settings menu.

8. Open the Cardfile accessory by double-clicking its program item, which usually appears in the Accessories program group in the Program Manager.

9. Choose Open from the File menu, select the .CRD file you want to use in the File Name list box, and then click OK.

10. Choose Printer Setup from the File menu.

11. Click Option.

12. Select the No Page Break check box and click OK twice to return to the document.

13. Choose Print All from the File menu.

14. When prompted for a filename, enter the Cardfile's name with a .TXT extension (instead of .CRD).

15. Open the .TXT file in Word. By default, this file is stored in the WINDOWS directory.

Figure 8-6 shows a Cardfile list and the data it contains in a Word for Windows document. As you can see, you need to format the Cardfile data after you import it into Word.

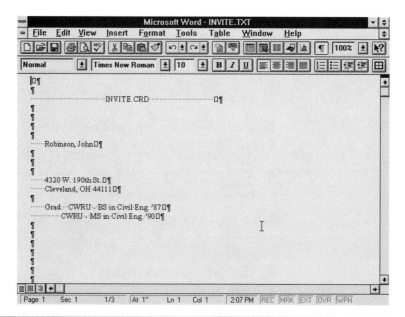

FIGURE 8-6   A Cardfile list imported into Word

I installed Norton File Assist version 3.0 on my computer and now I'm having trouble saving my Word documents. How do I save my files?

Word uses the WordBasic FileSave command to save your documents. Because Norton File Assist version 3.0 interferes with this command, you may encounter problems when you try to save documents in Word.

Norton File Assist installs four macros: FileOpen, FileSave, FileSaveAs, and FileAssist. These macros were originally written for Word 2.0. Since the Word 6.0 macro language is slightly different than the language used in both Word 2.0 and Norton File Assist, the macros do not function properly. To fix this problem, disable Norton File Assistant and then rename your NORMAL.DOT file by following these steps:

1. Exit Word, if necessary.

2. Double-click the File Manager program item, which is in the Program Manager's Main program group.

3. Display the contents of the WINWORD\TEMPLATE subdirectory. (If Word for Windows 6.0 is not installed in the WINWORD directory, substitute the name of your directory instead.)

4. Select the NORMAL.DOT file.

5. Choose Re**n**ame from the **F**ile menu.

6. Type a new filename in the **T**o text box, for example, **NORMAL.OLD**.

7. Click OK to rename the file.

8. Exit the File Manager and restart Word.

Word creates a new NORMAL.DOT file with the original default settings. This new NORMAL.DOT does not include any of the Norton macros and should function correctly.

When I try to access drive A or B from Word 6.0, I am thrown out to the DOS prompt. What is happening?

When you use Norton's Anti Virus software or Norton Desktop for Windows, problems may occur when you try to access floppy drives. If you cannot open files from your A or B drive and you are running Norton Desktop, you must disable it by following these steps:

1. Choose <u>R</u>un from the <u>F</u>ile menu in the Program Manager.

2. Type **SYSEDIT** and click OK.

3. Switch to the SYSTEM.INI window and change the Shell= line to read

```
Shell=progman.exe
```

3. Switch to the WIN.INI window.

4. If the LOAD= statement references Norton Desktop, insert a semicolon (;) in front of it.

5. Switch to the AUTOEXEC.BAT window and remove any references to the Norton Desktop directory in your Path statement.

6. Choose E<u>x</u>it from the <u>F</u>ile menu and then click <u>Y</u>es at the prompts displayed by the System Configuration Editor.

7. Close Windows.

8. If you made any changes to the AUTOEXEC.BAT, reboot the computer.

9. Restart Windows and reopen Word.

Proofing Tools

Experienced proofreaders train themselves to look for subtle problems in the text they review. A spelling mistake, missing or incorrect punctuation, or an incorrect verb tense is quickly noted by the proficient proofreader.

You can catch many of these mistakes yourself by consistently using Word's proofing tools. When you use these features, Word helps you produce professional, well-written documents. Word includes a Spelling feature, which identifies potential misspellings; a Thesaurus, which provides synonyms for an overused word; and a Grammar checker, which looks for incorrect tense use and other such problems. Of course, you will still need to read your final document; for instance, there are always situations in which words are spelled correctly but misused. You can only uncover these mistakes by reviewing your document.

Familiarizing yourself with the wide range of options offered by Word's Spelling, Grammar, and Thesaurus features will let you take advantage of their full, optimal functionality. The Frustration Busters box highlights some important, but infrequently used options.

FRUSTRATION BUSTERS!

Many users work with Word's proofing tools, but only use their standard options. If you're one of these people, take a look at these options to see if you could be reaping additional benefits from these tools.

Spelling

Many users who use the spelling feature frequently use only the Ignore and Change buttons. Several other important options can make your task easier:

- *Ignore All* tells Word to ignore all of the remaining occurrences of the currently flagged word during the current spell check.

- *Change All* tells Word to change all of the remaining occurrences of the flagged word to the current suggested spelling.

- *AutoCorrect* adds a misspelled word and its correct spelling to the AutoCorrect entries. The AutoCorrect feature corrects these entries as you type.

- *Options* lets you control whether or not Word offers spelling suggestions, and whether they are restricted to entries in the main dictionary. You can also designate whether Word ignores words that appear in all uppercase or contain numbers. In addition, you can specify which custom dictionaries Word uses.

Thesaurus

Most people use the thesaurus to find synonyms for over-used words in their documents. Other options allow you to get additional use from this proofing tool.

- *Antonyms* in the Meanings list box finds words with the opposite meaning.

- *Related Words* in the Meanings list box finds words with the same root. For example, it may display "operations" when you look up "operate."

- *Look Up* finds words related to the current entry in the Replace with Synonym text box.

Grammar

Many users work with the grammar feature without changing any of its options. One important change you might want to make is to change the rule group used when checking your document. You can use one of the three existing rule groups, with or without changes, or you can create up to three new rule groups that are fully customized. The predefined rule groups are available on the Grammar tab in the Options dialog box, which you display by choosing Options from the Tools menu. These options include:

- *Strictly (All Rules)* strictly enforces all grammar and style rules.

- *For Business Writing* enforces all grammar rules, but relaxes some of the style rules.

- *For Casual Writing* enforces most grammar rules, but suspends many of the style rules.

Can I skip a portion of text when I check spelling?

Word 6.0 provides a format called "no proofing" that you can apply to any text. This format tells Word not to check this text for spelling or grammar. You might want to use it when a section of the document contains many terms, formulas, or abbreviations.

To apply the No Proofing feature to text:

1. Select the text.

2. Choose Language from the Tools menu.

3. Choose (no proofing) in the Mark Selected Text As list box, as shown in the following:

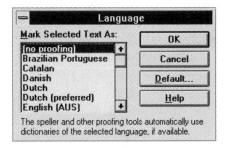

4. Click OK.

When you perform a spelling or grammar check, Word excludes this text from the proof.

When I perform a spelling check, Word displays the message "The spelling check is complete. Text formatted with (no proofing) was skipped." There are words that I know are spelled wrong in the document that were not corrected. What is wrong?

You can format text for a language just as you do for other formatting, such as font and line spacing. This formatting determines which language Word uses to check a document's spelling and grammar. One of the language options is (no proofing), which tells Word to ignore the text when it proofs the document. This selection is appropriate for unusual strings of letters, such as part names, and phone numbers displayed alphanumerically, such as 1-206-936-MSDL (the Microsoft Download Library).

The message you see simply indicates that some of your text is formatted as (no proofing). To reformat it:

1. Choose Select All from the Edit menu to select the entire document.

2. Choose Language from the Tools menu.

3. Select the desired language, such as English (US).

4. Click OK.

I am pleased with Word's grammar feature when writing business documents, but the rules seem too formal for my personal writing. Can I relax the rule checking process?

Word provides up to six rule groups that you can select when performing grammar checks. By default, it uses the For Business Writing rule group. However, you can relax the rules by designating the For Casual Writing group, or rigorously implement them by selecting Strictly (All Rules). You can also develope custom rule groups by "mixing and matching" the predefined rules.

To select a rule group:

1. Choose Options from the Tools menu.
2. Click the Grammar tab, as shown in Figure 9-1.
3. Select the desired rule group in the Use Grammar and Style Rules list box, then click OK.

To customize settings for any of the six rule groups:

1. Choose Options from the Tools menu.

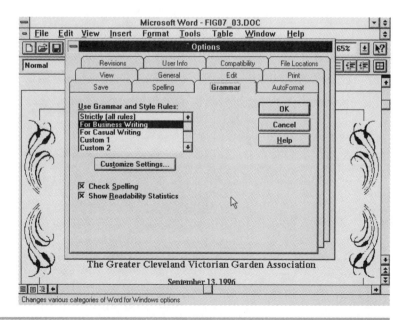

FIGURE 9-1   The Grammar tab in the Options dialog box

2. Click the Grammar tab.

3. Select the set of rules you want to modify in the Use Grammar and Style Rules list box.

4. Click the Customize Settings button.

5. Select the Grammar or Style option button.

6. Clear or select check boxes for the various options, as shown in Figure 9-2.

7. Use the drop-down list boxes in the Catch section of the dialog box to indicate how strictly you want Word to enforce the rules.

8. Click OK.

The Catch section in the Customize Grammar Settings dialog box lets you specify how stringently Word applies the grammar and style rules. The items in each of the three drop-down list boxes are similar, as described in Table 9-1.

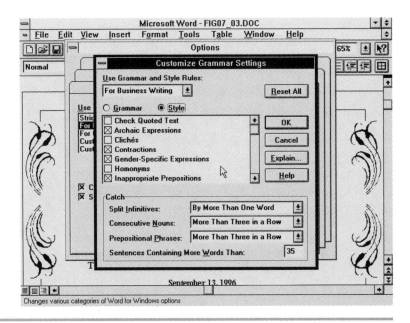

FIGURE 9-2   You can individually select style options

Rule Group	Setting	Default
Formal	Split Infinitives	By More Than One Word
	Consecutive Nouns	More Than Three in a Row
	Prepositional Phrases	More Than Three in a Row
Business	Split Infinitives	By More Than One Word
	Consecutive Nouns	More Than Three in a Row
	Prepositional Phrases	More Than Three in a Row
Casual	Split Infinitives	By More Than Two Words
	Consecutive Nouns	More Than Four in a Row
	Prepositional Phrases	More Than Four in a Row

TABLE 9-1   The Catch settings

After I run a grammar check, I don't see the Readability Statistics. Why?

If Readability Statistics, shown in Figure 9-3, do not appear after you check a document's grammar, you need to reselect this option.

To turn on this option:

1. Choose <u>O</u>ptions from the <u>T</u>ools menu.
2. Click the Grammar tab.
3. Select the Show <u>R</u>eadability Statistics check box and then click OK.

I prefer the spelling "theatre," but Word insists on changing it to "theater." How can I instruct Word to exclude this spelling and that of some other words?

If you don't like the spelling Word uses for certain words, you can create an exclude dictionary. Word stops at words that appear in an exclude dictionary just as it does at a misspelled word. In this case, you would add the word "theater" to the exclude dictionary; Word would then flag each occurrence of this word and give you an opportunity to edit it.

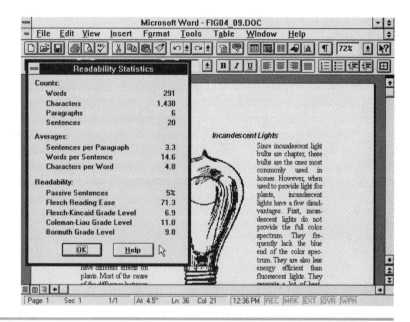

FIGURE 9-3   Sample Readability Statistics

Follow these steps to create an exclude dictionary:

1. Choose <u>N</u>ew from the <u>F</u>ile menu to create a new document.

2. Type each word you want to exclude from Word's spell check and press ENTER.

3. Choose Save <u>A</u>s from the <u>F</u>ile menu.

4. Select Text Only in the Save File As <u>T</u>ype drop-down list box.

5. Select the directory that contains your other dictionaries in the <u>D</u>irectories list box. Usually, this directory is C:\WINDOWS\MSAPPS\PROOF.

6. Type a file name in the File <u>N</u>ame text box that is the same as the main dictionary's, except add .EXC. as the extension.

    For example, enter **MSSP2_EN.EXC** as the name of your exclude dictionary if your main dictionary is MSSP2_EN.LEX.

7. Click OK to save the exclude dictionary.

Is there any way that I can check the grammar of my document without checking the spelling?

You can review your document for grammar only by following these steps:

1. Choose <u>O</u>ptions from the <u>T</u>ools menu.

2. Click the Grammar tab.

3. Clear the Check <u>S</u>pelling check box and then click OK.

Tech Tip: Alternatively, you can choose <u>G</u>rammar from the <u>T</u>ools menu to begin the grammar check and then click the <u>O</u>ptions button to display the Grammar tab.

How do I use a custom dictionary?

A custom dictionary contains words that Word would ordinarily identify as misspelled, such as acronyms and proper names. When you enter these terms in a custom dictionary, Word accepts their spelling as correct and no longer flags them.

To use a custom dictionary when spell checking:

1. Choose <u>O</u>ptions from the <u>T</u>ools menu.

2. Click the Spelling tab.

3. Select the check box to the left of the dictionary that you want to use in the Custom <u>D</u>ictionaries list box.

4. Click OK.

Word uses all the custom dictionaries selected. When you no longer want to use one of the custom dictionaries, simply clear the appropriate check box.

Is there a shortcut key that I can use to check the spelling of my document?

To check the spelling of a document, you can press F7. You can also click the Spelling button on the Standard toolbar, shown here:

I have British spellings in my document. Will Word recognize these words as correct?

Word's dictionary for the English language contains both American and British spellings. However, you must format the text as English (UK) so Word recognizes the entry as British.

To format the text:

1. Select the text you want to format.

2. Choose Language from the Tools menu.

3. Select English (UK) in the Mark Selected Text As list box, then click OK.

Can I edit the words in my custom dictionaries?

Yes, you can open and edit a custom dictionary as a Word document. To do so:

1. Choose Options from the Tools menu.

2. Click the Spelling tab.

3. Select the dictionary you want to edit in the Custom Dictionaries list box.

4. Click Edit.

5. Choose Yes when Word asks if you want to open and edit the custom dictionary as a Word document.
    Word opens a document like the one shown in Figure 9-4.

6. Click OK to close the Options dialog box.

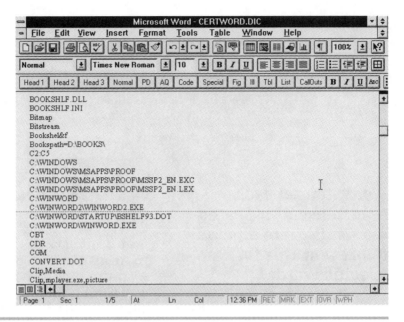

┌──┐
│ **Microsoft Word - CERTWORD.DIC**   │
│ <u>F</u>ile <u>E</u>dit <u>V</u>iew <u>I</u>nsert F<u>o</u>rmat <u>T</u>ools T<u>a</u>ble <u>W</u>indow <u>H</u>elp │
│   │
│ Normal │ Times New Roman │ 10 │ B I U │ ...   │
│ Head 1 │ Head 2 │ Head 3 │ Normal │ PD │ AQ │ Code │ Special │ Fig │ Ill │ Tbl │ List │ CallOuts │ B │ I │ U │ ABC │
│   │
│ BOOKSHLF.DLL   │
│ BOOKSHLF.INI   │
│ Bitmap   │
│ Bitstream   │
│ Bookshel&f   │
│ Bookspath=D:\BOOKS\   │
│ C2:C5   │
│ C:\WINDOWS   │
│ C:\WINDOWS\MSAPPS\PROOF   │
│ C:\WINDOWS\MSAPPS\PROOF\MSSP2_EN.EXC   │
│ C:\WINDOWS\MSAPPS\PROOF\MSSP2_EN.LEX   │
│ C:\WINWORD   │
│ C:\WINWORD2\WINWORD2.EXE   │
│ C:\WINWORD\STARTUP\BSHELF93.DOT   │
│ C:\WINWORD\WINWORD.EXE   │
│ CBT   │
│ CDR   │
│ CGM   │
│ CONVERT.DOT   │
│ Clip,Media   │
│ Clip,mplayer.exe,picture   │
│ Page 1 │ Sec 1 │ 1/5 │ At │ Ln │ Col │ 12:36 PM REC MRK EXT OVR WPH │
└──┘

FIGURE 9-4   Custom dictionary opened as a Word document

7. Edit the custom dictionary. You can insert, delete, and modify entries.

Tech Tip: Remember, you should only enter one entry on each line in a custom dictionary.

8. Save the document.

Can I delete a word from my custom dictionary?

To delete a word from the custom dictionary:

1. Choose <u>O</u>ptions from the <u>T</u>ools menu.

2. Click the Spelling tab.

3. Select the dictionary you want to edit in the Custom <u>D</u>ictionaries list box.

4. Click <u>E</u>dit.

5. Choose Yes when Word asks if you want to open and edit the custom dictionary as a Word document.

6. Click OK to close the Options dialog box and edit the dictionary.

7. Delete the lines that contain the words you want to remove from the dictionary.

8. Save the document.

Word stops at each occurrence of repeated words. Is there any way to prevent this for specific words?

Repeated words may be part of a company name, as in Baker, Baker & Jones. During a spell check, Word flags these duplications as incorrect and you must click either Ignore or Ignore All to accept them. To prevent Word from finding specific double or repeated words in the document, you can format them as (no proofing) and create an AutoText entry to insert them in your text. Follow these steps to create the AutoText entry:

1. Choose New from the File menu to open a new document.

2. Type the words you know will be doubled or repeated, such as **Baker, Baker & Jones**.

3. Select the words.

4. Choose Language from the Tools menu.

5. Select (no proofing) in the Mark Selected Text As list box and click OK.

6. With the text still selected, choose AutoText from the Edit menu.

7. Type a name for your AutoText entry in the Name text box, then click Add.

You can then insert these words at the appropriate places in your document:

1. Place the insertion point at the location where you want the words to appear.

2. Choose AutoText from the Edit menu.

3. Select the AutoText entry's name in the <u>N</u>ame list box.

4. Click <u>I</u>nsert.

Alternatively, you can insert an AutoText entry by typing its AutoText entry name in the document. Then, press F3 or click the Insert AutoText button on the Standard toolbar, shown here:

When you spell check the document, Word skips the AutoText entries because of their (no proofing) format.

I've always used F3 to add an AutoText entry, but it no longer seems to be working. What is wrong?

AutoText lets you type a short word or entry, and have Word replace it with graphics or a string of text. By default, you can insert the contents of an AutoText entry by typing its name and then pressing F3. If this shortcut no longer works, you either turned on the WordPerfect Help option, which reassigns keys to match WordPerfect's key combinations, or changed the keys assigned to the AutoText command.

If the WordPerfect Help feature is turned on, either "WPH" or "WP" appears in the status bar. To turn off WordPerfect Help:

1. Choose <u>O</u>ptions from the <u>T</u>ools menu.

2. Click the General tab.

3. Clear the Help for <u>W</u>ordPerfect Users and the Na<u>v</u>igation Keys for WordPerfect Users check boxes, then click OK.

If the WordPerfect Help feature is not turned on, then it is likely that you modified your key assignments. To reassign F3 to the AutoText command:

1. Choose <u>C</u>ustomize from the <u>T</u>ools menu.

2. Click the <u>K</u>eyboard tab.

3. Select Edit in the <u>C</u>ategories list box.

4. Select InsertAutoText in the Co<u>m</u>mands list box.

5. Move the insertion point to the Press <u>N</u>ew Shortcut Key text box and press F3.

6. Select Normal.dot in the Sa<u>v</u>e Changes In drop-down list box.

7. Click OK.

Word saves this key assignment in the Normal template, which makes it available in all documents.

I created a glossary of specialized terms. I placed A-/Baa at the top of the first page to indicate its contents. When I spell check the document, Word stops at this entry and won't continue. What can I do?

Word stops whenever it encounters a misspelling. In this case, it doesn't recognize the dash and slash characters together and leaves the misspelled word field blank. Unfortunately, this difficulty also causes the spell checker to "hang." (This problem occurs in version 2.0c of Word, but not in earlier releases of Word for Windows.) At this point, the best thing to do is cancel the spell

checker, add the word to your custom dictionary, and restart the spell check. Word now bypasses this word combination.

Tech Tip: This problem is fixed with the Word 6.0a update.

My document contains some text in another language. When I check its spelling, Word displays a message that says it cannot find the dictionary. What's wrong with my document?

Your document is fine. However, there are several ways you can ensure that Word handles the foreign text correctly:

- Verify that the text is formatted as the correct language. To check this, move the insertion point to the text and then choose <u>L</u>anguage from the <u>T</u>ools menu.
- Purchase and install the proper foreign language dictionary.

■ Make sure that the foreign language dictionary is installed in the same directory as the other proofing and editing tools.

Tech Tip: If you do not have the proper foreign language dictionary, you will want to set the foreign language text to "no proofing" so that Word skips over this foreign text when it searches for spelling errors

How do I obtain foreign language dictionaries?

Alki Software offers foreign, legal, and medical dictionaries for Microsoft Word for Windows. The foreign languages include British English, Dutch, French, German, Italian, Swedish, and Spanish. For more information about these dictionaries, contact Alki Software at (206) 286-2600. To order a dictionary, call (800) 669-9673.

I am going to a foreign country for a while. Does Microsoft offer foreign language versions of Word for Windows 6.0?

Word for Windows 6.0 is available in a variety of foreign versions. For more information about them, contact Microsoft International Sales at (206) 936-8661.

I have a need to type a document in a foreign language. Inserting symbols for foreign characters is too cumbersome. Is there a better solution?

You can customize Windows so that you can work in another language. When you change the international settings, it affects all of your Windows applications. These options include the language used; the keyboard layout; the default measurement system; the character used to separate lists and numbers; and date, time, and currency formats.

To change your international options in Windows:

Tech Tip: You may need to obtain special fonts for the language in which you are working. Various third-party vendors offer Windows fonts for foreign languages.

1. Start the Control Panel by double-clicking its program item, which is normally located in the Main program group of the Program Manager.

2. Choose International from the Settings menu or double-click the International icon to display the International dialog box, shown in Figure 9-5.

3. Select the country you want to use in the Country drop-down list.

4. Select the appropriate settings in the Language, Keyboard Layout, and Measurement drop-down list boxes.

5. Enter a new list separator, if desired.

6. Modify the date, time, currency, and number formats, if necessary, by clicking the Change buttons.

7. Click OK.

For more information about the effects of changing the International settings, see the online Windows Help.

FIGURE 9-5   The International dialog box

Tables

Word's table feature makes it easy to create tabular arrangements of data with entries in columns and rows. Once you define the number of rows or columns you want to appear in your table, Word inserts a grid in your document to separate your entries. You can apply table formatting to entries in individual cells, entire rows or columns, or the whole table all at once. For instance, you can change column width or row height; you can also insert and delete rows or columns. The width and color of the border around a table as well as the lines between cell entries are up to you. This formatting can be applied either before or after you enter data in your table. You can also create formulas that work with the table entries.

FRUSTRATION BUSTERS!

In addition to the standard methods for selecting text and graphics in a Word document, you can use the methods listed in the following table to select various table elements.

Action	Method
Select the cell	Click the selection bar (the space to the left of the cell's contents) within the cell, or triple-click the cell's contents
Select the next cell	Press TAB
Select the previous cell	Press SHIFT+TAB
Select the row	Click the row selection bar (the space to the left of the row, outside the table's border), or place the insertion point anywhere in the row and choose Select Row from the Table menu
Select the column	Click the column's top border when the mouse pointer becomes a downward arrow, or place the insertion point anywhere in the column and choose Select Column from the Table menu
Select multiple cells, rows, or columns	Drag the mouse from one selection bar to another or across the top borders of columns
Select all cells, rows, or columns between the current position of the insertion point and another location	Hold down SHIFT while you click another cell, row, or column
Select the entire table	Press ALT+5 (on the numeric keypad) or choose Select Table from the Table menu

Selection bar ———
Row selection bar ———

| Name | Department | Extension |
| Albee, Jan | Marketing | 1023 |

How do I create a table in my document?

You can add a table to a Word document in four different ways:

- Choosing commands from the Table menu
- Using the Table wizard
- Clicking a toolbar button
- Converting text that is already separated with tabs or another character

To create a table with a menu command:

1. Choose Insert Table from the Table menu.
2. Enter the number of columns for the table in the Number of Columns text box.
3. Enter the number of rows for the table in the Number of Rows text box.
4. Click OK to insert the table into the document.

For example, an empty table with two columns and four rows might look like this:

To create a table with the Table Wizard, you can either:

- Choose Insert Table from the Table menu, and click the Wizard button.
- Choose New from the File menu, select Table Wizard in the Template list box, then click OK. This method creates

a new document to contain the table you build with the wizard.

The Table Wizard walks you through the design process; all you have to do is respond to the prompts. You specify the table layout, column headings, row headings, table cell contents, the direction in which to print the table, and the Help display options. Once you've selected the options you want, click Next to move onto the next step. When you are done, Words adds your table to the existing document or the beginning of the new document, depending on how you originally accessed the wizard.

To create a table using a toolbar button:

1. Click the Insert Table button on the Standard toolbar, shown here:

2. Drag the mouse across the squares grid until you have highlighted the number of rows and columns you want in your table. Word indicates the size of the table at the bottom of the drop-down box, as shown here:

To create a table by converting text that's already separated with tabs or another character:

1. Select the text to turn into a table.

2. Choose Convert Text to Table from the Table menu.

3. Verify that the information in the Convert Text to Table dialog box is correct. Check that the entry in the Number of Columns text box is correct and that the character

selected in the Separate Text At section is the one that appears between the data you want split into columns.

4. Click OK.

If your text contained a different number of separators than the number of columns you specified, you may need to move entries between columns after Word creates the table.

Are there shortcut keys for moving around in a table?

You can still use the same key combinations that you normally do to edit a document. In addition, you can use the following key combinations that are specifically designed for tables.

Action	Shortcut
Move to the next cell	TAB
Move to the previous cell	SHIFT+TAB
Move to the beginning of the cell	HOME
Move to the end of the cell	END
Move to the first cell in a row	ALT+HOME
Move to the last cell in a row	ALT+END
Move to the first cell in a column	ALT+PGUP
Move to the last cell in a column	ALT+PGDN

In Word 2.0, I could right-click a single column in a table created with tabs to select it. Why doesn't this work in Word 6.0?

Unlike Word 2.0, clicking the right mouse button in Word 6.0 displays a shortcut menu. You therefore cannot use the right mouse button to select a column of text. To select a tabular column in Word 6.0, press ALT as you drag your mouse. This selects only the rectangle of text across which you drag your mouse.

How do I select an entire table?

To easily select an entire table, position your insertion point anywhere in the table then choose Select Table from the Table menu. Any commands or Word features you then use will affect the entire table.

Tech Tip: You can also select the table by pressing ALT+5 (on the numeric keypad). You may need to press NUM LOCK to toggle the keypad from moving the insertion point to entering numbers.

I selected a table and pressed DEL but the table is still there. How do I delete the table?

When you press DEL, Word deletes the contents of the table cells but leaves the table structure with all of its formatting in place. If you want to delete the table, select the table and then choose either Delete Rows from the Table menu or Cut from the Edit menu. These methods delete the table's structure as well as its contents.

Can I hide the gridlines in a table?

To display or hide gridlines that mark the divisions between rows and columns, choose Gridlines from the Table menu. When a check mark appears in front of the command, the gridlines are displayed; choosing this command again clears the check mark and hides the gridlines. Gridlines never print.

Tech Tip: When you display nonprinting paragraph marks, Word marks the ends of cells and rows with a special symbol (¤)

How can I get the table's gridlines to print?

The gridlines that you see when you insert a table are not designed to print. To print lines around the cells in a table, you need to apply borders to the cells, just as you might to paragraphs.

To apply borders to the whole table:

1. Choose the Select Table command from the Table menu.
2. Choose Borders and Shading from the Format menu.
3. Click the Borders tab.
4. Click the Grid button in the Presets section.
5. Click OK.

You can also add a border to a section of a table, such as an individual cell, row, or column. Figure 10-1 shows a table with borders and shading added selectively. To achieve this effect, simply select the appropriate cells, row, or column and then choose the same Borders and Shading command in the Format menu.

You may also add borders and shading to your table by using the buttons on the Borders toolbar. To display this toolbar, right-click any toolbar, and choose Borders from the shortcut

Accounting		
Name	Phone	Job Title
Brian, Samuel	x8739	Junior Accountant
Carter, Jane	x7893	Senior Accountant
David, Sharra	x9830	Senior Clerk
Fried, Cara	x5930	Junior Clerk

Production		
Name	Phone	Job Title
Fish, Kirk	X4894	Foreman
Martin, Gina	X4301	Stock Clerk
Paul, Steve	X4837	Electrician
Polk, Sara	X4834	Design Engineer
Robinson, James	X4300	Machinist
Witte, Doreen	X4305	Machinist Apprentice

FIGURE 10-1   Borders and shading added to a table

menu. You can click these buttons on the Borders toolbar to add or remove borders.

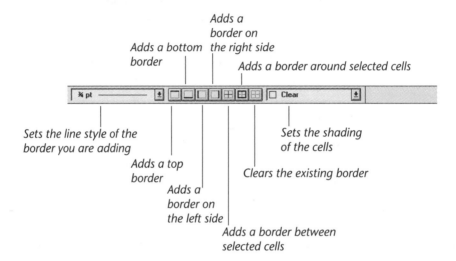

Adds a border on the right side

Adds a bottom border

Adds a border around selected cells

Sets the line style of the border you are adding

Sets the shading of the cells

Adds a top border

Clears the existing border

Adds a border on the left side

Adds a border between selected cells

Tech Tip: To remove borders from a table using the Borders toolbar, select None from the Line Style box, then click the button that adds the border you want to remove.

Tech Tip: When you add table formatting with either the Table wizard or the Table AutoFormat feature, Word automatically adds borders and shading for you.

How do I apply shading to table cells or paragraphs?

You can easily apply shading to table cells or paragraphs.

1. Select the table cells or paragraphs that you want to shade.

2. Choose <u>B</u>orders and Shading from the F<u>o</u>rmat menu.

3. Click the <u>S</u>hading tab.

4. Select the percentage of gray in the Sha<u>d</u>ing list box.

5. Click OK.

6. Click anywhere outside of the selection to remove the highlight and see the shading.

Shading within table cells fills the cells; shading of selected paragraphs extends from the left indent to the right indent.

Tech Tip: The appearance of shading in your printed output depends on your printer. Your printer may support more or fewer levels of shading than Word.

What is the quickest way to format a table?

Word includes a Table AutoFormat feature that quickly applies formatting to sections of a table. You can also use the Table AutoFormat feature when you create a table.

To use Table AutoFormat to modify an existing table:

1. Move the insertion point to the table you want to format.

2. Start Table AutoFormat with one of these three methods:

   ■ Right-click the table, and choose Table AutoFormat from the table's shortcut menu.

   ■ Move to the table and choose Table Auto<u>F</u>ormat from the T<u>a</u>ble menu.

   ■ Click the <u>A</u>utoFormat button, which is available when you create a table by choosing <u>I</u>nsert Table from the T<u>a</u>ble menu. (This method is only applicable for new tables, not existing ones.)

3. Select one of the predefined table formats in the Forma<u>t</u>s list box.

4. Select or clear the <u>B</u>orders, <u>S</u>hading, <u>F</u>ont, <u>C</u>olor, or AutoF<u>i</u>t check boxes to selectively apply the elements of the predefined style to your table.

For example, you can omit the font changes that a predefined style would add by clearing the Font check box.

5. Select the Heading Rows, First Column, Last Row, and Last Column check boxes to specify the areas to which Word should apply additional formatting.

You can use this additional formatting to distinguish your headings and totals from the other cells in the table. Clearing a check box removes the formatting from the specified part of the table.

1. Click OK to apply the formatting to the table.

Figure 10-2 shows a table that was formatted by using the Table AutoFormat feature. This table is formatted with the Grid 8 style with all check boxes selected.

Tech Tip: You can apply a heading style to the row in which the insertion point is located by pressing ALT+SHIFT and then pressing the LEFT ARROW or RIGHT ARROW to select the heading style you want to use.

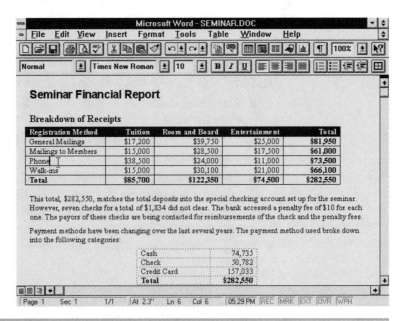

Seminar Financial Report

Breakdown of Receipts

Registration Method	Tuition	Room and Board	Entertainment	Total
General Mailings	$17,200	$39,750	$25,000	$81,950
Mailings to Members	$15,000	$28,500	$17,500	$61,000
Phone	$38,500	$24,000	$11,000	$73,500
Walk-ins	$15,000	$30,100	$21,000	$66,100
Total	**$85,700**	**$122,350**	**$74,500**	**$282,550**

This total, $282,550, matches the total deposits into the special checking account set up for the seminar. However, seven checks for a total of $1,834 did not clear. The bank accessed a penalty fee of $10 for each one. The payors of these checks are being contacted for reimbursements of the check and the penalty fees.

Payment methods have been changing over the last several years. The payment method used broke down into the following categories:

Cash	74,735
Check	50,782
Credit Card	157,033
Total	$282,550

FIGURE 10-2   A table formatted by using Table AutoFormat

I have a table that appears on more than one page. I want a header row to appear at the top of each page of the table to identify the columns. Can Word do this?

Word can repeat one or more rows at the top of every page on which the table appears. To add this header:

1. Select the row or rows you want to use as a table heading.

2. Choose <u>H</u>eadings from the T<u>a</u>ble menu.

If the table splits across a page, Word automatically repeats the table heading rows at the top of the next page. However, if you insert a hard page break within the table, Word does not display the heading rows.

How can I add more rows or columns to my table?

Although you initially set the number of columns and rows in a table when you first create it, you can always add more later, as needed. Word offers two ways to insert additional columns in your table:

- Select cells in the same number of columns as you want to add to the table, then choose <u>I</u>nsert Cells from either the T<u>a</u>ble menu or the shortcut menu that appears when you right-click the table. Click the Insert Entire <u>C</u>olumn option button, then click OK.

- Drag the mouse across the tops of the same number of columns as you want to add, where you want to add them. Then, choose <u>I</u>nsert Columns from either the T<u>a</u>ble menu or the shortcut menu that appears when you right-click the table.

Word adds the new columns to the left of the columns you selected.

To add more rows to a table:

- Select cells in the same number of rows that you want to add, then choose <u>I</u>nsert Cells from the T<u>a</u>ble menu or from the shortcut menu. Select the Insert Entire <u>R</u>ow option button and then click OK.

■ Drag the mouse down the left side of the same number of rows you want to add. Then, choose Insert Rows from the Table menu.

■ Press TAB when you are in the last cell of a table to add a new row at the end of the table.

The first two methods add the new rows above those you selected.

Tech Tip: Another way to insert cells is to select the same number of cells, columns, or rows as you want to add, and then click the Insert Table button on the Standard toolbar. If you selected entire columns or rows, Word automatically inserts the same number of columns or rows to the left of them, respectively. Otherwise, you enter your specifications in the Insert Cells dialog box that appears.

Can I move rows around within my table?

You can easily reorganize your table by moving rows without cutting and pasting them. To do so:

1. Select the rows you want to move.

2. Hold down ALT+SHIFT and press UP ARROW or DOWN ARROW until the row appears at the desired location.

Alternatively, you can select the rows with the mouse and then drag them to the beginning of the row before which you want them to appear. To use this method, make sure the Drag-and-Drop Text Editing check box on the Edit tab is selected. (Choose Options from the Tools menu to display the Edit tab.)

You can also copy and paste rows within a table by using the same Copy, Cut, and Paste commands that you use to rearrange text in the document.

Tech Tip: You can also rearrange rows by sorting them based on the entries in one of the table's columns.

How can I move and copy text and graphics from one table cell to another?

Word provides three ways to move and copy text and graphics from one table cell to another. Select the item you want to move or copy, then:

- Click the Cut or Copy button on the Standard toolbar, move to the location where you want the text or graphics to appear, and click the Paste button on the Standard toolbar.

- Choose Cut or Copy from the Edit menu, move to the location where you want the text or graphics to appear, and choose Paste from the Edit menu.

- Use the mouse to perform drag and drop editing. (To use this method, make sure the Drag-and-Drop Text Editing check box on the Edit tab is selected.)

My table currently appears right at the beginning of my document. How do I add text above it?

To add text before the table, move to the beginning of the first cell and press ENTER. Word adds a blank paragraph mark above the table.

How do I split cells within a table?

You can separate a single cell into several cells in different columns or redivide cells that you previously joined together.

To divide one or more cells:

1. Select one or more cells that you want to split.
2. Choose Split Cells from the Table menu.
3. By default, Word divides a cell in two. If desired, you can enter a different number in the Number of Columns text box to generate more than two cells from each of the originals.
4. Click OK.

Word splits the text within a table cell based on the number of paragraph marks it contains. If only one paragraph mark is in the cell, Word places the text in the leftmost cell and inserts empty cells to the right. For example, suppose your table originally appeared like the one shown here:

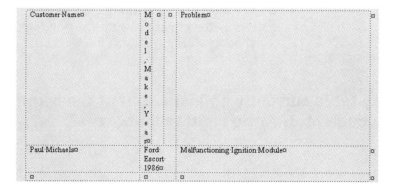

After splitting the cell in the first row of the second column into three, your new table would look like this:

In this example, you would then move "Make" and "Year" from the second cell to the two empty ones.

If the selected cell contains more than one paragraph mark, Word divides the paragraphs among the new cells. Suppose your invoice form looks like the one shown here:

After you split the cell in the first row, it would look like this instead:

Sam·Catering¶		216/762-4039¶	
Name:□		Phone:□	:c
Address:□			:c
□			:c
Item□	Quantity□	Price□	:c
□	□	□	:c

How do I make a single table cell span across several columns?

You can join several cells that are side-by-side to create a table entry that spans several columns. First, select the cells you want to unite and then choose <u>M</u>erge Cells from the T<u>a</u>ble menu. Word connects all of the selected cells in the same row. The contents of the original cells are separated by paragraph breaks in the new one. For example, you might want to combine the cells in the first row of this table:

Tamarac Community Sports			
Softball Signup		**Teams will be assigned May 1, 1995**	
Name	Phone Number	Position	Mitt (Y/N)

When you join the cells, the roster would look like this one:

Tamarac Community Sports			
Softball Signup **Teams will be assigned May 1, 1995**			
Name	Phone Number	Position	Mitt (Y/N)

Tech Tip: You can only split or merge cells horizontally, not vertically.

How can I easily insert a tab character in a cell?

In a table, pressing TAB moves the insertion point from one cell to another. To insert the tab character in a cell, move the insertion point to the position in the cell at which you want the tab to appear and then press CTRL+TAB.

How do I change the alignment of text in my table?

Paragraph formatting determines the alignment of table entries just as it does normal text in a document. You can therefore realign table entries in the usual manner:

1. Select the cells, columns, or rows whose alignment you want to change.

2. Choose Paragraph from the Format menu

3. Click the Indents and Spacing tab.

4. Select the alignment you want to use in the Alignment drop-down list box.

5. Click OK.

Tech Tip: You can make your selection and then click the Align Left, Center, Align Right, or Justify button on the Formatting toolbar.

In Word for Windows 2.0, I switch to table mode before inserting tabs stops in a table. Word 6.0 doesn't seem to have this mode so how can I add tabs?

Word for Windows 6.0 automatically switches to table mode whenever your insertion point is in a table. Therefore, you simply need to select the tab type by using the Tab Alignment button on the left end of the ruler, as shown here, then click the ruler to add a tab at the new location.

Tab Alignment button

You can also set tab stops within a table by using the <u>T</u>abs command in the F<u>o</u>rmat menu.

As I'm typing text in a table cell, it's disappearing. Where is it going?

The paragraph formatting for the table cell may apply indents that shift the text out of the table cell. To redisplay the text, you need to change or remove the indents by following these steps:

1. Choose <u>P</u>aragraph from the F<u>o</u>rmat menu.
2. Click the <u>I</u>ndents and Spacing tab.
3. Specify different indentation measurements; usually, you should set these at 0.
4. Click OK.

You can also position the insertion point in the cell, then drag the indent markers on the ruler to change them, accordingly.

If indents aren't the source of the problem, you may have an exact row height set in your table. Part of the text may simply extend below the cell. In this case, you can make the row taller to accommodate the entries.

How do I change the height of a row in a table?

Word initially sets the height of a row based on its contents; as you add more text to the cells, the row "grows." You can also specify a different row height or, after changing it, revert to the default setting. To change the height of a row:

1. Select the row or rows whose heights you want to set.

2. Choose Cell Height and <u>W</u>idth from the <u>T</u>able menu.

3. Click the <u>R</u>ow tab.

4. Set the row height in one of three ways:

   - Let Word automatically adjust the row's height to fit the text or graphics in it by selecting Auto in the H<u>e</u>ight of Rows drop-down list box.

   - Specify a minimum height for the row by selecting At Least in the H<u>e</u>ight of Rows drop-down list box. In the <u>A</u>t text box, type or specify the row's height in points. You can enter the distance using a different measurement by including a quotation mark (") or "in" for inches, "cm" for centimeters, or "li" for lines. If the contents of the cell exceed the minimum height, Word adjusts the height accordingly.

   - Specify a fixed row height by selecting Exactly in the H<u>e</u>ight of Rows drop-down list box. In the <u>A</u>t text box, type or specify the height as measured in points. You can also enter the distance using a different measuring system, as described in the previous paragraph. If the contents of the cell exceed the fixed height, Word cuts them off.

5. Click OK.

Tech Tip: If a row's height is set to Exactly and it cannot fully display the contents, the additional text or graphics may appear below it when you print the table. This "spillover" may occur even though it's not apparent on the screen. Whether it does so depends on the printer you are using.

You can also change the height of the rows using the vertical ruler in page layout view by dragging the bottom of the row up or down. Figure 10-3 shows a table with both rulers displayed. You can see the dividing points for the columns and rows in the table. When you drag one of these dividing points to a new location, the column or row's boundary changes accordingly.

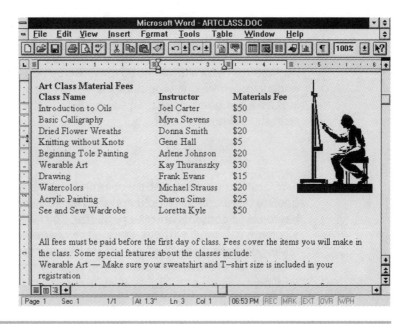

FIGURE 10-3   The rulers indicate the column and row boundaries in a table

How do I change the width of a column in a table?

Initially, Word sets equal column widths to produce a table that spans from margin to margin. However, your entries in the different columns are probably not all the same length. You can readjust the column widths to achieve a more effective and efficient page layout. You can specify the column widths yourself or let Word do so based on the columns' contents.

To change the width of a column in a table:

1. Move the insertion point to the column whose width you want to change. If you select more than one column, their widths will be identical.

2. Choose Cell Height and Width from the Table menu.

3. Click the Column tab.

4. To set the column width to an exact measurement, enter it in the Width of Column text box, and then click OK. Alternatively, you can click AutoFit to let Word set the width based on the column's contents and the page size.

When you display the ruler, you can resize a column by dragging the column divider to the left or right. Figure 10-3 shows the column dividers that separate columns in a table. You can also resize a column with the mouse by pointing to a gridline or where one would appear. When the mouse pointer looks like the one below, drag the gridline to the left or right to reset the column's width.

Class Name	Instructor
Introduction to Oils	Joel Carter

You can automatically size a column by double-clicking a gridline or where one would appear. Word adjusts the width based on its contents and the page size. To change the width of a column in a table without altering the overall width of the table, you hold down SHIFT or CTRL while you drag the gridline. Pressing SHIFT resizes the column immediately to the right of the gridline; pressing CTRL causes all columns to the right to be resized evenly.

Tech Tip: You can set the width of a cell in one row independently of the column's width in other rows. You simply select the cell and then drag the boundary to a new location. Most users discover this feature inadvertently when they change the width of one cell and find that the rest of the column didn't change.

Can I change the spacing between columns?

When you create a table, Word initially leaves some space between columns so that the entries in one do not butt up against those in the next. To change the spacing between columns:

1. Select the area of the table to format.
2. Choose Cell Height and Width from the Table menu.
3. Click the Column tab.
4. Type the distance you want between the current column and the next one in the Space Between Columns text box.
5. Click OK.

Is it possible to break a table row across a page break?

Word for Windows 6.0 has a new feature that allows a table row to break across pages. To activate this setting:

1. Select the row you want to divide.
2. Choose Cell Height and Width from the Table menu.
3. Click the Row tab.
4. Select the Allow Row to Break Across Pages check box and click OK.

When the Allow Row to Break Across Pages check box is cleared and Word cannot fit all of a row onto a page, the entire row moves to the next page. When Word breaks a row within a table across a page break, a dotted line appears through one or more cells in the table.

How can I prevent rows in a table from splitting across a page break?

To prevent selected rows from splitting across a page break:

1. Select the rows within the table you want to change.
2. Choose Cell Height and Width from the Table menu.
3. Click the Row tab.
4. Clear the Allow Row to Break Across Pages check box.
5. Click OK.

How can I center a table horizontally on a page?

To center a table horizontally:

1. Move the insertion point to the table.
2. Choose Select Table from the Table menu.
3. Choose Cell Height and Width from the Table menu.
4. Click the Row tab.

5. Select Center in the Alignment section.

6. Click OK to shift the table to the right so it is centered across the page.

Tech Tip: To center a table vertically, repeat steps 1 and 2. Select Insert Frame, then Format Frame. In the Vertical Selection box, choose position and select Center. In the Relative to box, choose Page. Click OK and your table will be vertically aligned on the page.

Is there any way to total the numbers in a column of my table?

Word makes it easy to set up a formula that totals the values in a column or row. Suppose you create a table like the one shown here:

Registration Method	Tuition	Room and Board	Entertainment	Total
General Mailings	$17,200	$39,750	$25,000	
Mailings to Members	$15,000	$28,500	$17,500	
Phone	$38,500	$24,000	$11,000	
Walk-ins	$15,000	$30,100	$21,000	
Total				

Tech Tip: When you are adding a formula to total a row, you may need to change =SUM(ABOVE) to =SUM(LEFT) in the Formula text box. As long as the cell above the one in which the insertion point is located contains a value, Word assumes that you want the =SUM(ABOVE) formula, even if you are in the last column of the table.

You can quickly add a formula to the cells in the last row of the table to total the values in the columns. You can use the same Word feature to quickly total the values in the rows. To total these values, you enter a formula in a cell that sums the values above or to the left of it.

To add this formula:

1. Move the insertion point to the cell in which you want to insert the formula.

2. Choose Formula from the Table menu.

Word automatically enters the formula =SUM(ABOVE) or =SUM(LEFT) in the Formula text box. You can also enter =SUM(BELOW) and =SUM(RIGHT) when you want to total values at the top or left side of the table.

3. Click OK.

Can I perform calculations using the data in my table?

You can add formulas that perform calculations. These formulas are especially useful when you want to calculate results based on other values in the table. You can create formulas yourself using the operators +, –, *, and / for addition, subtraction, multiplication, and division, respectively. You can use some of Word's predefined formulas, called *functions*.

You perform calculations in a table by inserting an = field and then adding the formula as the field's code. You can add these formulas three ways:

- By pressing CTRL+F9, typing = then the formula.

- By choosing Fi**e**ld from the **I**nsert menu, typing = and the formula to perform in the **F**ield Codes text box, then clicking OK.

- By choosing F**o**rmula from the T**a**ble menu and typing the formula to perform after the = sign that appears automatically in the **F**ormula text box.

Tech Tip: You can see the formulas rather than their results in your Word document by displaying field codes. Press ALT+F9 to toggle between field results and field codes.

I added a formula that sums a column in my table. However, it's also adding the year that identifies the column into the final sum. How do I prevent this?

You're probably using the =SUM(ABOVE) formula to total the values in the column. In this case, you need to replace ABOVE with the cells you want to total. To add this specification to the formula:

1. Move the insertion point to the cell that contains the formula.

2. Press ALT+F9 to display the field code, if necessary.

3. Replace ABOVE with the names of the table cells you want totaled.

4. Press ALT+F9 again to display the field results.

5. Press F9 to update the field's results.

A cell name consists of a letter that indicates the column and a number that indicates the row. In other words, C5 is the name of the fifth cell in the third column in a table. You can use a colon to separate the names of the first and last cells in a range you want to total. For example, to total the cells in the third column shown below, you can replace ABOVE with C2:C5. Because the formula doesn't include cell C1, the year does not contribute to the total. The formulas that total columns B and C omit the year in the first row; the formula in column D still needs to be corrected.

Projected Sales			
Store Location	1994	1995	1996
Mentor	450,000	500,000	600,000
Bedford Heights	500,000	525,000	550,000
Brooklyn	300,000	350,000	400,000
Westlake	500,000	600,000	700,000
Total	{=SUM(B2:B5)}	{=SUM(C2:C5)}	{=SUM(ABOVE)}

Tech Tip: You can total an entire row or column by including just the row numbers or column letters on either side of the colon. For example, 2:5 indicates rows 2 through 5, and D:G includes the fourth through seventh columns.

 Does Word provide any features to make entering formulas in a table easier?

Word includes a TABLES.DOT template in the WINWORD\MACROS sub-directory. This template contains a macro called TableMath that can help you set up the required math functions.

You can access the TABLES.DOT template by making it available globally to all of your documents or by attaching it to the current document.

To make the TABLES.DOT template available globally:

1. Choose <u>T</u>emplates from the <u>F</u>ile menu.

2. Click the A̲dd button.

3. Select the TABLES.DOT file in the WINWORD\MACROS subdirectory.

4. Click OK twice.

Tech Terror: If you installed Word using the Typical or Minimal installation options, you may not be able to find TABLES.DOT. It is only added to your system when you perform a Complete Installation of Word.

Use this option when you don't want to change the template that the current document uses and you want to make the TABLES.DOT macros available in other documents.

To change the template the current document uses to TABLES.DOT:

1. Choose T̲emplates from the F̲ile menu.

2. Enter **\WINWORD\MACROS\TABLES.DOT** in the Document T̲emplate text box.

3. Click OK.

To enter a formula by using the macros:

1. Move to the table in which you want to add the formulas.

2. Choose M̲acro from the T̲ools menu.

3. Type **TABLEMATH** in the M̲acro Name text box and then click R̲un to display the Math dialog box, as shown in Figure 10-4.

4. Select the function you want the formula to perform in the C̲alculation Type drop-down list box.

5. Select the cells from the table to include in this formula in the L̲ist list box. The table cells are identified by their column letter and row number. Word labels columns in the table starting with the letter A and rows with the number 1, as you can see here:

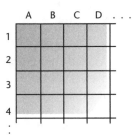

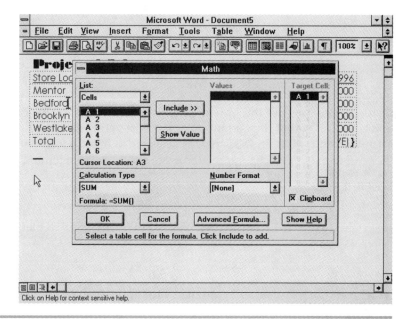

FIGURE 10-4 The Math dialog box

Tech Tip: To make sure you selected the correct cell in the list box, select it and then click the Show Value button. Word displays the current value of the selected cell.

6. Indicate where Word should store the results of the formula. By default, Word places them on the Clipboard so you can paste them into any cell you want. However, if you already know where you want to display the formula's results, clear the Clipboard check box and select the cell in the Target Cell list box.

7. Click OK to add the formula.

8. If you left the Clipboard check box selected, Word prompts you to move to the cell in which you want to place the formula and then choose Paste from the Edit menu. When you do so, Word inserts a formula field code into the document.

Tech Tip: Remember, Word is not designed to be a spreadsheet application—some math functions may be unavailable or limited in scope.

Once the TABLES.DOT template is available, you can display the Tables toolbar. This toolbar contains the Fill Down, Fill Right, Number, Math, and Access Exporter buttons shown below. These toolbar buttons perform the TableFillDown, TableFillRight, TableNumber, TableMath, and AccessExporter macros, respectively.

In WordPerfect, I used floating cells to add formulas in normal text. How do I add this feature in Word?

WordPerfect lets you add formulas to regular text by adding floating cells to your document. In Word, you create these formulas with the = field, which can be added in any location.

Tech Tip: When you use the = field to reference a number that is not in a table, you must add a bookmark to the number's location. You then enter the bookmark's name in the formula so that Word can find the correct value.

I added a formula to my table but I don't like the dollar signs nor number of decimal points that Word displays. How do I remove them?

Word for Windows applies a format to formula results that determines whether and what special symbols appear. It also sets the number of digits that display after the decimal point. Formulas can use either the default format or one of their own.

The default format is set in the International dialog box, which you access from the Windows Control Panel. If the values in a formula do not have any digits after the decimal point, the results display as few decimal digits as possible; if the values include formatting characters, such as commas to separate thousands or dollar signs, the results display them, too.

You can change the format of the formula's results by the following:

1. Move to the formula with the results you want to format.

2. Choose Formula from the Table menu.

    Windows displays the formula in the Formula text box.

3. Select a format in the Number Format drop-down list box or enter one of your own design.

    The drop-down list box includes several formats for currency and percentages. A # indicates where digits may appear; a 0 indicates that a zero will display if no digit appears at that location.

    To easily create a custom format, select one of the pre-defined ones and then modify it. For example, you might change $#,##0.000;($#,##0.000) to $#,##0;($#,##0) if you do not want any digits to display after the decimal point. This format includes two parts that apply to positive and negative numbers, respectively.

4. Click OK to apply the format to the formula.

I adjusted my document margins. Will this affect my tables?

When you alter your document margins, existing tables do not change. However, they may shift left or right depending on the new size of the left margin.

To modify the table's size, you can either change it manually or use the AutoFit option. To use AutoFit to quickly adjust columns widths:

1. Select the table by choosing Select Table from the Table menu.

2. Choose Cell Height and Width from the Table menu.

3. Click the Column tab.

4. Click the AutoFit button.

Word analyzes the table and resizes the columns according to their contents.

Tech Tip: If you change your document margins, an existing table may not print in its entirety. In this case, follow the steps to adjust the column widths so that the table fits within the new margins.

How do I reposition my table on the page?

You can position a table anywhere on a page by placing it in a frame. To do so, select the table, and then choose _F_rame from the _I_nsert menu. Respond to any prompt Word displays about switching to page layout view. Once the table is in the frame, use the Fra_m_e command on the F_o_rmat menu to move the table. You can also drag the frame with the mouse.

Tech Terror: If you attempt to insert a frame within a table (rather than around the table), the gridlines will not wrap around the frame. As a result, Word splits the table wherever a frame is located. The solution is to add as many paragraph breaks as necessary to accommodate the height of the frame and then insert a text box to hold whatever you want to enclose in the frame.

I placed a frame around my table but now I want to get rid of it. How do I eliminate the frame without deleting my entire table?

To remove a frame around a table:

1. Place the insertion point in the table.
2. Choose Select T_a_ble from the T_a_ble menu.
3. Choose Fra_m_e from the F_o_rmat menu.
4. Click _R_emove Frame.

Word removes the frame and keeps the table and its contents intact.

How can I number the columns and rows in my table?

You can number columns and rows in a table by clicking the Numbering button on the Formatting toolbar. To add these numbers:

1. Select the row or column you to want to number.

2. Click the Numbering button, as shown here, to display the Table Numbering dialog box:

3. Select Number <u>A</u>cross Rows if you want to number cells from left to right, or Number <u>D</u>own Columns if you want to number cells from top to bottom.

   You may also want to select the <u>N</u>umber Each Cell Only Once check box to avoid placing more than one number in a cell when some of the cells have more than one paragraph.

4. Click OK to add the numbers.

Figure 10-5 shows a table with numbers. As you add rows to this table, the new rows will also display numbers.

A few points about this feature will help you produce the desired results:

- If you have heading rows or columns, select all of the cells in the column or row except those that contain the headings. You can also select the entire row or column, add the numbers, select the heading, and then click the Numbering button again to remove the heading's number.

- If you want to add a column of numbers instead of placing them in the cells with the entries themselves, add a new column and then number it.

- Instead of using the Numbering button on the Formatting toolbar, you can add numbers by choosing the Bullets and <u>N</u>umbering command from the F<u>o</u>rmat menu or the shortcut menu for the selected cells. When

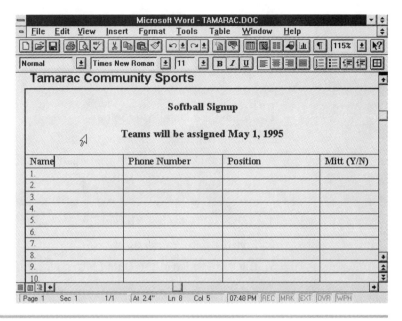

FIGURE 10-5   You can add numbers to rows in a table

you click the <u>N</u>umbered tab, select a numbering format, then click OK, Word displays the Table Numbering dialog box. When you add numbers in this way, you can also change their format.

Tech Tip: Word's TABLES.DOT template includes a TableNumber macro that inserts a column or row filled with numbers in your table. You cannot remove these numbers by using the Numbering button on the Formatting toolbar.

I have a lot of data in my table. Is there any way I can work with it like a database?

You can display a data form dialog box to work with the data in a table. This dialog box displays a single row's data in a different way than the table. Figure 10-6 shows a data form dialog box with the table whose data it uses.

When you use a data form to work with table data, you may notice that Word calls each row in the table a record and each column in the table a field. Records and fields are the same terms that databases and Word use to describe the data that you use for a mail merge.

To display the Data Form dialog box using the data from a table:

1. Display the Database toolbar.

2. Place the insertion point in the table.

3. Click the Data Form button, which looks like this:

4. Edit the data, as necessary.

5. Click OK to leave the Data Form dialog box.

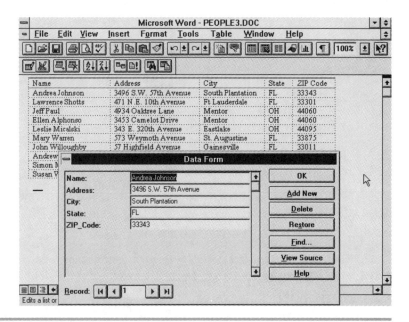

FIGURE 10-6   You can use the Data Form dialog box to display data in a table

You can make changes such as the following to data displayed in the Data Form dialog box:

- Select which record appears in the data form by clicking the buttons next to <u>R</u>ecord to move to the first, previous, next, and last record in the table, respectively. You can also type a record number in the text box to go directly to that record.

- Edit the data in the table by modifying the entries in the text boxes. If you change your mind, click the Re<u>s</u>tore button to return to the original data.

- Add more data to the table by clicking the <u>A</u>dd New button and typing new information in the text boxes.

- Delete a row from the table by displaying the data in the dialog box, and then clicking <u>D</u>elete.

- Find a row of data in the table by clicking the <u>F</u>ind button. In the Find in Field dialog box that appears, type the entry you want to find in the Fi<u>n</u>d What text box, select the field in the In Fiel<u>d</u> drop-down down list box, and click OK. Word displays the record with the designated entry in the Data Form dialog box.

How do I save a table as a delimited text file so that I can import it into a database?

In Word, you can save table data in a text delimited file and then import it into other programs, such as database and spreadsheet applications.

To create this type of file:

Tech Tip: While you can choose another delimiter, tabs usually work best.

1. If the table you want to convert appears in a document that includes other information, open a new document and copy and paste the table to it.

2. Choose Select T<u>a</u>ble from the T<u>a</u>ble menu, or press ALT+ 5 (on the numeric keypad).

3. Choose Con<u>v</u>ert Table to Text from the T<u>a</u>ble menu.

4. Select the <u>T</u>abs option button and click OK when Word prompts you to select a delimiter.

5. Choose Save As from the File menu.

6. Select Text Only in the Save File as Type drop-down list box.

7. You may want to enter an entirely different file name in the File Name text box to make it easy to distinguish this version from the original.

8. Change the directory in which the file will be stored, if desired.

9. Click OK to save the file.

Now, all you have to do is open your database application and import the file!

Merges

Word's merge feature is a powerful productivity tool. The personalized advertisements and announcements you undoubtedly receive in the mail is evidence of the power of merging.

At its most basic level, merging creates multiple, individualized documents by inserting data from one document, called a *data source*, into the text of another document, called a *form file*. Merging makes it possible to quickly create many documents to communicate with hundreds or thousands of people.

Word includes a Mail Merge Helper to walk you through the steps of performing a merge. The Mail Merge Helper can also help you select which records you want to use in a merge. By selecting specific types of records to merge, you can increase this feature's usefulness and flexibility.

You can also use Word's advanced programming commands to move beyond the basic level of simply combining two files. Word's advanced merge commands let you create documents that vary based on different entries within records. You can also use these commands to perform a keyboard merge in which the person conducting the merge, usually referred to as the merge's *user*, enters data directly during the merge process. A careful study of advanced merge techniques can quickly pay off in increased productivity.

FRUSTRATION BUSTERS!

Merging itself is a very simple process. However, you have probably heard other people describe how frustrating and complicated it can be. The strange, and sometimes confusing, terms used to describe different merge operations and objects often contribute to this misconception. Insufficient preparation when setting up the data source is also a common source of problems.

For new users, the first trick is to become familiar with the various merge terms, most of which are defined here:

- A *data source* is the file that contains the data that will be merged into the main document during the merge. For example, if you are using Word to print the envelopes for your wedding invitations, the data source would contain the name and address of each guest. Word can use data sources in a variety of formats, including data from databases or spreadsheets.

- A *record* consists of the data for a single entity and is stored in a data source. For example, if your data source contains the names and addresses of the people you are inviting to your wedding, you would store all of Aunt Jane's data, including her name, address, and the number of guests she's bringing, in one record.

- A *field* is a single piece of data in a record. For example, Aunt Jane's record contains a field for her first name, one for her last name, another for her street address, and so on. For Word to correctly perform a merge, each record must contain the same fields in the same order.

- A *main document*, or *form file*, is the document that contains the text, graphics, or other information that does not change in each copy of the final merge document. For example, the main document for your wedding envelopes would contain the formatting for the envelopes and your return address. It also contains merge fields.

- *Merge fields* are the codes in a main document that tell Word where to place the data from the data source when you merge.

Each merge field indicates the position of a single data source field. For example, you would enter a merge field to indicate where to place the name of your guest on an envelope.

- The actual process of taking the variable data from the data source and combining it with the constant data in the main document is the *merge*. For example, when you merge the guest list with the envelope document, you merge them to produce one envelope for each record in the data source. The final merge documents each look exactly like the main document, except that the data appears instead of the merge fields. When you merge, you can merge to a new document or directly to the printer. When you merge directly to the printer, you never actually see the new document on the screen.

Merging is a powerful tool, but only if you plan how you're going to use it in advance. Even expert Word users experience frustration when they don't properly prepare for a merge. You need to carefully design your data source to contain all information you need for current and future projects. If you tailor your data source to only today's mailing label needs, it may not include the entries you need to create form letters tomorrow. To get the most mileage from a data source, follow these simple rules.

- Before creating a data source, consider what information may be useful to you.

- Break this information down into the smallest reasonable components to give you the most flexibility. For example, if you enter a person's name into first and last name fields, you can then reference the first name in the salutations in your letters.

- Invest the time in asking other people what future uses they may have for the data source.

Whether your data source will be used for simple or complex merges, be sure to thoroughly consider how the data needs to be merged. Take into consideration such issues as whether your data includes entries in each of the fields you plan to use in every record. If not, what happens to records with missing entries?

If you carefully plan your data source and main document to take into account most possibilities, you are much more likely to perform a successful merge that yields consistent and the expected results. When you initially develop your data source, you can expect to spend time adding fields, rearranging fields, and altering how it's set up. But remember, planning ahead will greatly reduce the amount of time, if any, that you spend editing later.

How do I insert merge fields into my main document?

Merge fields tell Word where to insert what data in the main document to create your final output. To create your main document and add the merge fields:

1. Choose Mail Merge from the Tools menu to open the Mail Merge Helper dialog box, shown in Figure 11-1.

2. Click Create under Main Document and then select the type of main document you want to use: form letters, mailing labels, envelopes, or catalogs.

3. Choose where Word creates the main document by clicking either Active Window or New Main Document.

4. Choose Open Data Source from the Get Data Source drop-down menu under Data Source in the Mail Merge Helper dialog box. You will open the document containing the data in the background so you do not see it even though the data is available to your Word documents.

5. Choose the file that contains the data you want to use.

6. Click Edit Main Document when Word prompts you to do so.

7. In the main document:

- Enter the text and graphics you want to appear in each copy of the merge document.

- Place the insertion point where you want to insert information from the data source and then click the Insert Merge Field button on the Mail Merge toolbar to select the field.

8. After editing the main document, save it, then complete the merge as usual.

Tech Tip: Make sure that you include any desired spaces or punctuation between or after merge fields.

Tech Tip: To insert a merge field directly press CTRL+F9 to insert field braces. Then, type **mergefield** followed by a space and the name of the field you want to insert.

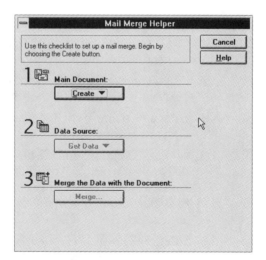

FIGURE 11-1 The Mail Merge Helper dialog box

How do I create a data source for a merge?

Although you can create a data source from a table or tab-delimited text in a document, it's much easier and foolproof to let Word guide you through the process. You can use Word's Mail Merge Helper to help you create your data source by following these steps:

Tech Tip: If you had previously created the data source, you could choose Open Data source from the Get Data drop-down menu and then select that document.

1. Choose Mail Merge from the Tools menu to display the Mail Merge Helper dialog box.

2. Click Create under Main Document and choose the type of main document to create.

3. Specify where you want to create the main document by clicking either Active Window or New Main Document.

4. Choose Create Data Source from the Get Data drop-down menu under Data Source to open the Create Data Source dialog box.

5. Add the fields you want to appear in your data source by selecting or entering them in the Field Names in Header Row list box. This list box includes the most common fields you might use, as shown in Figure 11-2.

   You can delete an entry by selecting it and then clicking Remove Field Name. To move a field name, select it and then click the Move buttons to the right of the list.

6. To add a field, if desired, enter its name in the Field Name text box and then click Add Field Name. Repeat this step for each additional field.

7. When the list reflects the fields you want, click OK to display the Save Data Source dialog box.

8. Enter a filename in the File Name text box and then click OK to save your new file.

9. Choose Edit Data Source when prompted. The Data Form dialog box, which makes adding data to the data source easier, appears. Each Data Form dialog box is individualized to match the fields in the data source you are editing.

10. Enter the information for each field in the first data record in the appropriate text boxes, as shown in Figure 11-3.

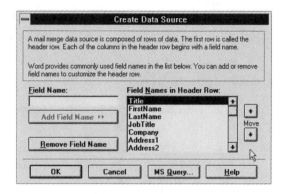

FIGURE 11-2   The Create Data Source dialog box

11. Click <u>A</u>dd New to add the current record in the document.

12. Repeat steps 10 and 11 for each record you want to add to your data source, then click OK.

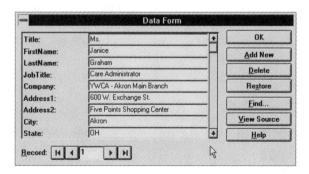

FIGURE 11-3   The Data Form dialog box

How do I merge my data source with the main document?

Before you merge the main document and the data source, verify the following:

■ You have entered all of the data you want to use in the data source file.

■ You inserted the merge fields in the main document in the locations where you want the variable data to appear in the final document.

To merge the data source with the main document:

1. Display the main document in the active window.

2. Click one of the merge buttons on the Mail Merge toolbar to merge the two documents and specify where the output appears:

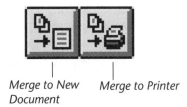

Merge to New   Merge to Printer
Document

Alternatively, click the Mail Merge button to display the Mail Merge dialog box. Specify where to send the output of the merge, how to treat blank lines created by missing field entries, which records you want to merge, and other options. Choose OK to perform the merge.

How do I create a main document for labels or envelopes?

Word 6.0's Mail Merge feature lets you easily create a variety of main documents, including labels and envelopes. The process is the same regardless of the main document type.

To create a label main document:

1. Choose Mail Merge from the Tools menu.

2. Choose <u>M</u>ailing Labels from the <u>C</u>reate drop-down menu under Main Document in the Mail Merge Helper dialog box.

3. When Word prompts you, click <u>A</u>ctive Window to make the current window a main document or <u>N</u>ew Main Document to open a new document as the Main document.

4. Choose <u>C</u>reate Data Source from the <u>G</u>et Data drop-down menu under Data Source in the Mail Merge Helper dialog box. Alternatively, choose <u>O</u>pen Data Source if you've already created the data source you want to use.

5. Create the data source file.

6. Choose <u>S</u>et Up Main Document when Word prompts you.

7. Select the appropriate options to define the type of label you want in the Labels Option dialog box and then click OK:

   - Specify the printer type by selecting the Dot <u>M</u>atrix or <u>L</u>aser option button.

   - If you are using a laser printer, select where the labels are being fed from in the <u>T</u>ray drop-down list box.

   - Select the type of labels in the Label <u>P</u>roducts drop-down list box. (If your brand is not listed, select one of the standard sets of label descriptions, such as Avery Standard. Most labels, regardless of who manufactured them, are marked with Avery equivalent numbers.)

   - Select the specific label format in the Product <u>N</u>umber list box, such as Avery 5371 - Business Cards.

Tech Tip: You can create a custom label definition by choosing <u>D</u>etails, entering the necessary measurements, and then clicking OK.

8. Enter the text and merge fields you want to use on the labels in the Sam<u>p</u>le Label text box in the Create Labels dialog box.

   You can add paragraph marks by pressing ENTER, or add merge fields by clicking In<u>s</u>ert Merge fields and choosing the field from the drop-down menu.

9. When you are satisfied with the label, click OK.

You can now execute the merge, as usual. Alternatively, you can return to the main document to perform additional editing, add graphics, and apply formatting, as shown in Figure 11-4, before merging the labels.

You perform almost the same steps to create an envelope main document. There are only three differences:

- In step 2, choose Envelopes from the Create drop-down menu under Main Document in the Mail Merge Helper dialog box.

- In step 7, select the envelope's size in the Envelope Size drop-down list box, specify the fonts for and precise location of the mailing and return addresses in the Delivery Address and Return Address section, and indicate how the envelope is fed into the printer and where it is fed from on the Printing Options tab.

- In step 8, enter the text and merge fields you want to use on the envelope in the Sample Envelope Address text box in the Envelope Address dialog box.

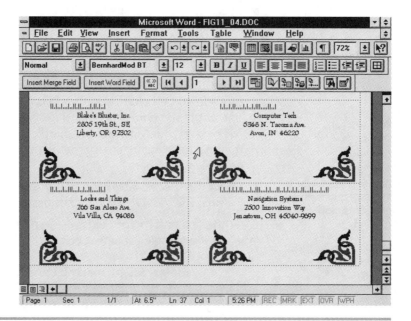

FIGURE 11-4   A formatted mailing label main document

What is a catalog main document?

In a catalog main document, Word does not insert page breaks between copies of the main document in the final merge output. In other words, instead of producing separate form letters or labels, the merged data all runs together. This type of merge is often used to create lists, directories, or catalogs of information, as shown in Figure 11-5.

How can I display the Mail Merge Helper dialog box during the merge process?

You can click the Mail Merge Helper button shown below on the Mail Merge toolbar to display the Mail Merge Helper dialog box at any time during the mail merge process.

Can I merge only some, but not all, records from a database and then sort them?

You can use Word's query feature to select and order only the records you want to use in the merge from a database. To query your source of data for specific records and sorting:

1. Open your main document and select your data source using the Mail Merge Helper, as you normally do.

Tech Tip: When you select an Access database as your data source, you must also select the particular table or query from the database you want to use.

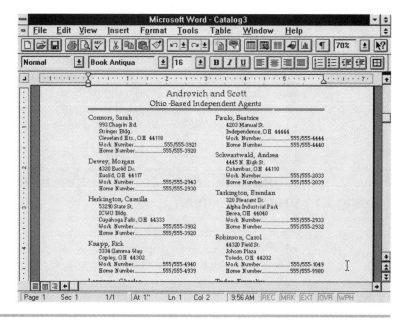

FIGURE 11-5   A catalog main document lets you create a single document that contains many records

2. Click Query Options in the Mail Merge Helper dialog box to open the Query Options dialog box.

3. Select the appropriate tab for the type of query you want to perform. The Filter Records tab selects which records you want to include in the merge while the Sort Records tab defines how you want to sort these records, as described in the following:

- On the Filter Records tab, select one or more fields from the data source in the Field list boxes, comparison operators in the Comparison list boxes, and enter the values to which to compare the fields in the Compare To text boxes.

  For example, to include the records for anyone whose first name is Peter in the merge, select the FirstName field in the Field text box, = in the Comparison list box, and enter **Peter** in the Compare To text box. If the fields in a record satisfy the criteria, Word includes the record in the merge.

■ On the Sort Records tab, you can select up to three
fields from drop-down list boxes by which to sort the
records included in the merge. Select the appropriate
option button to indicate if you want Word to sort the
records in ascending or descending order based on the
designated field.

4. Click OK to return to the Mail Merge Helper dialog box
and complete the merge process.

On the Filter Records tab, you can specify several comparison
operations and then indicate how they should interact by
making selections in the unlabeled drop-down list boxes at
the beginning of each row. Select And to include the record in
the merge only if both comparisons evaluate as true; select Or
if only one of the comparisons must be true. For example,
the following illustration depicts a filter that would include
only those records with Cleveland as the city and 44114 as
the ZIP code.

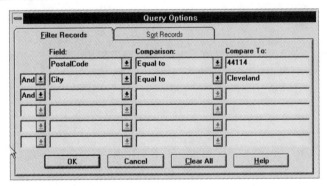

How do I input a postal bar code in a form letter or catalog main document?

Tech Tip: Consult
your post office
for the proper
placement of a
postal bar code.

Including a postal bar code on your
envelopes and labels expedites mail
delivery. Word 6.0 can automatically
produce these codes so that the
documents you send may get to their
destinations faster.

To add a postal bar code to your merge documents:

1. Create your envelope or mailing label main document.

2. Move the insertion point to the location at which you want the postal bar code to appear in the main document.

3. Choose Field from the Insert menu.

4. Select Numbering in the Categories list box, select BarCode in the Field Names list box, and then click OK.

   If the BarCode field does not appear in the document, press ALT+F9 to display field codes instead of field results.

5. Place your insertion point after the word "BARCODE."

6. Click the Insert Merge Field button on Mail Merge toolbar and select the field containing the ZIP code from the drop-down menu.

7. Type **\U** after the merge field, to indicate that the postal code is a U.S. ZIP code. Your field should now look something like this:

```
{BARCODE <<ZIP_CODE>> \U}
```

Tech Tip: Your code may also include *MERGEFORMAT if the Preserve Formatting During Update check box is selected in the Field dialog box.

8. Press ALT+F9 again to display field results instead of field codes.

   The BarCode field will probably display Error!; at this point, there is no ZIP code to display as a bar code.

9. Continue editing your main document as you normally would.

   When you merge the main document with the data source, the bar code appears, as shown in Figure 11-6, based on the ZIP code entered in that record.

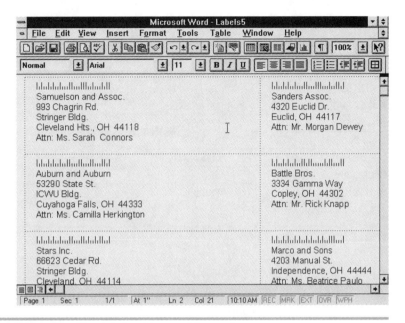

FIGURE 11-6 Merged mailing labels with postal bar codes

What does the Insert Word Field button on the Mail Merge toolbar do?

You can use this toolbar button to insert one of several Word fields that are useful in completing a merge. These fields perform special operations during the merge process. By using Insert Word Field, you can make your merges more complex with just a click of the button. The fields offered by this button's drop-down menu are listed in Table 11-1.

Each of these fields has a different function. You can use each of these fields to help program your merge to make it a more sophisticated and useful tool.

ASK   The ASK field prompts the person performing the merge to enter information at the keyboard, which is then assigned to

Option	Field Inserted
Ask	ASK
Fill-in	FILLIN
If...Then...Else	IF
Merge Record #	MERGEREC
Merge Sequence #	MERGESEQ
Next Record	NEXT
Next Record If...	NEXTIF
Set Bookmark	SET
Skip Record If...	SKIPIF

TABLE 11-1   The options available when you click the Insert Word Field button

a bookmark in the merge document. This field uses the format {ASK *bookmark "prompt"*} where *bookmark* is the name that Word assigns to the text and *prompt* is the message that Word displays to the user. You can display the text assigned to the bookmark by inserting a REF field or using the text with another field.

FILLIN   The FILLIN field prompts the person performing the merge to enter information at the keyboard, which then appears as the results of the FILLIN field. The field uses the format {FILLIN *"prompt"*}.

IF   This IF field compares two expressions and chooses a resulting action based on the results. The field uses the format {IF *expression operator expression "TextIfTrue" "TextIfFalse"*}, in which *expression* is a number, text, calculation, or merge field and *operator* defines how Word compares the two expressions. *TextIfTrue* and *TextIfFalse* are the text strings that Word displays depending on whether the comparison is true or not. You can choose from among the comparison operators found in Table 11-2.

MERGEREC and MERGESEQ   The results of the MERGEREC and MERGESEQ fields indicate the current record in the data source. MERGEREC returns the actual number of the record in the data source, whereas MERGESEQ returns a number indicating the position of the record in the set of records to be merged from the data source.

Operator	Meaning
=	Equals
>	Greater than
<	Lesser than
>=	Equals or greater than
<=	Equals or less than
<>	Not equal

TABLE 11-2   Operators to use in an IF field expression

NEXT   The NEXT field merges the next record into the current document rather than into a new merge document.

NEXTIF   The NEXTIF field compares two expressions. If the comparison is true, NEXTIF merges the next record into the current document rather than into a new merge document. It uses the format {NEXTIF *expression operator expression*}, in which *expression* is a number, text, formula, or merge field and *operator* is one of the comparison operators.

SET   The SET field assigns a value to a bookmark in the document. The field uses the format {SET *bookmark "data"*}. *Bookmark* is the name that Word assigns; *data* is the text to which Word assigns the bookmark.

SKIPIF   The SKIPIF field compares two expressions, and then skips or merges the record depending on the results of that comparison. It uses the format {SKIPIF *expression operator expression*}, in which *expression* is a number, text, formula, or merge field and *operator* is a comparison operator. No matter where the SKIPIF field appears in the main document, if the expression evaluates as true, the record will not appear in the final merge document.

The Insert Merge Field button doesn't display the list of merge fields. Why?

If you have a large number of merge fields, or the merge field names are very long, Word cannot display the list. However, if you press ALT+SHIFT+F, a dialog box appears with a list of the fields in the data source as well as the other fields you can add to a main document to change how Word performs the merge.

 Can I change which data source I use with a main document?

Yes, you can change the data source a main document uses. To do so:

1. Display the main document as the active document.
2. Click the Mail Merge Helper button on the Mail Merge toolbar.
3. Choose Open Data Source from the Get Data drop-down menu under Data Source, and then follow the usual steps for selecting the data source file.

Another way to switch to a different data source is to use a header file instead of a data source. A *header file* is a Word document that lists the field names, but contains no data. You can use a header file with different data sources, including those without header rows, such as databases and other non-Word application files. Header files make it easy to use a variety of data sources with one main document. As long as the data is arranged in the same order in each file, it doesn't matter whether the field names are exactly the same.

 Can I test a merge without actually performing it?

Yes, Word has a feature that lets you do a "test run" without actually running the merge. You can use this method to verify that the merge is set up correctly. For example, Word checks that all the merge fields in the document actually exist in the data source file.

To check the merge for errors:

1. Prepare for the merge as usual.
2. Click the Check for Errors button on the Mail Merge toolbar, shown here:

3. Select the appropriate option button in the Checking and Reporting Errors dialog box to indicate how you want Word to perform the check.

Tech Tip: Select the <u>S</u>imulate merge and report errors to a new document option button to discover any problems without performing the merge; use either of the other two options to actually complete the merge as well as report any errors. The other two options are <u>C</u>omplete the merge, pausing to report each error as it occurs, and Complete the <u>m</u>erge without pausing. Report errors in a new document.

4. Click OK.

Depending on the option you select, Word either simulates or actually runs the merge. Each time it encounters an error, Word displays a dialog box, such as the one shown here, so you can fix the error:

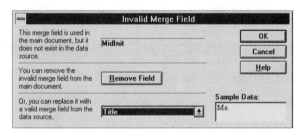

When the merge or simulation is complete, Word opens a new document that lists all of the errors it found.

Can I number the records in my data source, as I did in Word 2.0?

If the data in your Word 6.0 data source file is arranged in a table, you can number the records. To do so:

1. Open the data source in Word.
2. Select the first column of the table.

Tech Tip: You can also click the Numbering button on the Formatting toolbar to apply the default numbering style to the column.

3. Choose Insert Columns from the Table menu to add a new column at the left-hand side of the table.

4. Enter a field name in the first row of the new column.

5. Select the entire first column except for the first row.

6. Choose Bullets and Numbering from the Format menu.

7. Click the Numbered tab.

8. Select the type of numbering you want to use and then click OK.

9. When prompted, select the Number Down Columns check box and click OK again.

Numbering the column in this way allows Word to update the numbers whenever you add or delete records. Figure 11-7 shows a data source with numbered rows.

Tech Tip: In Word 6.0, you may not need to number the records in your data source. When you use the Data Form dialog box to edit your data source, you can move to a specific record by number even though the number doesn't actually appear in the record itself. Rather than adding another column to your table, you might just want to use this dialog box to access records by number.

	Title	First Name	Last Name	Job Title	Company	Address1	Address2	City	State	Postal Code	Country	Home Phone	Work Phone
1.	Ms.	Sarah	Connors	Hardware Manager	Samuelson and Assoc.	990 Chagrin Rd.	Stringer Bldg.	Clevel and Hts.	OH	44118		555/555-3920	555/555-3921
2.	Mr.	Morgan	Dewey	Programmer	Sanders Assoc.	4320 Euclid Dr.		Eucli d	OH	44117		555/555-2930	555/555-2943
3.	Ms.	Camilla	Herkington	Senior Analyst	Auburn and Auburn	53290 State St.	ICWU Bldg.	Cuyah oga Falls	OH	44333		555/555-3920	555/555-3902
4.	Mr.	Rick	Knapp	Programmer	Battle Bros.	3334 Gamma Way		Cople y	OH	44302		555/555-4939	555/555-4940
5.	Mr.	Charles	Lawrence	Systems Maintenance	Stars Inc.	666-23 Cedar Rd.	Stringer Bldg.	Clevel and	OH	44114		555/555-6590	555/555-2049
6.	Mr.	Jaques	Moliere	Information Manager	Zola Freres	44320 Huron Church Rd.	Westside Plaza	Wind sor	Ontar io	M25 B3C	Canada	555/555-4240	555/555-9030
7.	Ms.	Beatrice	Paulo	Technical Writer	Marco and Sons	4203 Manual St.		Indep enden ce	OH	44444		555/555-4440	555/555-4444
8.	Ms.	Andrea	Schwartzwald	Systems Analyst	Middle Systems Inc.	4445 N. High St.		Colu mbus	OH	44110		555/555-2039	555/555-2033
9.	Mr.	Brendan	Tarkington	Technical Writer	Johnson Co.	320 Pleasant Dr.	Alpha Industrial Park	Berea	OH	44040		555/555-2932	555/555-2933
10.	Ms.	Carol	Robinson	Hardware	Antaes Co.	44310 Field	Johnson	Toled	OH	44202		555/555-	555/555-

FIGURE 11-7 A data source with numbered rows

Can I suppress a blank space caused by an empty data field?

You can suppress a blank space caused by an empty data field by using an IF field. For example, to avoid displaying a blank space in the middle of a name that doesn't have an initial, you could enter these merge codes:

```
<<FIRSTNAME>> {IF <<MIDDLEINIT>> = "" "<<LASTNAME>>"
"<<MIDDLEINIT>>. <<LASTNAME>>"}
```

In this case, Word merges the Firstname field, then determines whether the Middleinit field contains an entry. If it does have an entry, Word merges both the Middleinit and Lastname fields; if the field is empty, Word merges only the Lastname field.

You could use this statement to check for an empty field before merging the data:

```
<<FIRSTNAME>> {IF <<MIDDLEINIT>> <> "" "<<MIDDLEINIT>>.
<<LASTNAME>>" "<<LASTNAME>>"}
```

Tech Tip: You can control whether Word skips an entire line if it only contains empty fields by making the appropriate selection in the Merge dialog box that Word displays when you start the merge process. The two option buttons that appear under When Merging Records determine whether Word removes blank lines.

Will Word 6.0 perform a mail merge with an dBASE database as the data source?

Word 6.0 can use dBASE databases as data source files. Word 6.0's Mail Merge feature can merge the data in these .DBF files by using the ODBC converters.

To use a dBASE database as a data source for a merge, open it from the Mail Merge Helper dialog box, just as you would any other data source. Word may prompt about opening specific tables or selecting a range of the database file. These prompts depend on the type of file and which ODBC converter you are using.

Tech Tip: Many different Microsoft applications install ODBC converters. Because all of Microsoft applications share these converters, two Word 6.0 users might be using different versions of the same converter, depending on the software installed on their individual computers.

Graphics, Drawing, and Pictures

Graphics can highlight important facts and add visual interest to everyday documents. You can create dazzling pages for any occasion by incorporating graphics from Word and other sources. These graphics can be modified with Word's drawing features, or you can add drawing objects directly to your documents.

You will put a *frame* around most graphics that you add to a document. A frame serves as a holder for the graphic and lets you move it easily around the page. Once text or a graphic is inside a frame, you can have the document text flow around or bypass the framed object.

You can also use drawing objects to add text and graphics anywhere on a page. Drawing objects such as lines, rectangles, squares, and callouts can be added using the tools on the Drawing toolbar. These drawing objects are placed on a layer on top of or below the text. You can think of drawing objects as items added to a transparency that lies either below or above the regular document text. You can display the Drawing toolbar the same way you display other toolbars, by either choosing Toolbars from the View menu and selecting the toolbars to display, or by right-clicking a toolbar and selecting another toolbar to open. Word also has another shortcut: click the Drawing button on the Standard toolbar and the Drawing toolbar appears. Click the button again and the Drawing toolbar disappears. The following Frustration Busters box briefly describes how the buttons in this toolbar are used.

FRUSTRATION BUSTERS!

Word's Drawing toolbar lets you add drawing objects to a document, modify them, and modify pictures added to a document. The buttons in the toolbar and how you use them are described here.

Button	How to Use
Line	Drag the mouse from where you want the line to start to where you want the line to end.
Rectangle	Drag the mouse from where you want one corner of the rectangle to where you want the opposite corner of the rectangle.
Ellipse	Drag the mouse from one corner of the rectangle that the ellipse will fill to the opposite corner.
Arc	Drag the mouse from where you want one end of the arc to where you want the other end.
Freeform	Click each endpoint of the shape you want to create and double-click the last point of the shape.
Text Box	Drag the mouse from where you want one corner of the box to where you want the other corner of the box. Then type the text in the box or add the picture.
Callout	Drag the mouse from the object the callout line will point at to where you want the callout box. (The placement of the line connecting the object and box depend on their relative positions.) Then, type the text in the box or add the picture.

Button	How to Use
Format Callout	Set those formatting options that only apply to callouts, for either the selected callout or all callouts you later create, including options such as how Word draws the line between the object and the callout.
Fill Color	Set the color used to fill rectangles, ellipses, free-form shapes, text boxes, and boxes for callouts. Setting the fill color sets the fill color of the currently selected drawing object and the ones you subsequently create.
Line Color	Set the line color for lines and arcs, and the border color for rectangles, ellipses, free-form shapes, text boxes, and boxes for callouts. Setting the line color sets the line color of the currently selected drawing object and the ones you subsequently create.
Line Style	Set the style of the line for lines and arcs, and the border of rectangles, ellipses, free-form shapes, text boxes, and boxes for callouts. Setting the line style sets the line style of the currently selected drawing object and the ones you subsequently create.
Select Drawing Objects	Select drawing objects that you will subsequently change with other buttons on the Drawing toolbar by dragging the mouse across the objects or clicking on them.
Bring to Front	Move the selected drawing objects on top of any other drawing objects in their location.
Send to Back	Move the selected drawing objects behind any other drawing objects in their location.
Bring in Front of Text	Move the selected drawing objects to the layer on top of the text.
Send Behind Text	Move the selected drawing objects to the layer behind the text.

Button	How to Use
Group	Group the selected drawing objects so they are later treated as a single drawing object.
Ungroup	Break up the selected drawing-object group so you can modify the drawing objects individually.
Flip Horizontal	Flip the selected drawing objects so what was on the left side is on the right and vice versa.
Flip Vertical	Flip the selected drawing objects so what was on the top is on the bottom and vice versa.
Rotate Right	Rotate the selected drawing object clockwise by 90°.
Reshape	Drag the endpoints of a selected drawing object to a new location.
Snap To Grid	Set the spacing of the grid Word uses for placing drawing objects on the document and specify whether drawing objects must start at the grid points.
Align Drawing Objects	Align the selected drawing objects relative to one another.
Create Picture	Create a picture in the newly opened window using the Drawing toolbar.
Insert Frame	Add a frame around the selected drawing objects, pictures, text, or combination of these.

How do I insert a picture into my document?

To insert a graphic image into a document, choose <u>P</u>icture from the <u>I</u>nsert menu, select the file, and choose OK. Word adds the selected image to the document. Once the graphic is inserted, you can use the Pictu<u>r</u>e command in the F<u>o</u>rmat menu to change the size and position of the picture. You can use the <u>F</u>rame command in the <u>I</u>nsert menu to insert a frame around the picture. You can also double-click the image to modify it using Word's drawing features.

Tech Tip: If you want to add drawing objects to a document, you can display the Drawing toolbar by clicking the Drawing button in the Standard toolbar shown here:

Can I see the graphic image before I add it to a document?

Previewing the graphic image you are about to add ensures that you select the correct graphic. After you select <u>P</u>icture from the <u>I</u>nsert menu, select the <u>P</u>review Picture check box. Figure 12-1 shows the Insert Picture dialog box with the contents of NOUVEAU2.WMF displayed. While the <u>P</u>review Picture check box is selected, you can continue to select different files in the File <u>N</u>ame list box and preview them.

I can see my graphics in all views except print preview, and they don't print, either. What is the problem?

More than likely, Draft Output has been selected as a printing option. Draft Output omits some of a document's formatting and contents to make the document print faster. What is printed when you print draft output depends entirely on the printer you are using. If you are using a dot-matrix printer, draft output

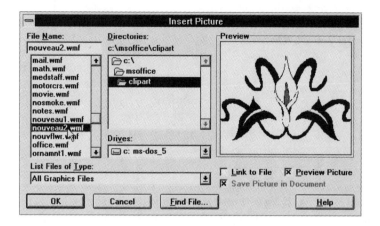

FIGURE 12-1 Preview of a picture to add to a document

eliminates all character formatting as well as graphics. Most laser printers, however, print the character formatting, but not graphics. Postscript printers, on the other hand, print both formatted text and graphics when printing draft output. To print your document without using Draft Output:

1. Choose Options from the Tools menu.
2. Click the Print tab.
3. Clear the Draft Output check box in the Printing Options section.
4. Click OK.

What graphics file formats can I use with Microsoft Word 6.0 for Windows?

The graphics formats that are supported by and shipped with Word 6.x are

.BMP	Windows Bitmaps	.PCX	PC Paintbrush
.DRW	Micrografx Designer/Draw	.TIF	Tagged Image File Format (TIFF)
.EPS	Encapsulated Postscript	.WPG	WordPerfect graphics (DrawPerfect)
.HGL	HP Graphics Language		

.CGM	Computer Graphics Metafile	.WMF	Windows Metafile
.PIC	Lotus 1-2-3 graphics	.PLT	AutoCAD Plot
.PCT	Macintosh PICT/Windows PICT filter	.DXF	AutoCAD Format 2-D
		.GIF	CompuServe GIF

You can see which filters are available to you when you select Picture from the Insert menu to add a graphic file to your document. The file formats you have available are listed in the List Files of Type drop-down list box. You may not have all of these graphics file formats available if you performed a minimal or custom installation.

Tech Tip: You can order a supplemental disk that includes additional and updated graphics filters. These filters include AutoCAD DXF (.DXF), AutoCAD plotter files (.ADI), CorelDRAW 3.0 (.CDR), HP Graphics Language (.HGL), Kodak Photo CD (.PCD), Lotus 1-2-3 graphics (.PIC), and Truevision Targa (.TGA).

How can I make a graphic image larger or smaller?

You can resize a graphic image using the keyboard or mouse. When you select a graphic object, its borders have small boxes called *handles* as shown here:

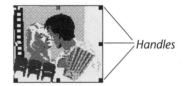

Handles

You select a graphic by clicking it or by holding down SHIFT while you use the arrow keys to select the graphic. To resize a graphic image with the mouse, drag one of these handles so the dotted outline is the size you want the graphic to become. Dragging the handle toward the center of the image makes the graphic smaller, and dragging the handle away from the center makes the graphic image larger. When you release the mouse button, the graphic box is resized to fit the dotted outline.

You can also set the height and width using the Picture command in the Format menu. From the Picture dialog box, you can set the size of the graphic in two ways.

- Set the size of the graphic by entering the height and width in the Width and Height text boxes below Size. Word adjusts the numbers in the Scaling section to match the new size of the graphic.

- Set the proportion of the graphic's original size that you want the graphic to appear in the Width and Height text boxes below Scaling. For example, if you want a graphic to be half as tall, you can type **50%** in the Height text box. Word adjusts the numbers in the Size section to match the physical size on the page.

Tech Tip: If you want to make sure that the aspect ratio of a graphic does not change, use the Picture command in the Format menu and set the values in the Scaling section to the same number. You can also keep the aspect ratio when you size a graphic with a mouse by holding down SHIFT while you drag one of the handles.

When I print graphics, I get only half a page or a memory error message. What can I do?

If a printed page has incomplete graphics, your printer might not have enough memory. You may also encounter a printer error message such as "Memory Overflow," or a message from Windows such as "Printer out of memory." Try the following solutions:

- Reduce the size of the graphic image. For example, if a graphic occupies the whole page, resize it so it uses only half the page.

- Change the document's fonts to printer fonts rather than fonts generated by software, such as TrueType fonts.

Tech Tip: You can tell which fonts are printer or TrueType fonts by the little icon that appears in front of the font name in the Font dialog box or in the Font box on the Formatting toolbar.

■ Reduce the graphics printing resolution. Follow these steps:

a. Choose Print from the File menu.

b. Click the Printer button.

c. Select the printer in the Printers list box and click Options.

At this point, you are looking at the same dialog box that you see from the Windows Control Panel application when you select the Printers icon, highlight the printer in the Installed Printers list box, and select Setup. The box you see depends on which printer you have selected. For example, the dialog box for a Hewlett-Packard LaserJet series III printer looks like Figure 12-2.

d. Set the graphics resolution. Since each printer has different settings, the one you choose depends on your printer. For the dialog box in Figure 12-2, you want to choose an option in the Graphics Resolution drop-down list box that has a setting lower than 300 dots per inch.

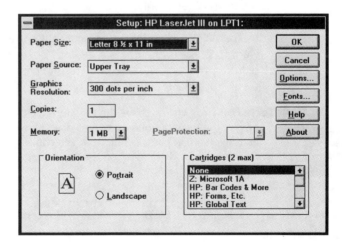

FIGURE 12-2   Printer options available for a Hewlett-Packard LaserJet series III

    e. Click OK, Close, and then either OK or Cancel depending on whether you want to print the current document immediately.

■ Increase the memory in your printer. If you plan to print a lot of graphics, this is the best long-term solution.

Can I hide and display the drawing objects in my Word document?

You can switch between hiding and displaying the drawing objects in a document. Hiding drawing objects can make working with the document's text easier. To switch between hiding and displaying drawing objects while in page layout view:

1. Choose <u>O</u>ptions from the <u>T</u>ools menu.

2. Click the View tab.

3. Clear the Dra<u>w</u>ings check box to hide the drawing objects, or select this check box to see them.

4. Choose OK.

    Drawn objects only appear in page layout view. These steps only hide or display the objects drawn using the Drawing toolbar. Pictures added to a document continue to appear. If you want to make the pictures appear as boxes rather than as the pictures, follow the preceding steps except that in step 3, select the <u>P</u>icture Placeholders check box.

Tech Tip: You will not have the Drawings check box on the View tab of the Options dialog box unless you are in page layout view. The choices on this tab vary depending on the current view.

How can I put text on top of a picture?

Most of the time when you add graphics to a file, you will want the document's text to flow around the text. However, there may be times when you want text and graphics to overlap. To get the text and graphic to overlap, you need to insert the art and the text into areas or objects that can be layered. For example, drawing objects can be put on a different layer than the document's text.

Imagine that your document consists of a series of transparencies such as you would use with an overhead projector. You need to get the art and text on different transparencies in order to put one on top of the other.

You have two options for printing text over a picture. You can add the text to the document, and then add a text box containing the picture. This text box, as a drawing object, can be put "behind" or underneath the layer of your document containing the text. You can also add the picture to the document, and then add drawing objects containing text that are formatted to appear on the layer above the document, so they are on top of the picture.

Figure 12-3 shows an example of text and graphics combined. In this case, the picture was added in a text box with the text added as regular document text. This document is created with these steps:

1. Add the text to the document. You can use any of Word's positioning and formatting options to create the look that you want for the document.

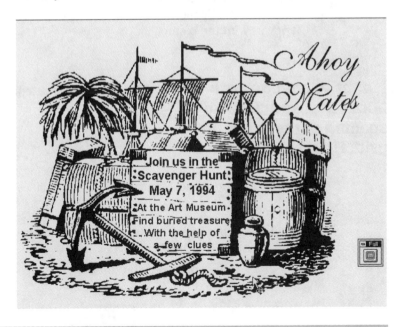

FIGURE 12-3   Document containing overlapping graphics and text
(clip art by A.J. Graphics)

2. Add a text box to the document, making the text box the size that you want the picture.

3. Choose Picture from the Insert menu for the text box's contents.

4. Select the image you want for the picture, and click OK to add it as the text box's contents.

5. Display the Drawing toolbar by clicking the Drawing button in the Standard toolbar.

6. Click the Send Behind Text button shown here:

You may need to change the size of the text box after you add the picture or change the text that is not in the text box. Remember that you can hide drawing objects such as the text box containing the picture when you want to work with the underlying document. This is also the case when you add the picture to the document and add the text to a text box so that it appears with the picture.

I want to change both the horizontal and vertical spacing of my drawing grid. How can I do this?

The drawing grid determines where objects are placed when you create or move drawn objects with Snap To Grid selected. By changing the drawing grid, you change the points where the objects are placed. To change the horizontal and vertical spacing between gridlines in the drawing grid:

1. Click the Drawing button on the Standard toolbar to display the Drawing toolbar.

2. Click the Snap To Grid button on the Drawing toolbar shown here:

3. Change the spacing between the gridlines across the page by typing or selecting a new measurement in the Horizontal Spacing text box.

4. Change the spacing between the gridlines up and down the page by typing or selecting a new measurement in the Vertical Spacing text box.

5. Select the Snap To Grid check box when you want the objects you create or move to start at an intersection of the horizontal and vertical gridlines, or clear it if you want the drawn objects to be placed anywhere.

6. Click OK.

You will not see the drawing grid even after you've set Snap To Grid on. The grid is always invisible. You can tell when it is on, and about how far apart the gridlines are set, by the way drawn objects move and place themselves.

I have other pieces of clip art. Can I use them in Word?

Word accepts many graphics file formats. You can use any clip art that is in one of Word's acceptable graphics file formats. For example, the documents in this book include graphics from CorelDRAW, Presentation Task Force, and A. J. Graphics. You can order clip art for your documents from many vendors. Many clip art companies create specialized clip art, such as medical symbols or pictures of well-known individuals. Purchasing clip art from outside sources can save you time and money. With the more elaborate drawings, the cost of the clip art is usually less than the value of the time you would use to draw it yourself. If you have a scanner, you can scan images into a computer file and use those images as clip art. You'll need to use another program that accepts scanned images and can save them in one of the file formats that Word can accept. See the question "What graphics file formats can I use with Microsoft Word 6.0 for Windows?" earlier in this chapter for a list of all the graphics formats that Word can accept.

How do I move drawing objects?

You can rearrange drawing objects by dragging the objects. You must be in page layout view, since drawing objects don't appear in other views. When you move a drawing object, you may notice that the object hops as you move it around on the page. This is because Snap To Grid is on. When Snap To Grid is on, the objects you move start at the intersection of the invisible gridlines. To move a drawing object:

1. Select the drawing object by clicking it.

2. Position the mouse pointer on the object. The mouse pointer includes a four-headed arrow as shown here:

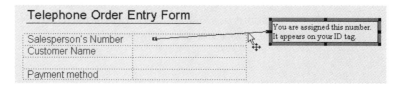

Make sure that the mouse isn't pointing to a handle, or you will resize the object instead of moving it.

3. Drag the object to a new location.

Can I make the same changes to a picture that I can make to a drawing object by using the buttons on the Drawing toolbar?

You can edit pictures in Word and make many of the same changes to the picture that you can make to drawing objects. These include colors, line shapes, positions, and size. When you edit a picture in Word, Word opens another window that contains only the picture. Figure 12-4 shows a picture window opened to edit a picture in a document. In a picture window, the picture includes the drawing objects such as shapes and lines that create the picture. You can modify the objects within the picture, and when you return to your document, the document contains the modified version of the picture. To modify a picture:

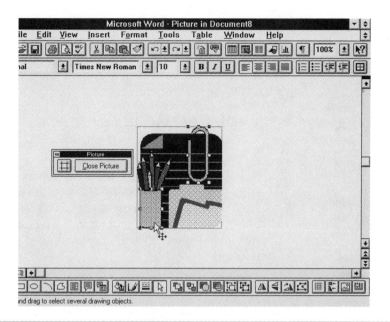

FIGURE 12-4   Picture window for editing a picture from a Word document

1. Double-click the picture to modify.

2. Word opens another window containing just the picture. The Drawing toolbar, if not already displayed, appears. At this point, you can work with the objects such as the lines and shapes that make up the picture by using the same buttons discussed in the Frustration Busters box at the beginning of this chapter.

3. Click the Select Drawing Objects button shown here:

4. Select the objects to modify. The steps you use depend on how much of the picture you want to change.

   ■ If you want to change just one object in the picture, click the object.

Tech Tip: If you move objects within a picture, you may need to resize the picture. Resize the picture by clicking the Reset Picture Boundary button in the Picture toolbar. The Reset Picture Boundary button is the button containing a # sign.

- If you want to change several objects in the picture, click the first object, hold down SHIFT, then click all the other objects you want to change.

- If you want to change the entire picture, drag the mouse pointer from above and to the left of the upper-left corner of the picture to below and to the right of the lower-right corner of the picture. This selects every object in the picture.

  When you select objects in the picture, each object has handles. You can use these handles to size objects within the picture the same way you can use handles to size the picture within the document. You can also drag objects to move them around in the picture. For the picture in Figure 12-4, the paper clip and the cup are selected.

5. Click the buttons in the Drawing toolbar to make the changes you want for the selected objects.

6. Create drawing objects to include in this picture using the Line, Rectangle, Ellipse, Arc, Freeform, Text Box, and Callout buttons from the Drawing toolbar.

7. Click the Close Picture button in the Picture toolbar or press CTRL+F4. Word closes the window and returns to the document displaying the modified picture.

Tech Tip: If a picture is an embedded object, double-clicking opens the application that supplied the embedded picture. Since this application is not Word, you must use the features of that application for modifying the picture. This other application may have additional editing features beyond what is available through Word.

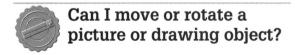

Can I move or rotate a picture or drawing object?

Pictures and drawing objects can be rotated, flipped, and moved. Figure 12-5 shows four copies of the same picture that are flipped and moved. The steps for doing this are slightly different when working with a picture versus a drawing object.

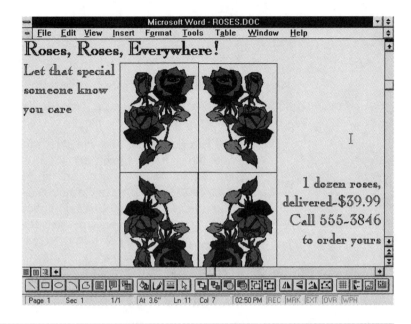

FIGURE 12-5   Graphics created by flipping and moving an image

To rotate, flip, or move a drawing object in a document:

1. Display the Drawing toolbar if it is not already displayed.
2. Select the drawing object.
3. Click one of these three buttons to flip or rotate the object:

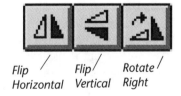

Flip   Flip   Rotate
Horizontal Vertical Right

The Flip Horizontal button flips the drawing object so
what was on the left side is on the right, and what was on
the right side is on the left. The Flip Vertical button flips
the drawing object so what was on the top is on the
bottom, and what was on the bottom is on the top. The
Rotate Right button rotates the drawing object 90° at a time.

To rotate, flip, or move a picture:

1. Double-click the picture to open the picture in its own window.

2. Click the Select Drawing Objects button.

3. Select the objects to rotate, flip, or move. The steps you use depend on how much of the picture you want to change.

4. Click the Flip Horizontal, Flip Vertical, or Rotate Right button to flip or rotate the object.
   The selected drawing objects are flipped or rotated according to the area the selected objects use. Therefore, if you do not select all the objects in a picture and flip the objects, they will not move from one side of the picture to the other, they only flip within the area that the selected drawing objects use.

5. Click the Close Picture button in the Picture toolbar to return to the document.

Tech Tip: When you want to rotate or flip an entire picture, you must edit it, select all of the objects, and then rotate or flip those objects. You cannot rotate or flip the picture as a whole.

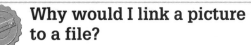

Why would I link a picture to a file?

A picture added to a document can either be stored in the document or in its own file. When a picture is linked to a file, the document containing the picture remembers which file the image came from. As the image in the file changes, the picture in the document also changes. Link a picture to a file when you always want the document to use the updated version of the picture. The document can even omit saving the image in the document to make the document file size smaller.

To link a picture to a file, select the Link to File check box when you insert the picture. If you do not want the document to save a copy of the image inside the document, clear the Save Picture in Document check box at the same time.

Tech Tip: When you link a picture to a file and do not save a copy of the picture in the document, you cannot edit it with Word by double-clicking it or by using the Drawing toolbar. If you edit a linked picture, Word converts the image so that it is now embedded in the document rather than linked.

I am importing a graphic in Word. However, when I bring it in, only part of it appears. How can I correct this problem?

Tech Tip: You can find out the size of the graphic with the Picture command in the Format menu. You can also click the Help button on the Standard toolbar, and then click the graphic. Word will display a box showing information about the image as shown in Figure 12-6.

When the top of a graphic does not appear, the line spacing of the paragraph containing the graphic is set to Exactly, and spacing specified is smaller than the actual height of the graphic. To correct this problem:

1. Select the graphic.

2. Choose Paragraph from the Format menu.

3. Click the Indents and Spacing tab.

4. Select Single in the Line Spacing drop-down list box.

If you want to use the Exactly setting here, you need to increase the measurement located in the At box to the height of the graphic.

5. Click OK.

Is it possible to use a different program rather than the Word 6.0 Draw program for editing drawing objects?

Word 6.0 ships with its own Drawing Editor. However, you may want to use another application as a drawing editor in Word:

1. Choose Options from the Tools menu.

2. Click the Edit tab.

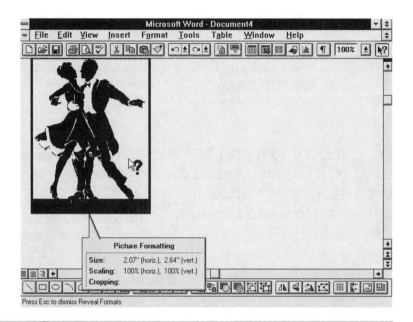

FIGURE 12-6 Using the Help button to get size information on a picture

3. Select the editor you would like to use when a drawing is double-clicked in the <u>P</u>icture Editor drop-down list box.

The drop-down list box shows the available applications that you can use to modify drawn objects.

4. Click OK.

I just inserted several clip art images into my document. Why can't I see them?

Two settings can prevent Word from showing pictures in a document. The setting that is preventing you from seeing your clip art depends on the view you are using to look at your document.

If you cannot see your clip art in normal, page layout, master document, or outline view and you do see a white box with a black border, Word is set to display pictures using placeholders. When you select the box, you will see the handles that you can drag to change the size of the clip art. To display the pictures, the Picture Placeholders option needs to be turned off. To turn off the Picture Placeholders option:

Tech Tip: Linked and embedded data that Word displays as a graphic will also change to display only picture placeholders when the Picture Placeholders check box is selected.

1. Choose <u>O</u>ptions from the <u>T</u>ools menu.
2. Click the View tab.
3. Clear the <u>P</u>icture Placeholders check box.
4. Click OK. Pictures will now appear in the document editing window.

If you cannot see the pictures when you are in print preview, Draft Output has been selected as a printing option, causing your printer to omit pictures when you print. Draft Output omits some of a document's formatting and contents to make the document print faster. To remove the Draft Output printing option:

1. Choose <u>O</u>ptions from the <u>T</u>ools menu.
2. Click the Print tab.
3. Clear the <u>D</u>raft Output check box.
4. Click OK.

Can I put text into frames just like I do with my pictures?

Word has few limits on what you put into a frame. You can put in a picture, text, or a combination of both. Simply select what you want in the frame before you select <u>F</u>rame from the <u>I</u>nsert menu. Figure 12-7 shows a document with text and graphics in a frame.

How do I put a graphics box on a different location on the page?

Pictures and drawing objects are positioned using *anchors*. When you first add a picture, the picture is added as if it were a character. This means that the height of the row containing the picture expands to fit the graphic and some character and paragraph formatting affects the image. The image's position reflects its position within the current paragraph. When you frame the picture, the frame has an anchor attached to the paragraph that controls where the image is placed. To set the frame's position:

1. Select the frame.

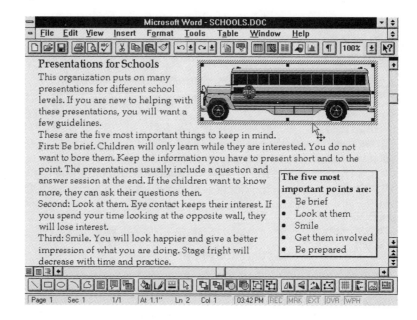

FIGURE 12-7 Pull-quote created by putting text into a frame

2. Choose Fra<u>m</u>e from the F<u>o</u>rmat menu or Format Frame from the frame's shortcut menu.

3. Select where you want the frame placed using the Horizontal and Vertical sections of the Frame dialog box. You can define a frame's position relative to the page edge, the margin, the column boundary, the top of the paragraph, or as an absolute distance from one of these points. Select a relative position from the Horizontal or Vertical Position drop-down list boxes, or type in an absolute measurement. Leave Paragraph, the default setting, selected in the Posi<u>t</u>ion drop-down list box under Vertical when you want the frame to move with the current paragraph. Select one of the other options to position the frame at a specific location on the page.

4. Click OK.

Figure 12-8 shows a newsletter that uses several frames to set where text and graphics appear. For example, the text in the upper-right corner is in a frame that has a horizontal position of right relative to the margin and a vertical position of top relative to the margin. The text and graphics in the lower-left corner are in a frame that has a horizontal position of left relative to the margin and a vertical position of bottom relative to the margin. The picture in the middle is in a frame with the horizontal and vertical positions of center relative to the margin.

Framed objects and drawing objects are anchored to paragraphs with anchors you can see in page layout view. When you display anchors, they look like this:

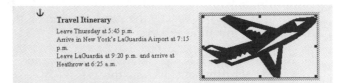

To display the anchors, follow these steps:

1. Choose Options from the Tools menu.

2. Click the View tab.

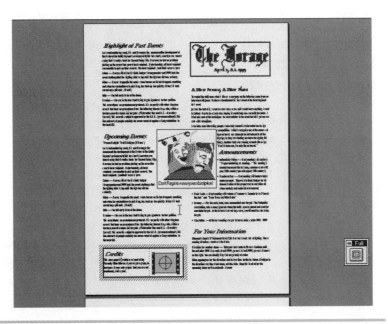

FIGURE 12-8   Multiple frames to show position options

Tech Tip: You can move frames and drawing objects by dragging them to a new location. When you do this, the vertical position may change, whether it is relative to the paragraph or the page.

3. Select the <u>O</u>bject Anchors check box.

4. Click OK.

You can move the anchor by dragging it to a new location. Move the anchor when the text the image is anchored to moves, and the anchored object does not. The framed or drawing object has the same position settings when you move the anchor. For example, suppose you have a drawing object that is set to appear at a specific position on the page. If the text the object is anchored to moves to the next page because of editing, the drawing object moves to the next page as well. However, it has exactly the same position on the new page as it had on the original page.

Tech Tip: If you change a drawing object's anchor and it still does not move with the text, select Drawing <u>O</u>bject from the F<u>o</u>rmat menu or select Format Drawing Object from the object's shortcut menu, and then select the Si<u>z</u>e and Position tab. Select Paragraph in the F<u>r</u>om drop-down list box, and then select OK.

How can I change the distance between a picture and the surrounding text?

When a picture or text is in a frame, you can specify how close the other text in the document is to the frame's contents. You can set the margin for the frame to increase or decrease the space between the edge of the frame and the surrounding document text. To set the distance between document text and the frame:

1. Select the frame.

2. Choose Fra<u>m</u>e from the F<u>o</u>rmat menu or the frame's shortcut menu.

3. Enter the distance from the left and right side of the frame to the surrounding text in the Distance from Te<u>x</u>t text box in the Horizontal section of the Frame dialog box.

4. Enter the distance from the top and bottom of the frame to the surrounding text in the Distance <u>f</u>rom Text text box in the Vertical section of the Frame dialog box.

You cannot use negative numbers for the distance to put the surrounding text into the frame's area. If you want text to overlap the frame's contents, add the text as callouts or in text boxes by using the Drawing toolbar.

5. Click OK.

If the frame has a border, this border has its own margin as well. The border's distance from text sets the distance from the border to the text inside the border. The border's margin affects anything that uses a border, even if the contents using the border are not within a frame. To change the amount of space in the border, follow these steps:

1. Select the text, graphics, table, or other document item with the border to change.

2. Choose Borders and Shading from the Format menu or the shortcut menu.

3. Set the distance that you want between the border and the contents of the border in the From Text text box.

4. Click OK to apply the new spacing for the border.

Can I put a frame inside a frame?

No, Word does not let you add a frame inside another frame. Instead use other options for how text and graphics are placed relative to one another. The following question describes some other possibilities.

How do I put graphics side by side with text?

Besides putting graphics in a frame and using the frame position options, Word has other ways that you can put graphics and text next to each other. Two other possibilities are using a table and using columns.

An example of using a table to place graphics is as follows:

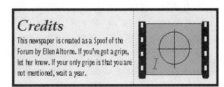

The reason a table is used is that both the text and graphics in the thick border are enclosed in a frame for the newsletter. As the newsletter text shifts, the text and graphics remain in place. By creating a table with one row and two columns, the text can be in the first cell and the graphics can be in the second. This table was created and then had a frame inserted around it.

You can also create columns and put a picture in one column and the graphic in another. When you use this approach, add a column break to separate the text and graphics that you want to appear in each column.

How can I move a picture when it is not in a frame?

The positioning options for inserted pictures that are not framed are more limited than when they are in a frame. However, you have some ways of changing the position. If you need a graphic raised or lowered and it is not in a frame, use Font in the Format menu, the Character Spacing tab, and Raised or Lowered in the Position drop-down list box. For example, the following document has the graphics lowered by 3 points so it looks aligned with the text next to it.

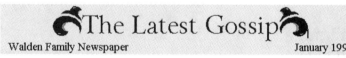

A graphic that is treated as a character is also affected by paragraph formatting, so you can set where the graphic appears across the page using paragraph formatting such as alignment and indentation. When you need to move the graphic slightly away from the text before or after it, you can add spaces or tabs to provide that distance.

Can I put graphics in a header?

You can place graphics in a document's header, as well as in footers, endnotes, comments, and footnotes. As you work in these sections of your document, you can add graphics using the same commands and features that you use when you are in the main part of your document. For example, you can add graphics to a header when you want to create a *watermark*, which is a drawing or text transposed behind other text or objects on a page. Placing a watermark in the header allows it to appear on every page. Figure 12-9 shows a watermark added to a document.

Tech Note: Watermarks started with designs imprinted into paper as part of the papermaking process that identified the paper content and maker. A watermark is similar to a letterhead, but is also used to create a design that appears behind the text of a document.

This watermark is added as part of the header:

1. Choose <u>H</u>eader and Footer from the <u>V</u>iew menu.
2. Display the Drawing toolbar if it does not already appear.
3. Add as a drawing object what you want as a watermark.

When you want to add a clip art file, add the clip art to a text box.

4. Choose <u>H</u>eader and Footer from the <u>V</u>iew menu, or choose Close in the Header and Footer toolbar to leave the header and footer.

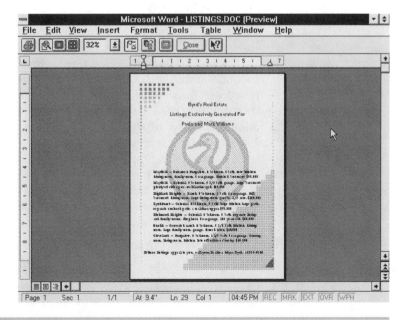

FIGURE 12-9   Watermark created by adding text and graphics to a header

In this example, the watermark is created by combining the images in VCONTBOX.WMF and BIRD.WMF, which are included with Word for Windows 6.0. The text box for VCONTBOX.WMF and the picture is sized to 7.5 × 10 inches and starting from one-half inch from the top and left edge. The picture in BIRD.WMF is edited so it is lighter than the original.

Tech Tip: Word includes many clip art files that you can add to your document using the same steps just described. These clip art files are a ready source of borders.

Is it possible to create an organizational chart in Word?

Yes. Word includes a macro called OrganizationalChartMaker. The macro will build an organizational chart based upon a document created using the built-in heading styles. To access and run this macro:

1. Display the nonprinting characters in the document. You will need to see where you have added line breaks and paragraph breaks.

2. Set up the document to contain the entries you want in the organizational chart.

    Figure 12-10 shows a document set up to create an organizational chart. Each entry is separated by a paragraph break (¶). Each entry can use up to three lines by separating the lines for the entry with a line break added by pressing SHIFT+ENTER (it appears as ↵ in Figure 12-10). The top level uses the Heading 1 style, the next level uses the Heading 2 style, and so on, for each of the entries. The order that the heading entries appear in the document is the order they appear in the organizational chart. You may want to use the outline view to see the heading levels you have added to the document.

3. Choose <u>M</u>acro from the <u>T</u>ools menu, and click <u>O</u>rganizer.

4. Click Close <u>F</u>ile from the left side of the dialog box.

5. Click Open <u>F</u>ile, select the WINWORD\MACROS directory, select MACRO60.DOT, and click OK.

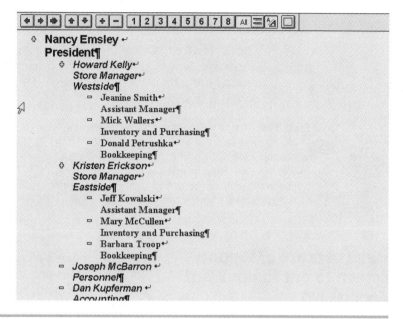

FIGURE 12-10 Entries created to generate an organizational chart

6. Select OrganizationalChartMaker in the list box listing the macros in MACRO60.DOT. Click Copy, then Close.

7. Choose Macro from the Tools menu.

8. Select OrganizationalChartMaker in the Macro Name list box and click Run. After the macro checks that the document is correctly formatted, the macro displays this dialog box:

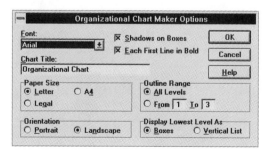

This dialog box specifies settings that change how the final chart will look.

9. Click OK twice to create the organizational chart in a new document. Figure 12-11 shows the organizational chart created using the data from Figure 12-10. The last level of entries is shown vertically.

Tech Tip: Make your entries for the organizational chart, then save the document. You will probably want to try the macro with different settings each time to test out the arrangement you want. You can return to the heading entries when you want to rearrange them.

 Can I capture a Windows screen to put in my Word document?

You can capture a picture of a Windows screen and store it in the Windows Clipboard. You can then paste the captured screen into a Word document. To capture a Windows

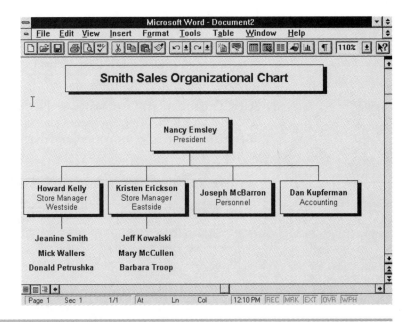

FIGURE 12-11 Organizational chart created with the OrganizationalChartMaker macro

Tech Tip: You can use the Windows Clipboard Viewer to open the Clipboard and save the screen capture as a file.

screen and put it into a Word document, follow these steps:

1. Set up the screen to capture.

2. Press PRINT SCREEN.

3. Switch to Word and the Word document where you want the screen.

4. Choose <u>P</u>aste from the <u>E</u>dit menu.

At this point, Word inserts a bitmap picture of the screen's contents when you pressed PRINT SCREEN. Figure 12-12 shows a Windows screen pasted into a Word document. It is cropped from all four sides using Pictu<u>r</u>e in the F<u>o</u>rmat menu so you only see the Clock window. You can change the image using the Drawing toolbar.

What is the difference between vector graphics and bitmap graphics?

A graphic image can be saved as vectors or bitmaps. Bitmap images are like the ones created with the Windows Paintbrush application, where you apply colors to any area of the drawing surface. Bitmap images remember an image by the dots of each color that make up the image. For example, when you draw a line, the program remembers the line by the series of dots that looks like a line. Vector graphics, on the other hand, record the lines and endpoints of shapes used in an image. For example, instead of remembering every

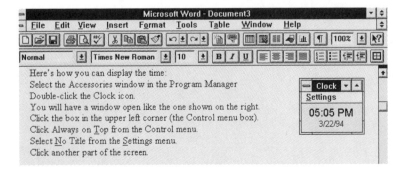

FIGURE 12-12 Windows screen pasted into a Word document

point on a line, a vector format remembers the endpoints of the line and the line's features, such as colors and styles. Vector graphics make certain types of editing easier, such as changing the line style, changing its size, or moving just the line without moving anything below it. Vector graphics look smoother than bitmap graphics, especially when enlarged. Vector graphics files usually also have the advantage of being smaller than bitmap files.

A third way graphic images are stored is using a Metafile format, such as .WMF or .CGM files. Metafiles store both vector and bitmap data used to create an image. Word includes its sample art as Windows Metafiles. However, Word can add many types of graphic image formats that are bitmap, vector, or Metafile images.

Envelopes and Labels

Printing envelopes and labels from a computer was once a tedious, time-consuming task. But now, Word automates so much of this process for you that frustration is almost a thing of the past! For example, Word can detect an address in a letter and enter it on an envelope for you. In addition, it can add your return address based on stored user information.

When you create labels, all you have to do is tell Word how big they are and it sets up a table in your document for you. Instead of getting out your ruler to measure the labels, you can just pick one of the predefined sizes that match the most popular brands.

FRUSTRATION BUSTERS!

To ensure that your letters are delivered promptly and properly, follow these commonsense guidelines when printing envelopes:

- Place the return address in the upper-left corner.

- Position the recipient's address in the center of the envelope.

- Make sure the address is easy to read; fancy fonts look impressive but can be difficult for the mail carrier to read at a glance.

- Remember the ZIP code. You can contact the U.S. Post Office if you need a ZIP code for a specific address. Post offices and libraries often include books containing ZIP codes for the entire country.

- Add the correct postage.

How can I create an envelope for a document?

When you create an envelope, you add a new section on its own page in the document that contains the relevant text and formatting. To add an envelope to a document:

1. Choose Envelopes and Labels from the Tools menu.

2. Click the Envelopes tab.

3. Type the address to which you are sending the document in the Delivery Address text box.

4. You only need to change the address in the Return Address text box if your update differs from the address that appears based on your user information.

5. Click the Add to Document button.

Word places the envelope at the beginning of the document and correctly positions the addresses for you, as shown in Figure

13-1. The status bar shows you that the envelope's page number is zero.

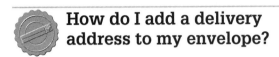

How do I add a delivery address to my envelope?

If Word finds three to five short lines of text at the beginning of the document, it automatically selects the paragraph as a delivery address. However, if Word picks the wrong text or you want to use a different address, you can always modify it.

To add a delivery address:

1. If necessary, select the delivery address in the document.
2. Choose <u>E</u>nvelopes and Labels from the <u>T</u>ools menu.

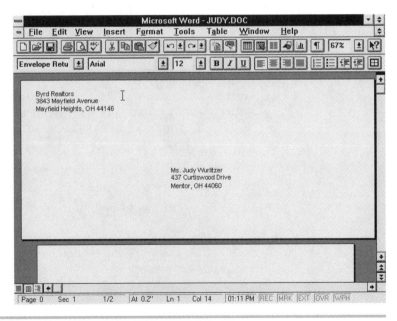

FIGURE 13-1   An envelope added to a document

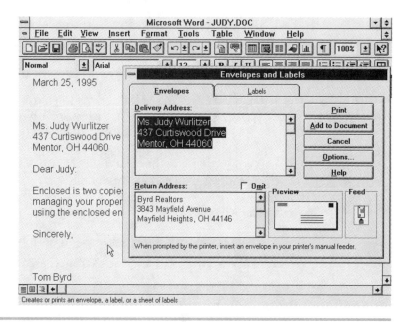

FIGURE 13-2   Word picks up the delivery address from the document

3. Click the Envelopes tab.
   The selected delivery address appears in the Delivery Address text box. (If it appears near the beginning of the document, Word may automatically highlight it for you.)

4. Edit the addresses as needed.

5. Click Options to specify a different envelope size, address position, or font size, if desired.

6. Click Add to Document or Print to create the envelope.

   In Figure 13-2, Word enters the correct delivery and return addresses based on the entry at the beginning of the letter and the user information, respectively. In this case, all you need to do is select Add to Document to create the envelope.

How do I print just the envelope from a document?

You can print an existing envelope separately from the document using either of these methods:

- Choose Envelopes and Labels from the Tools menu and click Print.

- Choose Print from the File menu, select the Pages option button, type **0** in the adjoining text box, and then click OK.

Tech Tip: If you want to print a document without the added envelope, choose Print from the File menu, select the Pages option button, type **1–** in the adjoining text box, and click OK. Word skips page 0, which contains the envelope.

Can I change my envelope after I add it to a document?

Yes, you can edit the addresses on the envelope as well as specify a new envelope size and whether to include bar codes. When you choose Envelopes and Labels from the Tools menu, the Envelopes and Labels dialog box displays the current settings for the envelope. Make your changes and then click Change Document to apply them to the envelope in the document.

How do I put a graphic on my envelope?

You can add a graphic, such as your company logo, to enhance the appearance of your envelope. To add a graphic to an envelope:

1. Add the envelope to the document, as usual.

2. Click the Show/Hide button on the Standard toolbar to display paragraph marks.

3. If the envelope contains a return address, move to the end of it, and press ENTER to add a new line. Otherwise, simply move the insertion point to the beginning of the return address area.

4. Choose Picture from the Insert menu, select the picture you want to add, and then click OK. The graphic appears at the insertion point's location.

5. Select the picture so that small boxes, or *handles*, appear around it.

6. Choose Frame from the Insert menu. If Word prompts you to switch to page layout view, click Yes.

7. Move the frame and picture to the desired location. (Because Word automatically adds a frame to the delivery address, you cannot move the graphic to this location.)

Figure 13-3 depicts an envelope with a graphic.

Can I add the Envelope button I had on my Word 2.0 toolbar to my Word 6.0 toolbar?

You can add the Word 6.0 version of this button to your toolbar by following these steps:

1. Display the toolbar to which you want to add the Envelope button.

2. Choose Customize from the Tools menu, or click the toolbar with the right mouse button and choose Customize from the shortcut menu.

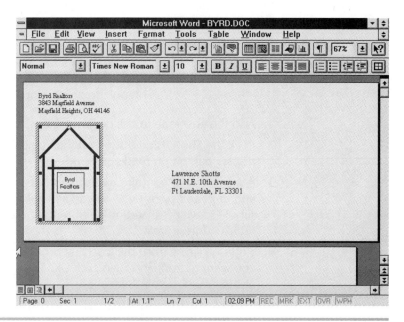

FIGURE 13-3   You can add a graphic to an envelope

3. Click the <u>T</u>oolbars tab, if necessary.

4. Select Tools in the <u>C</u>ategories list box.

The Buttons section displays the predefined toolbar buttons that correspond with the commands and features available on the <u>T</u>ools menu. The Envelope button looks much as it did in Word 2.0, except that it's in color. This toolbar button performs the ToolsCreateEnvelope command, which is the same command that Word performs when you choose <u>E</u>nvelopes and Labels from the <u>T</u>ools menu.

5. Click the Envelope button and drag it to the desired position on the toolbar.

6. Choose Close.

I use preprinted business envelopes. How do I tell Word not to print the return address?

To stop Word from printing a return address on an envelope:

1. Choose <u>E</u>nvelopes and Labels from the <u>T</u>ools menu.

2. Click the <u>E</u>nvelopes tab.

3. Select the O<u>m</u>it check box.

4. Verify or add the delivery address and make any other changes you wish.

5. Click <u>P</u>rint or <u>A</u>dd to Document.

Once selected, the O<u>m</u>it check box remains "on" until you clear it, even after you exit and restart Word.

I moved. How do I change the default return address?

To change your default return address:

1. Choose <u>E</u>nvelopes and Labels from the <u>T</u>ools menu.

2. Type a new address in the <u>R</u>eturn Address text box.

3. Click <u>A</u>dd to Document.

4. Choose <u>Y</u>es when Word prompts you to save the new return address as the default.

The current address in the <u>R</u>eturn Address text box becomes the default.

Tech Tip: You can also reset the default return address by choosing <u>O</u>ptions from the <u>T</u>ools menu, clicking the User Info tab, entering new information in the <u>M</u>ailing Address text box, and then clicking OK.

How can I change the font for my envelopes?

Tech Tip: You can also use the same character and paragraph formatting features with envelopes as you do with your other documents, by modifying the envelope address and the envelope return styles.

You can specify the font Word uses on your envelopes, and even use different ones for the delivery and return addresses. Envelopes initially use the Envelope Return style for the return address and the Envelope Address style for the addressee. These are system styles that Word automatically applies to text in envelopes. You normally do not see these style names unless you set Word to display all styles, including system ones.

You can select different fonts to use instead of the defaults by following these steps:

1. Choose <u>E</u>nvelopes and Labels from the <u>T</u>ools menu.
2. Click the <u>E</u>nvelopes tab.
3. Click the <u>O</u>ptions button.
4. Click the Font button in either the Return Address or Delivery Address section.
5. Select the font you want to use, just as you would in the Font dialog box.
6. Click <u>D</u>efault if you want to use this font on all envelopes you add in the future. Choose <u>Y</u>es when Word prompts you to confirm that you want to change the font for envelopes created with the same template.
7. Click OK.
8. Repeat steps 4 through 7 to change the font used for the other address, if desired.

9. Click OK.

10. Add the envelope to the document or print it with the new font.

How can I repeat text or a design on all of my envelopes?

You can take advantage of two AutoText entries to add this information to every envelope: EnvelopeExtra1 and EnvelopeExtra2. When the template (usually NORMAL.DOT) contains either or both of these entries, Word adds them to the upper-right corner of the envelope as if you did so yourself.

For example, the text and graphics on the envelope in Figure 13-4 were added as AutoText entries. The graphic is the EnvelopeExtra1 AutoText entry and the text is the EnvelopeExtra2 AutoText entry.

Tech Tip: To create these AutoText entries, follow the steps for adding graphics to an envelope if graphics and fancy text is what you want to add. Once the object or text is in the correct location, highlight it, select AutoText from the Edit menu, and set the name to EnvelopeExtra1 or EnvelopeExtra2. Now whenever you create an envelope, EnvelopeExtra1 and EnvelopeExtra2 will appear where you set them.

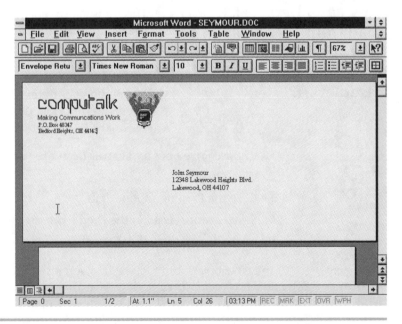

FIGURE 13-4   An envelope with graphics and text added with AutoText entries

An AutoText entry can be a framed object, which is desirable if you want to place it in a specific location on the envelope or in relation to the beginning of the return address. Chapter 6, "Special Features," describes how to create and add AutoText entries.

How do I print envelopes without producing a blank page in between them?

In this case, you must be printing the envelopes as the results of a merge. Follow these steps to print envelopes after a merge without producing blank pages between them:

1. Open your merged document.
2. Choose Print from the File menu.
3. Select the Pages option button and type **0-0** in the adjoining text box. This setting prints your envelopes only, without any blank pages.

How can I bypass the 'EC Load Com 10' message on the printer when I print envelopes with a HP LaserJet III?

This message occurs if Word is set up to feed from an envelope feeder and you are using version 31.3.89 of the HPPCL5A.DRV. You can bypass this message by pressing the Continue button on your printer. However, the addresses may now print too high on the envelope. To correct this problem:

Tech Tip: Include a paragraph mark in the AutoText entry if you want your return address to start on the following line, instead of the same one.

1. Choose Envelopes and Labels from the Tools menu.
2. Click Options.
3. Click the Printing Options tab.
4. Select Manual Feed in the Feed From drop-down list box.
5. Click OK and then click Cancel.

If the envelope doesn't feed when you insert it into the manual tray, hold down both the On Line and Form Feed printer buttons. The envelope should then feed properly. The other option would be to obtain an updated driver from Microsoft or HP which should resolve this issue.

What types of bar codes can I insert in my envelopes or labels?

The bar code feature of Word 6.0 is compliant with the U.S. Postal Service POSTNET Code. The bar code feature creates bar codes for Zip+4 digit and regulation 5 digit zip codes.

To include these bar codes on the envelopes or labels you create:

1. Choose Envelopes and Labels from the Tools menu.

2. Enter the correct return and delivery addresses, if necessary.

3. Click Options.

4. Select the Delivery Point Bar Code check box.

5. Select the FIM-A Courtesy Reply Mail check box if you want a facing identification mark that helps the U.S. Postal Service recognize the top of the envelope.

6. Click OK to return to the Envelopes and Labels dialog box.

7. Click Add to Document or Print to create the envelope.

Word generates the postal bar code based on the ZIP code information at the end of the delivery address.

Tech Tip: The delivery point bar code and any facing identification mark are field results. If you display the field codes in a document, you will see the field codes rather than the bar codes and marks. For example, a bar code may appear as {BARCODE \u "90210"}

What is the FIM-A Courtesy Reply Mail option that's available when I insert bar codes in my envelopes?

FIM is the acronym for the U.S. Postal Service's *Facing Identification Mark*. The FIM helps the Post Office to sort mail more efficiently. Word supports two types of FIMs: courtesy reply mail and business reply mail. FIM-A courtesy reply mail is often used when first-class postage is paid at the time it's mailed. Business reply mail requires a specific license from the Post Office and is not accessed with the Envelopes and Labels command on the Tools menu.

Tech Tip: You can add the FIM by choosing the Field command on the Insert menu, selecting BarCode in the Field Names list box, and typing the postal code in the Field Codes text box. After the postal code, enter **\b \u \f "A"** to create a courtesy reply mark.

When I create labels in a custom size, Word displays the message "The margins, label size, and number across or down values produce a page that is larger than the label page size." How do I get my labels to print?

You see this message when you have told Word to place more labels on a page than it can fit on the current paper size. You see this message for one of three reasons:

■ You have told Word to fit more labels across the page than can fit on the current paper size.

■ You have told Word to fit more labels down the page than can fit on the current paper size.

■ The page size required to fit the labels is larger than the default paper size; this problem often occurs when you are printing labels using a landscape orientation.

When this error message appears, double-check the measurements that you entered in the Custom Laser Information or Custom Dot Matrix Information dialog box. You see one of these dialog boxes when you click Options in the Envelopes and Labels dialog box when the Labels tab is selected, then click Details. Use the following formula to calculate the minimum paper width you need:

```
(number of labels across x horizontal pitch) + side margin =
minimum paper width
```

If the results are less than the paper width, the width of the page is not a problem. If the paper width is the problem, you either need to reduce the horizontal pitch or increase the page size setting.

To check whether the page length is the culprit, calculate the minimum height Word expects by using this formula:

```
(number of labels down x vertical pitch) + top margin = minimum
page height
```

Tech Tip: You can avoid this problem by using one of the predefined labels. When you select one of these label sizes, Word automatically sets the page size to the correct dimensions.

When the height and width match your label stock, more than likely your problem is that the paper size of the labels doesn't match the current paper size setting. Word adjusts the paper size when printing labels on a dot matrix printer. However, when you define labels for printing on a laser printer, the default label page size is the same as the default page size as any document created with the Normal template.

When the error message displays, follow these steps to resolve the problem:

1. Click OK in response to the error message.
   Word returns to the Custom Laser Information dialog box.

2. Write down the correct dimensions of your labels and how many there are across and down the actual page.

3. Reduce the size of the labels using the Label He̲ight and Label W̲idth text boxes. Depending on the number of labels across and down, adjust the label size to fit a standard 8 1/2 x 11 sheet of paper. Remember to leave room for the top and side margin.

4. Specify the correct number of labels across and down the page in the Number A̲cross and Number D̲own text boxes, respectively.

5. Click OK twice to accept the label size and close the Label Options dialog box.

6. Click New D̲ocument to add the labels to the document.

Word lays out the correct number of labels in the form of a table. Once the labels are laid out in the document, you can change the orientation to match the direction in which the labels will pass through the printer.

When printing labels landscape, the best thing to do is to set the labels manually, because when setting the labels using the label feature, Word automatically assumes portrait orientation. If you were to set up labels portrait first and then try to rotate to landscape, the labels would not rotate, just the page orientation.

To set up labels landscape, do the following:

Tech Tip: The measurement for the rows probably appears in points. If you prefer, you can enter the measurement in inches or centimeters. After the number, type **in** or " for inches; type **cm** for centimeters.

1. Open a new document.

2. Choose Page Setup from the File menu.

3. Click the Paper Size tab.

4. Select Landscape.

5. Make sure that Whole Document appears in the Apply To drop-down list box.

6. If the page size is incorrect, you select the correct one in the Paper Size drop-down list box.

7. Click OK. (Now you have a portrait piece at paper.)

8. Choose Select Table from the Table menu to insert a table. If your label sheet is 10 across and 3 down, insert a table with 10 columns and 3 rows.

9. Choose Cell Height and Width from the Table menu.

10. Click the Row tab and enter the correct vertical pitch measurement for the labels in the At text box, that indicates how high each label is.

11. Click the Column tab and enter the width of your labels in the Width of Columns text box.

12. Type **0** in the Space Between Columns text box.

13. Click OK.

You now have a custom label page. You can save this as a template for future use.

How can I change the font when I'm printing a single label?

Display the Labels tab in the Envelopes and Labels dialog box, select the text, and then click the right mouse button to display the formatting shortcut menu. Choose Font or Paragraph, depending on the formatting you want to change. You can also change the font by highlighting the text, pressing CTRL+D, selecting a font in the Font dialog box that appears, and then clicking OK. Similarly, you can press CTRL+D and select a font before you enter the label's text.

Once you add labels to a document, they use the font specified in the Normal style. You can modify this style to change the appearance of your labels.

My labels are an unusual size. Will Word let me print addresses on them?

If the labels can go through your printer, you can print addresses on them with Word. However, before you can print these labels, Word needs to know their exact dimensions, the number of labels in each direction on the page, and overall paper size. The dialog box in Figure 13-5 shows the measurements that Word uses. You should measure all of the distances that appear in the dialog box shown in Figure 13-5 and then enter them in the appropriate text boxes.

Tech Tip: Word recognizes commonly used, predefined label sizes. If your labels are a different type, check the package to see if they are identical to one of existing selections.

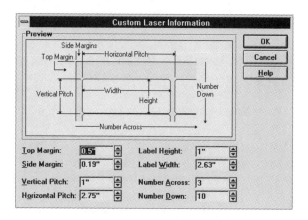

FIGURE 13-5 You can enter the measurements for a custom size label

I already created a main document for mailing labels. Now I want to use a new label size. Can I modify my existing document?

Tech Tip: If you want to save the original mail label document, select New Main Document at the prompt in step 4. Otherwise, Word replaces the original main label document with a blank labels merge document.

When you change to a different label size or to a different printer, you can use the same main document and simply set up the mail labels again by following these steps:

1. Open your main document.

2. Click Mail Merge Helper on the Mail Merge toolbar.

3. Select Create and Mailing Labels.

4. Select Change Document Type.

Word overwrites the existing document with a blank labels document.

5. Click the Setup button, which replaces the Edit button in the Mail Merge Helper dialog box.

6. Select a new label size and then click OK.

7. Redefine the label contents by adding your merge fields and then click OK.

The main document will now use the new label size and layout.

What types of mailing label main documents does Word recognize?

Word recognizes three types of main documents for mailing labels:

- A main document based on the MAILLABL.DOT template that came with Word for Windows version 2.x.

- A main document based on the label template provided with Word for Windows version 1.x; the first item in this document must be a data field that identifies the data you want to merge.

- A main document set up in Word for DOS or Word for the Macintosh; the first item in this document must be the data instruction that identifies the data with which you want to merge it.

Working with Large Documents

Large documents require a great deal of memory and organization. Word's master document feature makes it easy to optimize performance by letting you break large files into subdocuments. You can then edit these smaller files individually and, finally, recombine them into an easily formatted, large document. Word also provides tools to create other elements that you're likely to include only in large documents, such as indexes, tables of contents, and tables of authorities. In addition, Word provides a feature for adding footnotes and endnotes to your work.

FRUSTRATION BUSTERS!

Creating large documents can be frustrating, especially when many people work on different parts of the same document. It is easy to lose track of one section or file while juggling so much information. Here are a few suggestions for managing such a project:

- Before you start writing, outline the document in as much detail as possible. This outline can act as a "road map" for you and everyone else who may work with the file. Once you have an outline, it's easier to assign sections to different people and keep track of which ones are done and which ones aren't. Make sure each person involved in the project carefully reviews the outline and knows where his or her contribution fits into the "big picture."

- Create a table to record when each section of the document is written, edited, or reviewed. This will help you monitor your progress and ensure that nothing is falling behind schedule.

- Create and post a check list of what needs to be done to each section of the document, including formatting, spell checking, and grammar checking. Use this document to make sure each step is completed for each section before you declare a document finished.

What do section breaks do and why are there four types?

Word applies certain types of formatting, such as margins, columns, and paper size, to *sections* in a document. Section breaks let you divide your document so that you can apply different formatting to different parts of your document. For example, you might want to have a single column at the top of a newsletter page, three columns in the middle, and one column at the bottom, as in the newsletter shown in Figure 14-1. Each of these areas of the newsletter is a section.

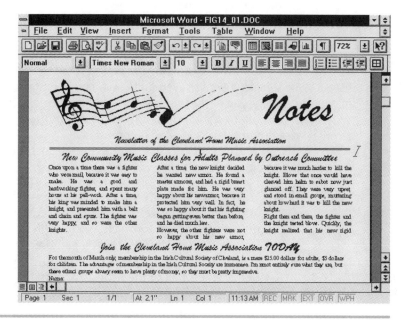

FIGURE 14-1   You can use sections to display different numbers of columns on the same page

Word 6.0 offers four section breaks: Next Page, Continuous, Odd Page, and Even Page. The type of section break determines the pagination that follows:

- *Next Page* starts the next section on the next new page.

- *Continuous* begins the next section at the insertion point's location, without starting another page.

- *Odd Page* starts the next section on the next odd numbered page.

- *Even Page* begins the next section on the next even numbered page.

To insert a page break:

1. Choose Break from the Insert menu.

2. Select the option button for the type of section break you want to insert.

3. Click OK.

Why would I use a master document?

Word's master document feature lets you manage long documents more easily by breaking them into parts. Each part, or *subdocument*, is saved in its own file. The master document combines all of these subdocument files into one. It also makes it possible to standardize formatting without setting these options and styles in each component.

Using subdocuments to create a master document has several advantages over working with one large file:

- You can easily divide up a task, such as producing a large annual report, between several people. When the individual files are complete, you simply assemble them into the master document. You can then create a common table of contents or index in the master document for all of the subdocuments.

- A very large document can cause Word to run very slowly because it uses so much memory. By working with smaller subdocuments, you can avoid compromising Word's performance.

How do I create a master document?

You can convert an existing document into a master document or you can create one from scratch. When you convert an existing document to a master document, you tell Word to divide a document into subdocuments based on heading levels. You specify a particular heading level as the beginning of each new subdocument. Then, Word saves all of the text between the specified heading levels to separate files.

Follow these steps to generate a master document:

1. Open a file formatted with heading levels or create an outline with heading levels in a new document.

2. Switch to master document view by choosing <u>M</u>aster Document from the <u>V</u>iew menu.

3. Select all of the text you want to include in the subdocuments. The first paragraph you select must be formatted with the heading level that is going to begin

each new subdocument. For example, if the first paragraph uses the Heading 1 style, Word will create a new subdocument every time it encounters this style in the document.

4. Click the Create Subdocument button on the Master Document toolbar, as shown here:

Word breaks the current document into subdocuments at the specified heading levels. Figure 14-2 shows a newly created document that is divided into subdocuments.

5. Choose Save from the File menu to save the master document and all of its subdocuments. Word automatically creates names for the subdocuments using the first eight characters in the first heading of the subdocument. If a heading is not unique, Word uses random letters or characters for the last four characters in the file name to make it so.

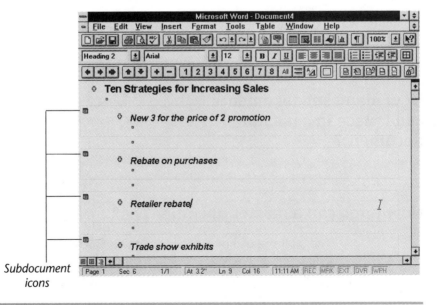

Subdocument icons

FIGURE 14-2 You can break a document into subdocuments

Can I add an existing Word document to a master document?

To add a Word document to your master document as a subdocument:

1. Open the master document to which you want to add the existing document.

2. Choose <u>M</u>aster Document from the <u>V</u>iew menu.

3. Move your insertion point to the location in the master document where you want to insert the existing document. (Make sure you are not inserting into a subdocument.)

4. Click the Insert Subdocument button on the Master Document toolbar, shown here:

5. Select the name of the document you want to insert in the File <u>N</u>ame list box, then click OK.

Word adds the subdocument to the master document, retaining the original file name.

How many subdocuments can I place in a master document?

You can insert up to 80 subdocuments in a single master document.

How large can a master document be?

The total size of a master document and all of its subdocuments cannot exceed 32MB. This figure does not include the graphics in the files.

Can I rearrange my subdocuments within the master document?

Yes, you can rearrange the subdocuments in your master document. To do so:

1. Switch to master document view by choosing <u>M</u>aster Document from the <u>V</u>iew menu.

2. Click the subdocument icon in the upper-left corner of the subdocument to select all of the subdocument.

3. Drag the icon to the location where you want the subdocument to appear.

Tech Tip: You cannot drag a subdocument icon to a locked subdocument in your master document. When you drag a subdocument to immediately above another one, the dragged subdocument becomes a part of the subdocument it is dragged to. You cannot do this with a locked subdocument because it would be editing the subdocument that is locked against editing. When moving a subdocument to before a locked subdocument, make sure there is a section or paragraph break before the locked subdocument, and that you are dragging the subdocument to before that break.

Why can't I print my master document the way I want to?

How your master document prints depends on the view displayed at the time. When you are in master document view, as shown in Figure 14-2, you can print the outline of the master document. To print the entire contents of the master document and its components, you must switch to normal or page layout view.

To print your master document to suit your needs:

1. Choose the appropriate view from the <u>V</u>iew menu.

If you switch to outline view, use the buttons on the Outlining toolbar to display the levels you want to print.

2. Click the Print button on the Standard toolbar, or choose <u>P</u>rint from the <u>F</u>ile menu, then click OK to print the document.

What happens to the header and footer in my subdocument when I assemble the master document?

Subdocuments either keep their existing header and footer or "borrow" them when assembled into the master document, as follows:

- A subdocument retains its headers and footers when it is inserted into a master document.

- If a subdocument contains neither a header nor footer, it inherits those of the previous subdocument.

- If the subdocument that contains neither a header nor footer appears first in a master document that has its own, the subdocument uses this header and footer.

- If the subdocument has only a header or only a footer, it keeps whichever one it contains and borrows the other from the previous subdocument.

- To modify a subdocument's header or footer, move the insertion point to the section to be changed and choose <u>H</u>eader and Footer from the <u>V</u>iew menu. Click the Same as Previous button on the Header and Footer toolbar to remove any link to the previous subdocument's header and footer. Delete the text in the header or footer and enter the new information.

When I try to save my master document, Word displays the message "Cannot save or create this file." What can I do?

This message sometimes appears when saving a master document. Usually, you'll either see it the first time you try to save the file or you won't see it at all. Unfortunately, there is no known cause of this error and there is little you can do to correct it without first exiting Word. If the message displays, try checking the following:

- Open your AUTOEXEC.BAT file and edit the line that loads SHARE.EXE to increase the /L: switch number to 1000.

- Edit your CONFIG.SYS file to increase the number of files and buffers.

- Verify that the Windows temp directory exists and contains no files. To check this, exit Windows, type **SET** and press ENTER at the DOS prompt to display the environmental variable settings, note the directory listed in the line that begins with TEMP=, switch to the temp directory and delete any files in it that have the .TMP extension.

- Make sure you have enough available hard drive space. You need to have at least three times the size of the document free, especially if you are working with graphics.

- Try saving each individual subdocument before saving the entire master document.

 My subdocument and the master document use different templates. When I open the subdocument in the master document, its formatting reflects the template on which the master document is based. Why does this happen?

Word does this by design. When you open a subdocument within a master document, Word applies the formatting from the template attached to the master document to all text, including the subdocument. If you print the master document, including the subdocuments, the master document's template formatting remains in effect and appears in the output.

If you open the subdocument independently, the formatting from the template attached to the subdocument remains in effect. If you print a subdocument separately, it retains this formatting.

Why don't chapter numbers appear with my page numbers in my master document? I formatted it to use chapter numbers.

At least one section in your master document is not formatted for chapter page numbering. Because of this, no chapter numbers appear anywhere, even in those sections that you formatted to use them. To solve this problem:

1. Open the master document.
2. Choose Select All from the Edit menu.
3. Choose Page Numbers from the Insert menu.
4. Click Format.
5. Select the Include Chapter Number check box.
6. Select the heading style applied to the chapter headings in the Chapter Starts With Style drop-down list box.
7. Click OK twice to return to your document.

Now that you have formatted all of the sections in your master document to include chapter numbers along with the page numbers, you should no longer have a problem.

I created a template which includes headers and footers to use with my master document. When I insert a subdocument, Word warns me that the master document's formatting will override the subdocument's. However, the subdocument still uses its own header and footer. What can I do to fix this?

This message tells you that any style in the subdocument that has the same name as one in the master document will be overridden by the master document style. However, it does *not* mean that all of the master document's template settings will prevail. When you insert a subdocument into a master document, Word formats it as its own section by inserting section breaks before and after it. It therefore retains its header and footer. If you want the master document's headers and footers to appear in a subdocument, you must insert it, then remove the surrounding section breaks.

How do I create a table of contents or other list of items in my document?

Word can create several types of "look-up" lists based on the entries in your document. Essentially, all of these lists indicate where particular items appear in your document. You can easily generate four types of lists that are commonly found with large documents:

- *Tables of Contents* provide an overview of the layout of a document. Figure 14-3 shows a table of contents created with Word.

- *Tables of Authorities* appear in legal documents to mark where citations to specific laws or court cases appear. You usually include a table of authority for each category or citation source. Each entry provides all of the citations for that particular case or law.

- *Indexes* indicate the location of specific information in your document. Indexes usually include references to meaningful bits of information in your document that might not be distinguished by headings. Index entries are arranged alphabetically rather than in the order in which the items appear in the document. You can find a good example of an index at the end of this book.

- *Tables of Figures* list charts, tables, illustrations, and other such elements that you might add to your document. For example, you might create one table that identifies and locates all of the graphs in your document and another that lists all of the photographs.

None of these lists have to be used exactly as described here—Word gives you the flexibility to create whatever type of look-up list you need. For example, you might produce a table of figures to reference all of your equations. You could also

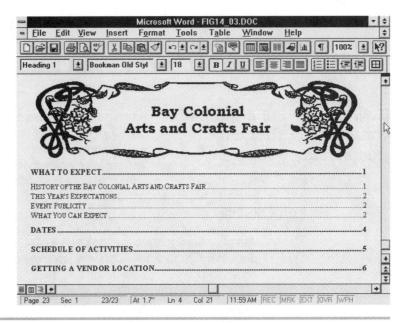

FIGURE 14-3   A table of contents helps readers locate useful information

create multiple tables of contents: one at the beginning of the document that lists the chapter titles, and one at the beginning of each chapter that indicates the sections it contains.

To create a look-up list:

1. Move your insertion point to where you want the list to appear in your document.

Tech Tip: To prevent Word from numbering the pages in the table of contents and reflecting them in the document's pagination, you can insert a next page section break before the first text in your document and start the page numbering again after it. To do so, choose Break from the Insert menu, select Next Page, and click OK. Then, choose Page Numbers from the Insert menu, click Format, enter **1** in the Start At text box, and click OK twice. An easier solution, of course, is to create the table of contents at the end of your document, format it without page numbering, and move the printed pages to the beginning of the document before you bind it.

2. Choose Inde**x** and Tables from the **I**nsert menu.

3. Click the appropriate tab for the type of list you want to create.

4. Preview and select the desired format.

5. Select and clear the other available options to indicate the entries to include, then click OK.

Because each look-up list is actually a field, you see its code rather than the list itself when you display field codes.

How do I update a table of contents in my document?

To update a table of contents:

1. Display field results, not field codes.

2. Position the insertion point in the table of contents.

3. Press F9.

4. Select Update Page Numbers Only or Update Entire Table. The first option retains any direct formatting you have applied to the table of contents.

5. Click OK.

When I inserted a Table of Contents in my master document, I got the message "Error! No Table Of Contents Entries Found." I inserted TC fields in my subdocuments and they appear on the screen. What's wrong?

Word can add two types of entries to a table of contents: headings and TC fields. By default, the table of contents only reflects text formatted as headings. To create a table of contents that uses TC fields:

1. Choose Index and Tables from the Insert menu.

2. Click the Table of Contents tab.

3. Click Options.

4. Select the Table <u>E</u>ntry Fields check box. If you don't want headings as entries in the table of contents at all, clear the <u>S</u>tyles check box.

5. Click OK twice to insert the table of contents.

Is there a shortcut for inserting TC fields for a table of contents?

Yes, Word provides a shortcut for creating TC fields to mark your table of contents entries.

1. Select the text you want to identify as a table of contents entry.

2. Press ALT+SHIFT+O to open the Mark Table of Contents Entry dialog box, shown here:

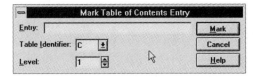

3. Edit the text, if necessary, in the <u>E</u>ntry text box. Whatever you type here appears verbatim in the table of contents.

4. If the document includes more than one table of contents, indicate the one in which to include this entry by selecting it in the Table <u>I</u>dentifier drop-down list box.

5. Select the level for this entry in the <u>L</u>evel drop-down list box. The level controls the text's indentation in the table of contents.

6. Click OK to insert the TC field.

Is there a shortcut for marking citations for a table of authorities?

The first occurrence of a citation in a Word document uses a long form that includes all of the information required to locate the cited law or case; later citations to the same source use a shorter form that identifies clearly it but doesn't repeat the details. With Word, you add the first, longer citation. You can then let Word mark the short citations for you.

Tech Terror: Nothing can be more frustrating to a legal student or professional than having to go back and re-mark all of the citations in a long and complicated brief. To prevent this situation, make sure that marking citations for the tables of authorities is the final task you perform when writing a brief.

To mark your citations quickly:

1. Highlight the first, long citation.

2. Press ALT+SHIFT+I to open the Mark Citation dialog box.

3. Edit the selected text so that it matches the required form for the tables of authorities entries.

4. Select the category for the current citation in the Category drop-down list box. Each category of citations appears in its own table.

5. Enter the text of the short citation in the Short Citation text box. This text must match the entries in your document exactly, including punctuation, spaces, and capitalization. A completed Mark Citation dialog box might look like this one:

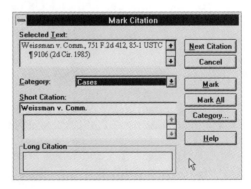

6. Click Mark All to let Word automatically mark all of the short citations in your document for inclusion in the tables of authorities.

7. Click Cancel to close the dialog box, or <u>N</u>ext Citation to move to the next text formatted as a long citation in your document.

Can I change the categories for which I can create tables of authorities?

You can use up to 16 categories of citations to create tables of authorities. By default, the first seven are named Cases, Statues, Other Authorities, Rules, Treatises, Regulations, and Constitutional Provisions. You can change these names or assign names to any of the remaining nine categories. To modify the categories to reflect the types of citations included in your document:

1. Choose Inde<u>x</u> and Tables from the <u>I</u>nsert menu.
2. Click the Table of <u>A</u>uthorities tab and click Mar<u>k</u> Citation. You can also press ALT+SHIFT+I to display the Mark Citation dialog box.
3. Click the Cate<u>g</u>ory button.
4. Select the category you want to rename in the <u>C</u>ategory list box.
5. Enter a new name for the category in the Replace <u>W</u>ith text box.
6. Click <u>R</u>eplace, then click OK to return to the document.

How can I easily update my table of authorities?

You can update your table of authorities using the menus or with a keyboard shortcut. To update a table of authorities using the menu:

1. Choose Inde<u>x</u> and Tables from the <u>I</u>nsert menu.
2. Click the Table Of <u>A</u>uthorities tab.
3. Click OK.

Word finds and selects any existing table of authorities, then prompts you to confirm that you want to replace it.

Tech Tip: You can switch a single field between showing field codes and results by moving to it and pressing SHIFT+F9. Pressing ALT+F9 is a shortcut for switching between displaying field codes and results for all fields in a document.

4. Choose Yes to update the table.

You can also update a table of authorities by positioning the insertion point anywhere in the table of authorities and pressing F9.

If the table of authorities does not update, verify that it is still a field by turning on field codes. To display field codes:

1. Choose Options from the Tools menu.

2. Click the View tab.

3. Select the Field Codes check box and then click OK.

If the table of authorities still appears as a list in the document, it is no longer a field and cannot be updated. You need to regenerate the table of authorities to make it current.

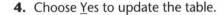

What is a concordance file and how would I use it?

You can create a list of words and phrases (one per line) that you want to appear as entries in your document's index and save it as a separate *concordance file.* You then tell Word to mark each occurrence of the concordance file's words and phrases for inclusion in the index.

To use a concordance file to mark your document for index entries:

1. Create the concordance file, just like any other Word document. Each word or phrase you want to index appears on its own line, as shown in Figure 14-4.

2. Save the concordance file.

3. Open the document you want to index.

4. Choose Index and Tables from the Insert menu.

5. Click the Index tab.

6. Click Automark.

7. Select or enter the name of the concordance file and click OK.

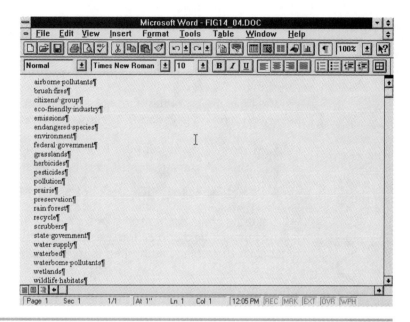

FIGURE 14-4   A sample concordance file

Word marks the designated text in your document with XE fields. Your final index, using the concordance file, might look like the one shown in Figure 14-5.

Tech Tip: While using a concordance file can help you create an index quickly, it is not a substitute for reviewing the document thoroughly to mark index entries. Often, the text in a document may not exactly match the contents of the concordance file. In this case, you need to flag these entries manually because the concordance file simply won't find them.

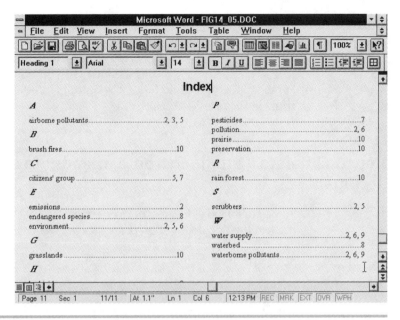

FIGURE 14-5 An index created using a concordance file

How do I update an index?

To update an index:

1. Choose Inde**x** and Tables from the **I**nsert menu.

2. Click the Inde**x** tab, then click OK.

3. Word finds and selects the index in your document. When Word prompts you to confirm that you want to replace the existing index, choose **Y**es.

You can also update all fields in a document, including the index, by choosing Select **A**ll from the **E**dit menu and then pressing F9.

Can I index text in my endnotes and footnotes?

In Word 6.0, you can index text that appears in endnotes and footnotes. To do so, simply mark the text for entry in the index as you normally would. For example, you could index the authors listed in the endnotes shown in Figure 14-6.

How do I delete a single footnote or endnote in my document?

To delete an individual footnote or endnote, select its reference mark in the document, then press BACKSPACE or DEL to delete it.

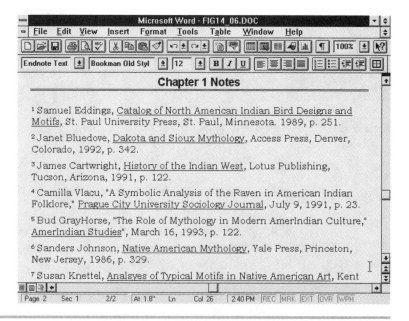

FIGURE 14-6   You can index text found in endnotes with Word 6.0

I have footnotes and endnotes in my document. Is there any way to delete them all at once?

To easily delete all your footnotes and endnotes:

1. Choose Replace from the Edit menu.
2. With the insertion point in the Find What text box, click Special and choose either Footnote Mark or Endnote Mark from the pop-up menu.
3. Delete any text that appears in the Replace With text box.
4. Click Replace All.

This procedure replaces your footnote or endnote references with nothing, thereby deleting them. Note that deleting these references automatically removes the associated footnotes or endnotes.

Is there any way to move directly to a particular footnote or endnote in my document?

To quickly move to a specific footnote or endnote:

1. Choose Go To from the Edit menu, or press F5.
2. Select Footnote or Endnote in the Go To What list box.
3. Enter the number or custom mark of the note in the Enter Footnote or Endnote Number text box.
4. Click Go To.
5. Choose Close to close the dialog box.

Tech Tip: You can also type values in the Enter Footnote or Endnote Number text box to move to an earlier or later footnote or endnote based on its position relative to the insertion point. For example, you could enter **+5** to move to the fifth footnote forward, or **–3** to move three backwards.

Is there a keyboard shortcut for inserting endnotes or footnotes?

Word provides shortcut keys to make it easy to insert footnotes and endnotes. When you press these shortcut keys, Word inserts the appropriate type of reference and opens the note pane, as shown in Figure 14-7, in which you enter the associated text.

- To insert an endnote, press ALT+CTRL+E.
- To insert a footnote, press ALT+CTRL+F.

How do I remove my footnote or endnote separator?

The footnote or endnote separator is the text or graphic that separates footnotes or endnotes from other text on the page. For example, Figure 14-8 shows a document that displays short lines between the document body and any notes.

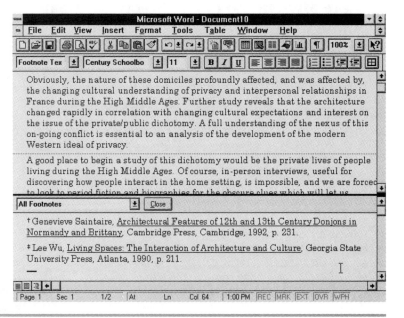

FIGURE 14-7   Enter endnotes and footnotes using the note pane

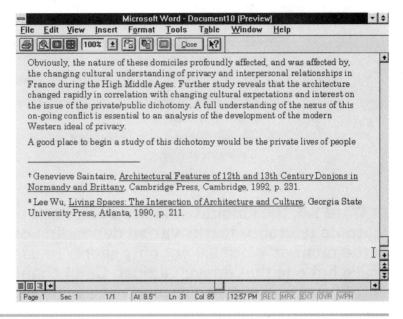

Obviously, the nature of these domiciles profoundly affected, and was affected by, the changing cultural understanding of privacy and interpersonal relationships in France during the High Middle Ages. Further study reveals that the architecture changed rapidly in correlation with changing cultural expectations and interest on the issue of the private/public dichotomy. A full understanding of the nexus of this on-going conflict is essential to an analysis of the development of the modern Western ideal of privacy.

A good place to begin a study of this dichotomy would be the private lives of people

---

† Genevieve Saintaire, <u>Architectural Features of 12th and 13th Century Donjons in Normandy and Brittany</u>, Cambridge Press, Cambridge, 1992, p. 231.

‡ Lee Wu, <u>Living Spaces: The Interaction of Architecture and Culture</u>, Georgia State University Press, Atlanta, 1990, p. 211.

FIGURE 14-8   A note separator separates the notes from the other text

To remove this separator:

1. Make sure you are in normal view by choosing Normal from the View menu.
2. Choose Footnotes from the View menu.
3. Select Separator in the drop-down list box in the note pane.
4. Select the separator in the note pane and delete it. If you just want to change the separator, enter a new one in this pane.
5. Choose Close in the note pane.

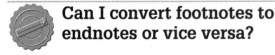

Can I convert footnotes to endnotes or vice versa?

To convert one or more footnotes to endnotes, or vice versa:

1. Choose Normal from the View menu, if necessary, to switch to normal view.

2. Choose Footnote from the View menu.

3. Select All Footnotes or All Endnotes in the drop-down list box in the note pane.

4. Select the footnotes or endnotes you want to convert.

5. Click the right mouse button to display the shortcut menu.

6. Choose Convert to Footnote or Convert to Endnote from the shortcut menu.

 In Word 2.0, the amount of space before and after my footnote reference marks varied depending on the size of the number. Word 6.0 not only seems to use a larger space but one that doesn't adjust. Can I change the size of this space so it doesn't stand out as much?

The footnote reference mark reserves a certain amount of space around the number that cannot be modified in Word 6.0. This problem is fixed in Word 6.0a, so that the space will once again vary appropriately based on the size of the number.

Forms

You can create a special type of document, called a *form*, that lets you control not only what but where information is entered into it. Word provides several features that make it easy to design your own custom forms. Once you define the form by adding *form fields*, you can fill it in using Word or by hand. If you have used any of the wizards, you have probably already used Word's form features. For example, the Fax Wizard includes check boxes added as check box fields. Documents created with the invoice template also use many form fields to ensure that you enter all of the information you need to complete an order.

FRUSTRATION BUSTERS!

Careful planning can greatly enhance a form's design—and a well designed form makes it much more likely that the user will enter the correct information in the correct locations. Consider these tips as you set up your form:

- If you are creating a form that will be filled out on paper instead of on screen, make sure the spaces for entering information are large enough to accommodate either handwritten or typewritten responses.

- Align the entries so that they are indented the same amount on the page.

- Use Word's table features to create grids of prompts and room for the expected responses. You can then select and add borders to cells in the table to create response boxes, if desired.

- Allow adequate white space around and within the text to make it easier to read.

- Organize the form entries in a logical arrangement. For example, place the entries for a sales invoice or customer inquiry in the order in which the information is provided to the person who enters it.

- Take your time and plan your form well. Designing a simple form can be straightforward, but you can also use features, such as bookmarks and macros, to create more complex ones.

Can I use Word to create my own forms?

Word offers many features and formatting capabilities to help you create custom forms that fit your needs. You can use borders, character and paragraph formatting, tables, and frames to achieve "the look" you want.

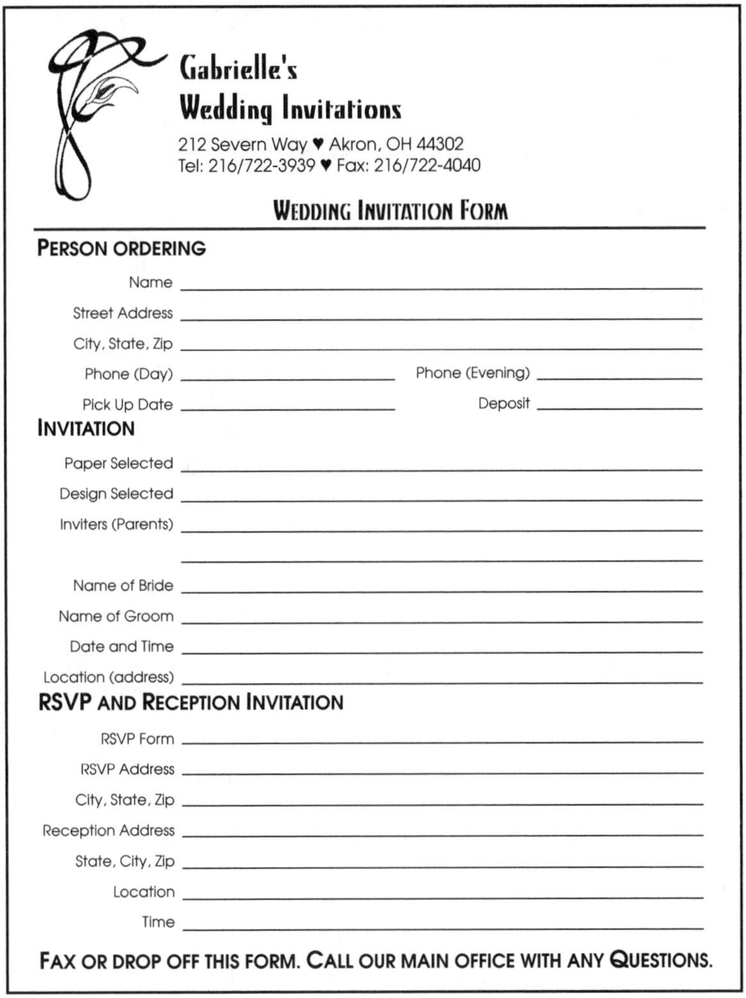

FIGURE 15-1 A form created using Word's formatting features

Figure 15-1 shows a form created in Word that's designed to be completed by hand. You can also use form fields to produce forms that you complete within Word. These forms only let you move to and enter information in the appropriate places in the document.

How do I use a form in Word that someone else set up for me?

You can use these steps to enter data into the form, which should have been saved as a template:

Tech Tip: When you design a form, you can set up a text form field so that it limits the number of characters it accepts or only allows a number or date and time entry.

1. Choose <u>N</u>ew from the <u>F</u>ile menu.

2. Select the name of the template that contains the form in the <u>T</u>emplate list box or type the name in the <u>T</u>emplate text box, then click OK.

3. Move to each field, in turn, and enter the appropriate type of entry.

To move to the next field, press DOWN ARROW, ENTER, or TAB. To move to the previous field, press UP ARROW or SHIFT+TAB.

Word has three types of form fields, as shown in Figure 15-2:

- You type your entry in a *text form field*.

- You can press SPACEBAR, type an **X**, or click a *check box form field* to toggle between selecting and clearing it.

- To display the list of options in a *drop-down form field*, you click the arrow or press either F4 or ALT+DOWN ARROW. You then click your choice, use the arrow keys, or type its first letter to select it.

4. Choose <u>S</u>ave from the <u>F</u>ile menu.

5. Enter a name for the completed document in the File <u>N</u>ame text box and select OK.

The saved version contains both the form's contents and all of your entries.

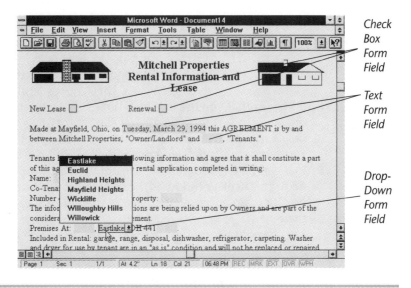

Check
Box
Form
Field

Text
Form
Field

Drop-
Down
Form
Field

FIGURE 15-2   Word includes three types of form fields

In Word for Windows 2.0, I could just type text in a Fillin field's dialog box and press ENTER to open the next dialog box. In Word 6.0, pressing ENTER just creates a new paragraph within the dialog box. How do I get to the next dialog box?

Word for Windows 6.0 lets you enter multiple lines within the dialog box, like the one shown here:

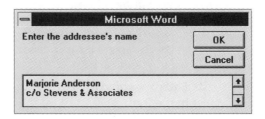

You press ENTER to move to the next line. To choose OK, you can click it with the mouse or press TAB once to activate the button, then press ENTER.

What are the types of form fields that I can add to a form?

Word includes three types of form fields: text, check box, and drop-down, as shown in Figure 15-2. These form fields are just like the text boxes, check boxes, and drop-down list boxes that you use in dialog boxes. You enter information directly into text form fields. You can set them up so they accept only a specific type of entry: text, numbers, or dates and times. You can supply a default entry as well as limit the amount of text that can be entered into this type of field. Text form fields can perform calculations just as the ones in Word's Invoice template do. They can also execute macros when you move to or from them.

A check box form field lets you select an option by placing an X in the box. You can control whether a check box form field is automatically selected, whether the user can change the selection, and the size of the check box.

Drop-down form fields let you select an entry from a predefined list of choices. Because this type of field has a set number of specific options, you may want to include None in the list to give users the flexibility to leave the field blank.

How do I create a form?

A form is a template that contains whatever standard text and formatting you want plus form fields in the locations where users can make entries. You create a template in order to store all of the AutoText entries and macros used by the form. A user can then open a new document based on this template to fill in the form.

To create your own form:

1. Choose New from the File menu, leave Normal selected in the Template list box, select the Template option button, and click OK.

2. Enter the standard text and graphics you want to appear in the form. Focus first on the part of the document that

does not include form fields. When needed, use tables to maintain alignment.

3. Move to the first location in the document where you want to be able to enter information. Add a form field by choosing For_m Field from the _Insert menu, selecting the type of field to add, and clicking OK. Alternatively, you can display the Form toolbar and click the Text Form Field, Check Box Form Field, or Drop-Down Form Field button, shown here:

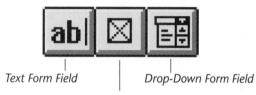

Text Form Field   *Drop-Down Form Field*

Check Box Form Field

4. Repeat step 3 for each form field you want to add.

5. Set the options for each form field in the document. Display the appropriate dialog box for each form field by double-clicking it, or by clicking it with the right mouse button and choosing Form Field Options from the shortcut menu. The options vary for each type of form field. These options are described throughout this chapter.

6. Choose _Protect Document from the _Tools menu and select the _Forms option button.
    Protecting a form prevents others from moving to and editing any part of the document that is not a form field. Once you protect the document, you cannot modify its form fields without first unprotecting it.

7. Type a password in the _Password text box if you want to make sure no one else can remove the protection.

8. Click OK to protect the form.

9. If you supplied a password, Word prompts you to retype it and click OK again.

10. Choose _Save from the _File menu to save your template. Type the name for your form in the File _Name list box and click OK.

Tech Tip: Make sure you keep a record of the password in a safe place; if you forget it, there is no way to unprotect the form. Usually, protecting a document without a password is as much protection as you need.

You can now use the form by choosing <u>N</u>ew from the <u>F</u>ile menu, selecting your template in the Template list box, and then clicking OK.

Tech Tip: To display the Forms toolbar, you can choose For<u>m</u> Field from the <u>I</u>nsert menu and click the <u>S</u>how Toolbar button. Alternatively, you can right-click any toolbar displayed on the screen and choose Forms from the shortcut menu that appears.

How do I insert a form field into my document?

Tech Tip: You can also display the Forms toolbar and click the Text Form Field, Check Box Form Field, or Drop-Down Form Field button to add a default form field. Once you add the form field, you can click the Form Field Options button to modify its settings.

You can add text, check box, and drop-down form fields to either a document or a form template. To add a form field:

1. Make sure that the document is not protected. If it is, choose Un<u>p</u>rotect Document from the <u>T</u>ools menu. You cannot modify form fields while the document is protected.

2. Move the insertion point to the location where you want to insert the form field.

3. Choose For<u>m</u> Field from the <u>I</u>nsert menu

4. Select the type of form field you want to add.

5. Click the <u>O</u>ptions button and specify the appropriate options depending on the type of form field you added. These options are described throughout this chapter.

6. Click OK.

How can I limit the type of entry a user can input into a form field?

You can limit a text form field's entries to just text, numbers, or dates and times. When you set or change the allowable entry type, the other options that you can set for the form field change.

To limit the types of entries made into a text form field:

1. Open the template file.

2. Unprotect the template, if necessary, by choosing Unprotect Document from the <u>T</u>ools menu, typing any password you set, and clicking OK. Alternatively, you can click the Protect Form button on the Forms toolbar (the button appears shaded), shown here:

3. Select the text form field.

4. Open the Form Field Options dialog box by double-clicking the field, choose Form Field Options from its shortcut menu, or clicking the Form Field Options button on the Forms toolbar, shown here:

5. The Form Field Options dialog box, shown here, displays the options you can set for the Text Form Field.

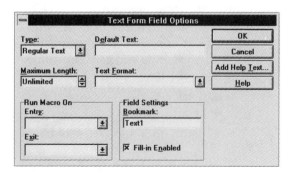

Select one of the following choices in the Type drop-down list box:

- *Regular Text* accepts any text as an entry. You can set the default entry that initially appears in the form in the Default Text text box. In the Text Format drop-down list box, you can select the case with which Word will format the entry in the form. You can also enter your own format.

- *Number* accepts any number as an entry. You can set the default number that initially appears in the form in the Default Number text box. Specify the format of the number by making a selection in the Number Format drop-down list box. You can also enter your own format using the same codes that you use for other numeric fields, such as the EQ field.

- *Date* accepts any date as an entry. You can enter a default in the Default Date text box and select a format in the Date Format drop-down list box.

- *Current Date* displays the current date in the text form field. You specify the date's format in the Date Format drop-down list box. When you pick this option, Word clears the Fill-in Enabled check box because you cannot change the entry when you use the form.

- *Current Time* displays the current time in the text form field in whatever format you select in the Time Format drop-down list box. If you pick this option, Word clears the Fill-in Enabled check box because you cannot change the entry when you use the form.

- *Calculation* displays the results of a formula. Enter the formula that the text form field will evaluate in the Expression text box and select the format of the results in the Number Format drop-down list box. If you pick this option, Word clears the Fill-in Enabled check box because you cannot change the entry when you use the form.

6. Click OK.

7. If there are additional changes you want to make to the form, do so before performing the following two steps.

8. Reprotect the template by choosing the Protect Document command from the Tools menu or clicking the Protect Form button on the Forms toolbar (the button appears shaded) .

9. Save the template again.

How do I add the items that appear in a drop-down form field?

You add the items that appear in a drop-down form field in the Drop-Down Form Field Options dialog box, as follows:

1. Open the template that contains the form.

2. Make sure the template is unprotected. If necessary, remove protection by choosing Unprotect Document from the Tools menu or clicking the Protect Form button on the Forms toolbar (the button appears shaded).

3. Insert a drop-down form field into your form or select an existing one.

4. Open the Form Field Options dialog box for this form field. If you are adding a new drop-down form field, click the Options button in the Form Field dialog box. For an existing drop-down form field, double-click the form field, choose Form Field Options from the shortcut menu, or click the Form Field Options button on the Forms toolbar.

5. Add a new item by typing it in the Drop-Down Item text box and then clicking Add. Repeat this step for each new option you want to add to the list.

6. Remove any incorrect entries by selecting them in the Items in Drop-Down List list box and then clicking Remove.

7. Arrange the items in the drop-down form field in the desired order. Select any item you want to move in the list and then click the up and down arrow buttons until it appears in the desired position. Repeat this step, as needed, to display the entries in the desired order. A completed list of entries for a drop-down form field might look like this:

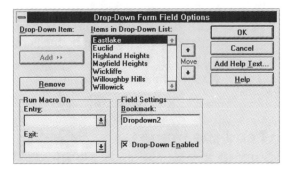

8. Click OK. If there are additional changes you want to make to the form, do so before performing the following two steps.

9. Reprotect the template by choosing the Protect Document command from the Tools menu or clicking the Protect Form button on the Forms toolbar (the button appears shaded) .

10. Save the template again.

When you open a document based on the template, it displays the correct options for the drop-down form field, as shown here:

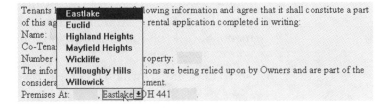

Is it possible to print only the data entered into a form?

Sometimes, you may want to print only the data in an online fill-in form, not all of the other text in the document. For example, you might create a form in Word whose design exactly matches a preprinted one. You can then print just the data to the preprinted form, as illustrated in Figure 15-3. Accounting applications often use this technique to print out information on tax forms.

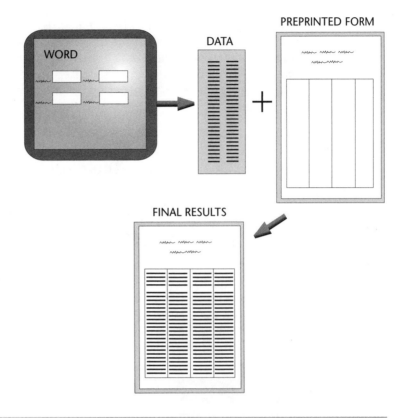

FIGURE 15-3   You can print only the form field data on preprinted forms

To print only the data entered on a form:

1. Create and complete the form document.
2. Choose Options from the Tools menu.
3. Click the Print tab.
4. Select the Print Data Only for Forms check box.
5. Click OK.

Word prints only the information entered in the form fields and places them in the exact same positions in which they appear within the document.

Selecting the Print Data Only for Forms option affects only the current document; you must reset it in each document from which you want to print just the form field contents. If you want to print only the form field data in every document based on a particular form, open the template in step 1 above and follow the same procedure to make this option the default.

 ## The form fields on my form are shaded and I don't like the way they look. Can I change their appearance?

You can toggle this shading on and off by clicking the Form Field Shading button on the Forms toolbar, shown here:

If you turn the shading off, however, you may want to add directions on the form to tell the user where to input the information. Figure 15-4 shows two versions of the same form, one without and the other with shading.

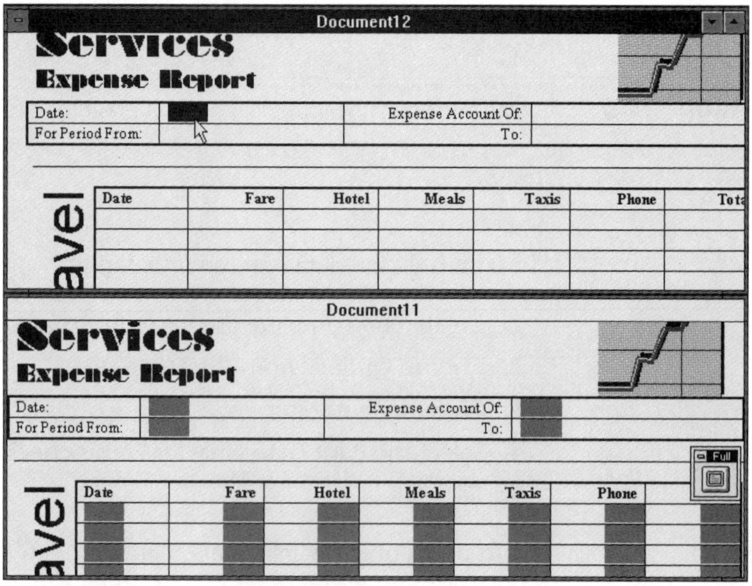

FIGURE 15-4 The same form without and with form fields shading

Tech Tip: If you see large brackets at the end of the fields, even after you turn off shading, they indicate bookmarks in the template. To hide them, choose Options from the Tools menu, click the View tab, clear the Bookmarks option, and click OK.

How can I change the appearance of form entries?

You can apply character formatting to form entries the exact same way you do to regular text. As with any other changes to a form template, you need to unprotect it before you can apply the formatting. Then, select the form field you want to format and modify the font, size, and attributes as you wish. When you are finished, reprotect the template and save the modified version. From now on, the character formatting will appear in any new document created with the template.

Tech Tip: The appearance of the items in a drop-down form field list doesn't change even though you apply character formatting to the field. However, the entries in the form itself will reflect these changes accordingly; they will also appear in the printed output.

Can I run a macro when entering or exiting a form field?

You can tell Word to execute a macro automatically whenever the insertion point enters or exits a particular form field. To specify a macro:

1. Double-click the form field, choose Form Field Options from the shortcut menu, or click the Form Field Options button on the Forms toolbar.

2. Select the name of a macro in either or both of the Entry and Exit drop-down list boxes in the Run Macro On section.

3. Click OK.

Tech Tip: Any macro you want to run when you enter or exit a text form field must either be available in the form template itself or in one of the global templates, such as NORMAL.DOT.

Documents based on the Invoice template demonstrate the effect of running a macro when you leave a form field. Figure 15-5 shows a section of a new document created using this template. All of the entries in the Amount column are text form fields that display the results of calculations. You cannot move the insertion point to these form fields. For most of the entries in this column, the text form field equals the quantity multiplied by the amount. In the Quantity and Amount columns, Word runs the Update macro whenever you leave one of the text form fields. This Update macro updates all of the calculated fields in the form. (You may want to use this macro as a basis for creating a similar one suited to your own needs.)

SALESPERSON	P.O. NUMBER	DATE SHIPPED	SHIPPED VIA	F.O.B. POINT	TERMS

QUANTITY	DESCRIPTION	UNIT PRICE	AMOUNT
1	Misty Night Sleeping Bag	$ 70.00	$ 70.00
5	Freeze-Dried Apples	$ 2.99	$ 14.95
1	Ever-Glo Flashlight	$ 15.99	$ 15.99
			$ 0.00
			$ 0.00
			$ 0.00
			$ 0.00
		SUBTOTAL	$ 100.94
		SALES TAX	
		SHIPPING & HANDLING	
		TOTAL DUE	$ 100.94

Enter the number of units purchased

FIGURE 15-5 A document created with the Invoice form template

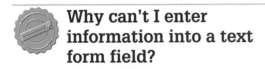

Why can't I enter information into a text form field?

If the form field contains the current date, the current time, or the results of a calculation, you cannot modify the contents. Also, you can only enter text into other types of form fields when the Fill-in Enabled check box in the Form Field Option dialog box is selected. To verify the status of this option, you can unprotect the document or template. Checking the form field in the document lets you test the settings but not change them permanently; to modify them in all documents, you must open and edit the template itself.

To enable the form field:

1. Remove protection from the document or template, if necessary, by choosing Unprotect Document from the Tools menu or clicking the Protect Form button on the Forms toolbar (the button appears shaded).

2. To open the Form Field Options dialog box, either double-click the appropriate form field, right-click it and choose Form Field Options from the shortcut menu, or select the field and then click the Form Field Options button on the Forms toolbar.

3. Select the Fill-in Enabled check box, if necessary, and then click OK.

4. Protect the document or template with either the Protect Document command on the Tools menu or the Protect Form button on the Forms toolbar.

   If you were testing this field in a document, now try moving to the form field. If you can, then you have found the reason you were unable to enter text in this form field, and now need to open the form's template to fix it by repeating these steps. This ensures that all forms based on the template will work correctly.

5. Save and close the document or template.

6. After fixing the template, choose New from the File menu, select the template in the Template list box, and then click OK.

You should now be able to enter text into the form field.

Can I prevent Word from resetting the form fields each time my macro protects my document?

When a macro protects or unprotects a document, it uses a WordBasic command. Unless you specify otherwise, the WordBasic command that protects your document again automatically resets the form fields to the default values. You can prevent Word from resetting the form fields by using this line in the macro to protect a document with form fields:

```
ToolsProtectDocument .Type = 2, .NoReset = 1
```

How do I make my text form fields longer?

When you add a text form field, Word sets it to either the default width or the width of the default entry. You can enlarge the shaded area in the blank form by entering a longer default entry in it. However, as you add text to the field, Word automatically expands or contracts the shaded area to accommodate your entry. The only way to permanently resize the form field is to turn off shading and add a box to indicate the location of the entry instead.

Can I add help text to my form fields?

You can add two types of help to form fields: status bar help, and F1 key help. Status bar help appears in the message area at the bottom of the screen whenever you select the field. As the name implies, F1 key help displays when you select the field and press the F1 key.

To add either type of help text to a field:

1. Open the template that contains the form.
2. Remove protection from the template, if necessary, by choosing Unprotect Document from the <u>T</u>ools menu or

clicking the Protect Form button on the Forms toolbar (the button appears shaded).

3. Move to the form field to which you want to add help text.

4. Open the Form Field Options dialog box by double-clicking the field, right-clicking it and choosing Form Field Options from the shortcut menu, or selecting the field and then clicking the Form Field Options button on the Forms toolbar.

5. Click the Add Help Text button.

6. Click the Status Bar tab or the Help Key (F1) tab, depending on the type of help text you want to add. (You can add one or both types of help to the same field.)

7. Select the option button for the source of the help text. You can select None for none, AutoText Entry to use an AutoText entry containing the text you want to appear as the help message, or Type Your Own to enter your own text.

8. Click OK twice.

9. Reprotect the template with the Protect Document command on the Tools menu or the Protect Form button on the Forms toolbar (the button appears lighter).

10. Save the template.

Figure 15-6 shows a form in which F1 key help was added to the selected text form field. The Help dialog box displays an AutoText entry that is part of the form's template.

Is there any way to set up a form so that users can modify part of the document that is not a form field?

Word can selectively protect sections of a document or template. In this case, you can leave the section that you want the user to be able to change unprotected and still protect the other sections.

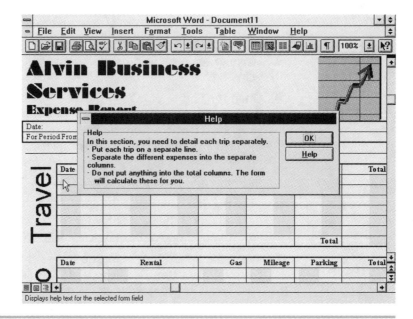

FIGURE 15-6   You can add two types of help information to a text form field

To protect only certain sections in a template:

1. Open the form's template if necessary, and remove any protection you applied previously by choosing Unprotect Document from the Tools menu or clicking the Protect Form button on the Forms toolbar (the button appears shaded).

2. Move to the location where you want to switch between protection and no protection.

3. Choose Break from the Insert menu, select the type of section break you want to insert, and then click OK.

4. Repeat steps 2 and 3 to add any additional section breaks.

5. Choose Protect Document from the Tools menu.

6. Click the Sections button in the Protect Document dialog box to display the Section Protection dialog box, which looks like this:

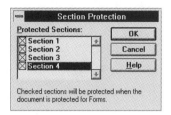

7. Select the check boxes for the sections you want to protect and clear the check boxes for those you don't.

8. Click OK twice.

Tech Tip: When you want to modify a form field, you need to remove protection from the template, even if the given field appears in an unprotected section of the form.

How can I use the results of a form field in a macro?

Word macros use two versions of a WordBasic function to return data that a user entered in form fields: GetFormResult(*bookmark*) and GetFormResult$(*bookmark*). Each version returns information about the form field marked with the specified bookmark. The results that these functions provide are shown in Table 15-1.

Form Field Type	Data returned by GetFormResult (*bookmark*)	Data returned by GetFormResult$ (*bookmark*)
Text	(You cannot use this function with this type of field)	The text entry in the text form field
Check Box	0 if the check box is selected, 1 if the check box is cleared	"0" if the check box is selected, "1" if the check box is cleared
Drop-down	The number of the item selected in the drop-down form field list	The text entry selected in the drop-down form field

TABLE 15-1   You can use a WordBasic function to use a form field's results in a macro

Fields and Macros

Macros are wonderful productivity tools that handle repetitive tasks with ease and efficiency. If you've had difficulties with macros or have heard of problems other people have encountered, take heart! The questions and answers in this chapter will help you achieve success whether you are creating your first macro or your fiftieth one. The Frustration Busters box describes some basics about macro construction.

FRUSTRATION BUSTERS!

If you are new to macros, you will want to learn a few basics of macros.

- Macros are stored within templates. When you select a template in which to store a macro, you limit which documents can use the macro. You can copy the macro between templates with the Organizer.

- Put a macro in NORMAL.DOT when you want the macro available to all documents.

- Macros are a collection of WordBasic *statements*. The first WordBasic statement is Sub MAIN and the last one is End Sub. Many of the WordBasic statements are followed by *arguments*. These arguments supply the information the WordBasic statement needs to perform.

- Lines in the macro that start with ` or REM are comments. Comments allow you to add text that is not processed as a WordBasic statement. You can also include comments after a WordBasic statement by putting a ` and the comment at the end of the WordBasic statement. Use comments liberally within your macros. This macro documentation will spare you headaches when you are looking for an error or making modifications.

- Many of the statements in a macro are for Word commands. To make entering these statements easier, Word can record them for you. Then you will have all of the arguments the statement uses in the correct order and you will reduce typing mistakes.

- A macro can include dialog boxes to receive and display information. To make creating dialog boxes easier, Word has a Dialog Editor that lets you create the dialog appearance you want; the Dialog Editor converts the dialog box design into WordBasic statements.

- Macros can call other macros. The called macro is called a *subroutine*. When Word finishes running the subroutine macro, Word continues running the next statement in the calling macro. Subroutines allow you to break up macros into smaller and more manageable sections.

In Word 2.0 for Windows, I viewed field codes by selecting Field Codes from the View menu. Where is this option in Word 6.0?

In Microsoft Word 6.0 for Windows, the Field Codes option has been removed from the main menus and moved to the View tab of the Options command in the Tools menu. To turn on field codes:

1. Choose Options from the Tools menu.
2. Select the View tab.
3. Select the Field Codes check box.
4. Select OK. Field codes will now appear where applicable.

Tech Tip: You can also switch between displaying field codes and field results with Word's key combinations. Press ALT+F9 to toggle between seeing field codes and results for a single document. Press SHIFT+F9 to toggle between seeing field codes and results for a single code.

You can add a button to a toolbar for turning on and off field codes. To do this:

1. Display the toolbar to add this button.
2. Choose Customize from the Tools menu.
3. Select the Toolbars tab.
4. Choose View from the Categories list box.
5. Drag the button containing a lowercase "a" to where you want the button positioned on the toolbar.
6. Release the mouse button. The {a} button now appears on the toolbar to toggle field codes.
7. Select Close.

This drag and drop procedure to add commands from the Customize dialog box to the toolbars can be used to add any command to any toolbar.

How do I update date and time fields?

To update a date that was inserted as a field using the Date and Time command in the Insert menu, place the insertion point on that date and press F9. Word adds a date or time as a field when the Insert as Field check box is selected in the Date and Time dialog box. Pressing F9 updates any field codes, not just date and time fields.

How do I create a foreign character that does not exist in any symbol set?

If the foreign character is composed of two characters combined, you can create this character with the EQ field. This field creates an equation without creating an embedded object as the Equation Editor does. For example, the field {EQ \o (A,E)} creates a Æ character. This field has the format of {EQ \o (*character 1,character 2*)}. The \o overlays the first character with the second. The parentheses enclose the two characters and the comma separates them.

I just finished writing a macro, and when I click the Start button in the Macro toolbar, I get an error message that says "Command Unavailable." Why?

When you write a macro, you are in a macro-editing window. Many Word features are not available in a macro-editing window. You may have noticed when you edit a macro that many of Word's commands are dimmed, indicating that these commands are unavailable. When you click the Start button, Word starts running the macro, but usually encounters some statement in the macro that Word cannot perform in a macro-editing window. The message you will see looks something like this:

To run the macro, you must be in a document window. You can switch to the document window or close the macro-editing window. If you switch to a document window, you can run the macro by clicking the Start button. The Macro toolbar remains available as long as you have a macro-editing window open. You can select which macro you will run by selecting the macro name from the Active Macro box in the Macro toolbar. You can also run the macro by choosing <u>M</u>acro from the <u>T</u>ools menu, typing the name of the macro in the <u>M</u>acro Name text box, and selecting <u>R</u>un.

How can I take what I have highlighted in the document and use it with macro statements?

A macro often operates on text in the document, for example, selecting some data and copying it to a new location. You can also take the selection and assign it to a variable. Once text is assigned to a variable, other WordBasic statements can use the variable name to represent the selected document contents. The Selection$() function assigns the selected part of a document to a variable. An example of a macro using this function might look like this:

```
Sub MAIN
Highlightedtext$ = Selection$()
MsgBox Highlightedtext$
End Sub
```

This example takes whatever is highlighted in the document and puts it into a string variable named Highlightedtext$. Then Word displays that text in a message box.

How do I edit my macro?

Word macros are stored in templates, so the template containing the macro you want to edit must be available. This means you need to open the template file or open a document that uses the desired template. Once the template is available, you can edit the macro as follows:

1. Choose <u>M</u>acro from the <u>T</u>ools menu.

2. Type the macro name in the <u>M</u>acro Name text box or select the macro from the list box.

3. Select <u>E</u>dit. Word opens a macro-editing window containing the macro instructions. This window will stay open until you close it using the same Word features you use to close any document window. Besides showing the contents of the macro, Word also displays the Macro toolbar that you can use to work with macros. Figure 16-1 shows a macro-editing window.

Can I use a mouse to record a macro?

Since Word records the results of what you are doing when you record a macro, rather than how you go about it, you can use either the keyboard or mouse in this process. For example, when you choose the <u>O</u>pen command in the <u>F</u>ile menu, Word records the FileOpen statement whether you used the keyboard or mouse to select the command. Recording the results also means that you can select commands with arrow keys or by typing underlined letters to record the same result.

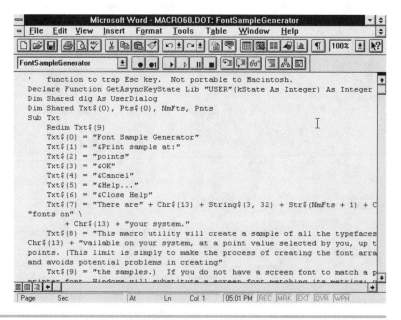

FIGURE 16-1   Macro-editing window to show the macro you are editing

How can I have a macro run every time I create a new document?

Each template can have an AutoNew macro. Any macro named AutoNew is run when a new document is created based on the template containing the AutoNew macro. Additional automatic macros are listed here:

Macro Name	When It Runs
AutoExec	When you start Word (this macro must be in NORMAL.DOT)
AutoNew	When you create a new document
AutoOpen	When you open an existing document
AutoClose	When you close a document
AutoExit	When you quit Word

Does Word have a shortcut for entering statements for menu commands?

Since the statements for Word's menu commands can include many arguments, use a shortcut to record the WordBasic statement for a command rather than remembering every parameter to include. You can record menu commands when you initially create a macro. When you want to subsequently add a WordBasic statement for another menu command to a macro, follow these steps:

1. Put the insertion point in the macro where you want the statement for the menu command added.

2. Switch to a document window.

3. Click the Record Next Command button in the Macro toolbar, shown here:

This button records the next command that you enter and adds it to the insertion point's location in the macro displayed in the Active Macro box in the Macro toolbar.

4. Perform the next command. Word records it and puts the WordBasic statement in the macro.

At this point, you continue performing steps 3 and 4 for as many commands as you want to record. You can return to the macro-editing window to see the WordBasic statements Word has added to the macro.

I'm having some problems with my macro. What are some mistakes I could be making?

Everyone makes mistakes when they first start writing macros. Although you probably feel a little frustrated when you make yours, it is part of the learning process. After you write a few, you will learn to be more careful. Here is a list of the most frequent sources of problems. Watch out for them when you are writing your code:

- Quotation marks missing from string values
- A reserved word used as a variable name
- Two subroutines with the same name
- A statement that requires multiple reserved words, such as If...Then, missing a reserved word
- A missing closing parenthesis in a function
- A dialog box option argument that does not have the initial period, or multiple arguments that are missing a comma separator
- A misplaced comma separator or extra comma
- A misspelled statement or function name
- A data type that is incorrect for an argument (type mismatch)

I wrote a macro that searches for a word in the document and replaces it with another word. But it only finds and replaces the first word. How can I make the macro repeat itself throughout the entire document?

Use a While...Wend loop and the CmpBookmarks function. A While...Wend loop repeats the statements between the While and Wend statements while a condition is true. The CmpBookmarks function compares two bookmarks and returns a value that indicates the relative location of the two bookmarks and their contents. This function frequently uses one of the many predefined bookmarks that every document has. The CmpBookmarks function can be the condition for the While...Wend loop to repeat statements until you reach the end of the document. An example of a macro using this statement looks like this:

```
Sub MAIN
StartOfDocument
'Takes you to the top of the document
While CmpBookmarks("\Sel","\EndOfDoc")
'Compares insertion point/end of document
EditReplace .Find = "Word", .Replace = "Word for Windows", .Direction = 0,
.MatchCase = 0, .WholeWord = 0, .PatternMatch = 0, .SoundsLike
= 0, .FindNext, Format = 0, .Wrap = 1
Finds "Word" and replaces with "Word for Windows"
Wend
'Completes the loop
End Sub
```

This macro finds and replaces every instance of "Word" with "Word for Windows". When you are creating your own macros that have statements to repeat until the end of the document, you will put your statements between the While and the Wend statements.

Table 16-1 lists Word's predefined bookmarks. These are bookmarks that every open document has. Statements and functions, such as CmpBookmarks, can include these without setting up these bookmarks first. Table 16-2 lists the values that CmpBookmarks returns.

 I want to open a document and then run a macro from the template that the document is based on when I start into Word for Windows 6.0. How can I do this automatically?

If there is a particular document that you want to open when you start Word and you want the macro to run automatically, you can modify the Word for Windows 6.0 icon's Command Line entry to open a document and run a macro. To do this:

Bookmark	Description
\Sel	Current selection or the insertion point
\PrevSel1	Insertion point's location or selection where previous editing occurred
\PrevSel2	Insertion point's location or selection where previous editing occurred before the location marked by PrevSel1
\StartOfSel	Start of the current selection
\EndOfSel	End of the current selection
\Line	Line containing the insertion point or the first line of the selection
\Char	Character after the insertion point or the first character of the selection
\Para	Paragraph containing the insertion point or the first paragraph of the selection
\Section	Document section containing the insertion point or the first document section of the selection
\Doc	The entire document except the final paragraph mark
\Page	Page containing the insertion point or the first page of the selection
\StartOfDoc	Beginning of the document
\EndOfDoc	End of the document
\Cell	Cell in a table containing the insertion point or the first table cell in a selection
\Table	Table containing the insertion point or the first table of the selection
\HeadingLevel	Heading containing the insertion point or selection along with any subordinate headings and text

TABLE 16-1   Bookmarks Automatically Defined to Use in Macros

1. Select the icon for Word for Windows in the Program Manager.

2. Choose Properties from the File menu or press ALT+ENTER.

3. Move to the end of the C:\WINWORD\WINWORD.EXE entry in the Command Line text box. Your entry may be different depending on where you installed Word.

4. Press SPACEBAR and type the complete path and file name of the document.

5. Press SPACEBAR, type **/m**, and the name of the macro.

6. Select OK. When you start Word with this icon, you will open the document and start the macro.

Value	Explanation
0 (zero)	Bookmark1$ and Bookmark2$ are equivalent
1	Bookmark1$ is entirely below Bookmark2$
2	Bookmark1$ is entirely above Bookmark2$
3	Bookmark1$ is below and inside Bookmark2$
4	Bookmark1$ is inside and above Bookmark2$
5	Bookmark1$ encloses Bookmark2$
6	Bookmark2$ encloses Bookmark1$
7	Bookmark1$ and Bookmark2$ begin at the same point, but Bookmark1$ is longer
8	Bookmark1$ and Bookmark2$ begin at the same point, but Bookmark2$ is longer
9	Bookmark1$ and Bookmark2$ end at the same place, but Bookmark1$ is longer
10	Bookmark1$ and Bookmark2$ end at the same place, but Bookmark2$ is longer
11	Bookmark1$ is below and adjacent to Bookmark2$
12	Bookmark1$ is above and adjacent to Bookmark2$
13	One or both of the bookmarks do not exist

TABLE 16-2   Values Returned by the CmpBookmarks Function

As an example, your entry in the <u>C</u>ommand Line text box might look like this:

```
C:\WINWORD\WINWORD.EXE C:\FORMS\FORM1.DOC /MFORMRUN
```

In this example, C:\WINWORD\WINWORD.EXE is the program path for Word for Windows, C:\FORMS\FORM1.DOC is the document path, /M is the switch to run the macro, and FORMRUN is the name of the macro.

Tech Tip: If you want to always run the macro when you start Word, name the macro AutoExec and put it in the NORMAL.DOT template.

What macros does Word provide?

Word includes many sample macros. These sample macros are in addition to the ones that run the wizards. These macros and a brief description of what they do are listed in Table 16-3. These sample macros are installed in the MACROS subdirectory of the directory containing your Word for Windows program files. Depending on the installation option you choose, you may need to run the Setup program to install the template files containing these macros.

Macro Name	Template	Macro Result
AccessExporter	TABLES	Transfers a table of data in Word into a table in the Access database you select
ArrangeAll	LAYOUT	Tiles all open windows when you select Tiled from the dialog box of the ArrangeWindows macro
ArrangeWindows	LAYOUT	Displays a dialog box for selecting how you want to display the open windows
AveryLNLBuilder	MACRO60	Creates a label and starts the address in a letter
BaseShiftDown	LAYOUT	Lowers selected text by a small increment each time the macro is run
BaseShiftUp	LAYOUT	Raises selected text by a small increment each time the macro is run
BatchConverter	CONVERT	Converts multiple documents
Cascade	LAYOUT	Cascades all open windows when you select Cascade from the dialog box of the ArrangeWindows macro
CharacterTrackIn	LAYOUT	Reduces character spacing in a selection a small amount each time the macro is run
CharacterTrackOut	LAYOUT	Expands character spacing in a selection a small amount each time the macro is run
CreateTips	MACRO60	Creates tips to show with the CustomTipOfTheDay macro
CustomTipOfTheDay	MACRO60	Displays custom tips like the Word tips that Word shows
DateCalculations	LAYOUT	Inserts a date that is the specified number of days, weeks, or years more or less than the current date
DecreaseFont	LAYOUT	Makes the selected text smaller by a small increment each time the macro is run
DecreaseLeftAndRightIndent	LAYOUT	Decreases the left and right indent on selected text

TABLE 16-3   Sample Word Macros

Macro Name	Template	Macro Result
DisableAutoBackup	MACRO60	Disables the EnableAutoBackup macro so you are no longer making automatic backups to a specified directory
EditConvertOptions	CONVERT	Sets conversion options
EnableAutoBackup	MACRO60	Turns on AutoBackup to make backups to a specified directory
ExitAll	MACRO60	Closes all open windows and exits Word. Displays a dialog box that lets you select which documents are saved before closing them
FindSymbol	MACRO60	Finds and substitutes symbol, using the Symbol dialog box to select the symbols
FontSampleGenerator	MACRO60	Creates a sample of each of the installed fonts
IncreaseFont	LAYOUT	Makes the selected text larger by a small increment each time macro is run
IncreaseRightAndLeft-Indent	LAYOUT	Increases the left and right indent on selected text
InstallTipOfTheDay	MACRO60	Installs the CustomTipOfTheDay macro so your custom tips will appear when you start Word
LineSpaceIn	LAYOUT	Decreases the line spacing on selected text
LineSpaceOut	LAYOUT	Increases the line spacing on selected text
MindBender	MACRO60	Runs a sample game similar to the card game where you have to remember where various symbols are placed
OrganizationalChart-Maker	LAYOUT	Creates an organizational chart out of the data already entered in a document
PresentIt	CONVERT	Exports the document's outline into PowerPoint
PrintableCharacters	MACRO60	Prints the available printable characters in a font
PrintSel2File	MACRO60	Prints selection to a DOS text file
RunWizard	MACRO60	Runs selected wizard to quickly create a desired type of document
SaveSelection	MACRO60	Saves the selected part of a document in another file
SectionManager	LAYOUT	Displays information about the current section and provides a series of dialog boxes that handle all of your section formatting
SuperDocStatistics	MACRO60	Shows more document statistics than when you select Statistics from the dialog box that the Summary Info command in the File menu displays
TableFillDown	TABLES	Fills selected cells in a table with the contents of the first cell in each column of the selection

TABLE 16-3   Sample Word Macros *(continued)*

Macro Name	Template	Macro Result
TableFillRight	TABLES	Fills selected cells in a table with the contents of the first cell in each row of the selection
TableInfo	TABLES	Returns information about a table and lets you select where you want to go in the table
TableMath	TABLES	Creates an interactive guide to select the table entries you want to include in a formula and the computations you want to perform on them
TableNumber	TABLES	Adds a column or row, and numbers the columns or rows you want
TileHorizontally	LAYOUT	Horizontally tiles all open windows when you select Horizontal from the dialog box of the ArrangeWindows macro
TileVertically	LAYOUT	Vertically tiles all open windows when you select Vertical from the dialog box of the ArrangeWindows macro
TipOfTheDay	MACRO60	Used by the CustomTipOfTheDay macro to display a custom tip
Watermark	LAYOUT	Creates a watermark for one or all pages using one of the graphics that comes with Word

TABLE 16-3   Sample Word Macros *(continued)*

Tech Tip: Use these sample macros as models for the macros you want to create. For example, you can look at the MindBender macro to see the statements it uses to manipulate a changing dialog box.

I would like to distribute a macro that I wrote to my coworkers. Where is the macro stored?

Word's macros are stored in templates. The easiest way to distribute the macro is to create a new template and add your macro to it, then distribute the template to your coworkers.

Your coworkers can add the macro to their template by using the Organizer. They will want to copy the macro to their

NORMAL.DOT template if they want to run the macro in any document. To copy the macro from the template file you provide them:

1. Choose Templates from the File menu.

2. Select the Organizer button.

3. Select the Macros tab.
   This lists the existing template's macros on the left. You can then open the template to copy the macro to (these are the files with the .DOT extensions).

4. Select your macro name.

5. Select the Copy button.

6. Select Close.

For example, one option you have is to create an auto macro that handles copying the new macro to their NORMAL.DOT template. The following macro, named AutoOpen, copies the example macro SaveAsRTF from a NEWMACRO.DOT template to the NORMAL.DOT template.

```
Sub MAIN
Organizer .Copy, .Source = "C:\WINWORD\TEMPLATE\NEWMACRO.DOT",
.Destination = "C:\WINWORD\TEMPLATE\NORMAL.DOT", .Name =
"SaveAsRTF", .Tab = 3
Organizer .Delete, .Source =
"C:\WINWORD\TEMPLATE\NEWMACRO.DOT", .Name = "SaveAsRTF",
.Tab = 3
MsgBox "The macro SaveAsRTF is copied to your Normal template.
Please delete your copy of the NEWMACRO.DOT file"
End Sub
```

Both the SaveAsRTF and the AutoOpen macros are now in the NEWMACRO.DOT template. You can distribute this template to your coworkers. When they open this document, the macro will copy the macro to their NORMAL.DOT template for them.

Tech Tip: Be cautious when distributing templates—you may accidentally overwrite another user's file. For instance, if you give a coworker a template named MYMACRO.DOT and they already have a template by the same name, they could overwrite their template and lose their previous information.

Can I create toolbar buttons to start other applications like the ones that Word has for other Microsoft applications?

Yes. If you display the Microsoft toolbar, you can see toolbar buttons that start other Microsoft applications. You can create buttons like these to start other applications from Word. To create these toolbar buttons:

1. Choose Macro from the Tools menu.

2. In the Macro Name text box, type a macro name, such as the name of the application you wish to start.

3. In the Description box, type a short explanation, such as "Starts Paintbrush."

4. Select Create to open the macro-editing window.

5. Between Sub MAIN and End Sub, enter the following:

```
If AppisRunning ("NameofApplication") then
AppActivate "NameofApplication"
Else
Shell "ExecutableFile"
End If
```

The NameofApplication in the first two statements is the name of the application in the Task List window. It should be as close as possible to what appears, although these statements can select one close to what you have entered if none matches exactly. In the Shell statement, include both the program name and the path. For example, to start the Paintbrush application, the statement is Shell "C:\WINDOWS\PBRUSH.EXE."

6. Choose Save Template from the File menu to save the macro to the template.

7. Choose Close from the File menu to close the macro-editing window.

8. Add the completed macro to the toolbar:

   a. Choose Toolbars from the View menu and select Customize.

   b. Select Macros from the Categories list box.

   c. Highlight the macro you just wrote from the Macros list box.

   d. Drag the macro name to the toolbar.

   e. Select a button appearance for the macro on the toolbar.

Tech Tip: The steps outlined here work for assigning any macro you have created to a toolbar button.

   f. Select Close to leave the Customization dialog box.

      As you drag the name, it changes into a button that you can place anywhere on your toolbars. After you let go of the macro on the toolbar, the Custom Button dialog box appears. You then can either choose from some preset buttons, write a text button, or, for the more creative, draw your own image by clicking on the Edit button.

9. Choose Save All from the File menu to save the customization to the template.

I am working on macros and getting WordBasic errors. The User's Guide doesn't give much information on these. Is there more information?

Word includes a separate help section just for WordBasic called Programming with Microsoft Word. This online Help can assist you as you work at creating a macro. This help includes a listing of the error messages and information on why you might be seeing them. Also, this help contains a list of all the WordBasic statements, their syntax, and examples of code that you can copy and paste into your macro and modify for your own needs. To access the online Help, press F1. If the title bar displays Word Help, select Contents, and select the Programming with Microsoft Word option. If you press F1 while you are in a macro-editing window, Word automatically displays the WordBasic Help. You can print any of the information you

Tech Tip: When you see the WordBasic Error message, you can go directly to the information on that error message in WordBasic Help by selecting the Help button.

see by selecting Print Topic from the File menu from the WordBasic Help window, or by selecting the Print button in the Examples window.

Once you are in the WordBasic Help, you can select Error Messages from the help window that displays Programming with Microsoft Word. You can also select Search, type **Errors and error trapping**, select Show Topics, select Macro Error Messages from the bottom list box, and select the Go To button. The window lists the WordBasic Error messages. Selecting one from the list changes the information displayed in the window to a description of the WordBasic Error message and its possible causes and solutions. When you want to learn about a specific statement, select Search, type the WordBasic statement or function you want more information on, select Show Topics, select Macro Error Messages from the bottom list box, and select the Go To button.

Tech Tip: When you get a WordBasic Error message for a macro that you have open in a macro-editing window, the statement that caused the error is highlighted when you switch to the macro.

If you want printed reference material about the macro language, ODBC and Workgroup extensions, and Microsoft Word APIs, Microsoft Press has published a Word Developers Kit.

 ## How do I convert my Word for Windows 2.0 macros to Word for Windows 6.0?

Word for Windows 6.0 converts Word for Windows 2.0 macros when you do any of the following:

- Change to the template containing the Word for Windows 2.0 macros.

- Create a document using a template containing Word for Windows 2.0 macros.

- Attach a template containing Word for Windows 2.0 macros to a document.

You will want to save the modified template so Word does not have to repeat converting the macros in the template into Word for Windows 6.0 macros. Most macros convert easily. After the conversion, if your macro does not perform correctly, check the WordBasic Help for a list of possible changes you may need to make to your macro. To see this information, open WordBasic Help, select Search, type **Converting**, select Show Topics, select Converting Word Version 2.x Macros from the bottom list box, and select the Go To button.

How can I pass a variable from one macro to another?

Passing a variable is how one macro sends a value to another macro. You can pass a variable to any subroutine of any macro. The subroutine of the accepting macro must be set up to accept the passed variable. For example, you may have one macro that will pass a variable to a second macro. This first macro may have statements like this:

```
Sub MAIN
Test$ = "Hello World!"
Macro2.Main(Test$)
'syntax = [macro name][period][subroutine](variable)
End Sub
```

Notice that this macro has no statements that will display the contents of Test$. This macro runs the Macro2 macro. An example of this second macro can look like this:

```
Sub MAIN(Catch$)
MsgBox Catch$
End Sub
```

Notice this macro does not set Catch$ to equal anything. This macro expects that the value of Catch$ is set by whatever macro calls it. Running the first macro sets Test$ to equal "Hello World!", then sends the variable to the second macro. This second macro accepts Test$, puts it into a variable called Catch$, and then it displays Catch$ in a message box.

How do I create my own dialog boxes?

Macros use dialog boxes to display and receive information from the macro's user. To make creating dialog boxes easier, Word includes a Dialog Editor. The Dialog Editor lets you lay out the appearance of the dialog box and generates the WordBasic statements that create the dialog box you designed. The Dialog Editor initially provides an empty dialog box for you to fill with *items* such as text, text boxes, check boxes, list boxes, option buttons, and other buttons such as OK and Cancel. To create a dialog box using the Dialog Editor:

1. Start the Dialog Editor. You can click the Dialog Editor button in the Macro toolbar as shown here, or you can start the Word Dialog Editor program item from the Program Manager.

In the Dialog Editor application, you have an empty dialog box. You can alter the size of the dialog box and where it appears on the screen. Change the size by dragging a side of the dialog box, just like you would size a document or application window. Change a dialog box's placement by dragging the dialog box's title bar to a new location. You can also have the dialog box sized based on the items you add to it and positioned so it remains centered on the application window.

Tech Tip: You may need to install the Dialog Editor before you create your own dialog boxes if you have less than a full installation of Word.

2. Add items by selecting them from the Item menu. Depending on the command you select, you may need to further clarify which type of item you want to add.

Word will add a default item of the type you select. This means that text items initially contain "Text," and the text for check boxes is initially "Check Box." To change the settings for the item, double-click it to show an Item Information dialog box like the following one for a text item.

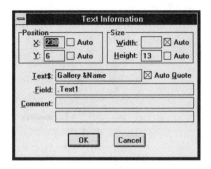

This dialog box is where you select the text that you see, the *identifier* that the Word macro will use for the dialog box item, and the item's size and position. You may find setting the size and position easier if you use the mouse to drag the item to a new location or its border to a new size. When you want a text item to have an underlined letter, put an ampersand in front of it. For example, to underline the N in Gallery Name in Figure 16-2, the contents of the Text$ text box for this text item are Gallery &Name.

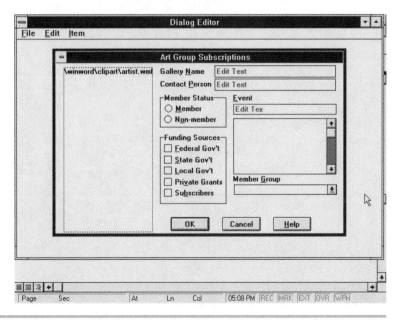

FIGURE 16-2   Dialog box created in the Dialog Editor

3. Choose Select Dialog from the Edit menu to select the entire dialog box when you have added all the items for the dialog box.

4. Choose Copy from the Edit menu to copy the entire dialog box to the Clipboard.

5. Move to where you want the dialog box in a Word macro. Switch to Word, display the macro-editing window, and move the insertion point to where you want the statements that create the dialog box.

6. Choose Paste from the Edit menu to paste the WordBasic statements that create the dialog box into the macro. Figure 16-3 shows the WordBasic statements pasted into the macro when you copy the dialog box from Figure 16-2 onto the Clipboard.

The WordBasic statements that create the dialog box items are listed in Table 16-4. After each of the statements are the arguments that set the same features for the item that you see when you double-click the item in the Dialog Editor. Once you

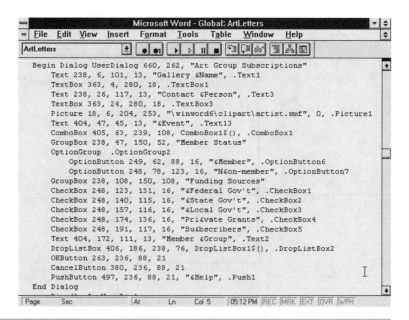

FIGURE 16-3   WordBasic statements that create the dialog box designed in the Dialog Editor

add the dialog box to the macro, your macro will need the following statements:

- Statements that set the initial values of the dialog box items. These statements identify the dialog box items using the identifier. For example, a macro might have the statement .Event$="Art for a Day" to set the initial value of the combo box.

- Statements that set the items that appear in combo boxes, drop-down list boxes, and list boxes. The macro partially shown in Figure 16-3 has these statements to set the values of the Member Group drop-down list box:

```
Dim DropListBox1$(5)
DropListBox1$(0) = "Ohio Arts Council"
DropListBox1$(1) = "Northeast Art Galleries"
DropListBox1$(2) = "New Age Art Assn."
DropListBox1$(3) = "Art for Artists Coalition"
DropListBox1$(4) = "Ohio State Art Assn."
```

- The Dim dlg As UserDialog statement. This statement tells Word that you are working with a user-defined dialog box. In this example, dlg is the name of the dialog box. Since you can have only one user-defined dialog box defined at a time, you do not provide a name for the dialog box with the statements that create the dialog box. This statement is after the End Dialog statement that defines the dialog box and before the Dialog statement or function.

- The Dialog dlg statement or the Dialog(dlg) function. This statement or function activates the dialog box. It is this statement or function that tells Word to take the statements like the ones in Figure 16-3 and display a dialog box like the one in Figure 16-4. If you are using the dialog box to return a single value, use the Dialog() function. Otherwise, use the Dialog statement. After the Dim dlg as UserDialog and Dialog dlg statements come the macro statements to perform when the user finishes using the dialog box.

- Statements that process the results of the dialog box use. These statements also use the identifier to represent the dialog box item. For example, if the Gallery Name text box has the identifier of GalleryName$, subsequent macro statements will use GalleryName$ to represent what was in the text box when you left the dialog box. Table 16-4 lists macro statements that create dialog box controls.

I am writing a macro and I want my user-defined dialog box to show an ampersand (&) in it. How can I do this?

This is easy. Just put two ampersands together in the text for the text item. For example, "City && State" in a text item appears as "City & State" in the dialog box.

I like the way the wizard dialog boxes look with the graphics and document previews. Can I do the same in my own macros?

Yes, you can add pictures to dialog boxes just like the ones you see in the wizard. Adding pictures to dialog boxes is a new feature of the WordBasic language. Your macros will include the PICTURE statement for the picture. Like other dialog box items, rather than entering the statements into the macro, create the

Dialog Box Item	WordBasic Statement
Cancel Button	CancelButton
Check Box	CheckBox
Combo box (a text box and list box)	ComboBox
Drop-down list box	DropListBox
Group box that encloses related controls	GroupBox
List box	ListBox
OK button	OKButton
Option button	OptionButton
Option button group	OptionGroup
Picture to show graphics	Picture
Preview window that shows the contents of a file or the current document	FilePreview or FilePreview()
Push button (other than OK or Cancel)	PushButton
Text	Text
Text box	TextBox

TABLE 16-4   Macro Statements that Create Dialog Box Controls

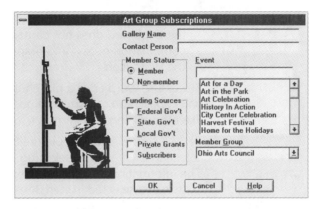

FIGURE 16-4   Dialog box created by the WordBasic statements in Figure 16-3

feature of the WordBasic language. Your macros will include the PICTURE statement for the picture. Like other dialog box items, rather than entering the statements into the macro, create the dialog box with the Dialog Editor. Figure 16-4 shows a picture added to a dialog box. To add a picture like this:

1. Start the Dialog Editor. You can click the Dialog Editor button in the Macro toolbar shown here, or you can start the Word Dialog Editor program item from the Program Manager.

2. Select the Picture command from the Item menu.

3. Select the source of the picture. Your choices and the subsequent selections you make include:

   ■ File—This option inserts a picture you have stored in a file into the dialog box.

   ■ AutoText Entry—This option inserts a picture Word has stored as an AutoText entry.

   ■ Bookmark—This option displays the graphical contents of a bookmark in the document that you use when you use the dialog box.

- Clipboard—This option displays the graphic contents of the Clipboard at the time the dialog box is used. If the Clipboard does not contain graphics or is a combination of text and graphics, Word will display the Word icon.

4. Select OK. Word adds a placeholder where the picture will appear. You can size and position this placeholder just like other dialog box items.

5. Set the contents for the picture by double-clicking it or by selecting the item and selecting Info from the Edit menu. The information you will add depends on the option button you selected in step 3.

    - If you selected File, type the filename in the Text$ text box.

    - If you selected AutoText Entry, type the AutoText entry in the Text$ text box.

    - If you selected Bookmark, type the bookmark in the Text$ text box.

    - If you selected Clipboard, leave the Text$ text box empty.

6. Select OK.

7. Continue making changes to the dialog box, such as adding the other items that you want the dialog box to have.

8. Choose Select Dialog from the Edit menu to select the entire dialog box.

9. Choose Copy from the Edit menu to copy the entire dialog box to the Clipboard.

10. Move to where you want the dialog box in a Word macro. You need to switch to Word, display the macro-editing window to hold the dialog box, and move the insertion point to where you want the statements that create the dialog box.

11. Choose Paste from the Edit menu to paste the WordBasic statements that create the dialog box into the macro.

The resulting WordBasic statements include the Picture statement that adds the graphic to the dialog box. The WordBasic statement that creates the picture shown in Figure 16-4 looks like this:

```
Picture 18, 6, 204, 253, "\winword\clipart\artist.wmf", 0, .Picture1
```

You can look at the macros in Word's wizards to see the WordBasic statements that the wizards use to operate. Looking at these macros will provide ideas on how you can create similar effects with your own macros. To see these macros:

1. Select <u>O</u>pen from the <u>F</u>ile menu.

2. Change to the TEMPLATE directory and show all files.

3. Select the <u>R</u>ead Only check box, since you want to be sure you do not accidentally change the wizards.

4. Select the wizard file to open then select OK. Wizard files have a .WIZ extension instead of the .DOT extension that is the default for templates.

5. Select <u>M</u>acro from the <u>T</u>ools menu.

   The list of macros will include AutoNew that the wizard uses to automatically start itself when you create a new document using the wizard as a basis. This AutoNew macro usually has only one statement, StartWizard, that starts what you see as the wizard. It is this StartWizard macro that contains the meat of the wizard's actions.

6. Select StartWizard from the <u>M</u>acro Name list box and select <u>E</u>dit to open a macro-editing window containing the macro statements the wizard uses to operate.

When I use a dialog box and I type underlined letters to move to dialog box items, I am moving to the wrong ones. What is wrong with my dialog box?

The problem with your dialog box is caused by having the statements that create your dialog box in the wrong order. Every dialog box item, such as a list box or text box, has a separate label item. This label item is the one that has the underlined letter, but it is actually the item *next* to it that you want to select by typing the underlined letter. WordBasic assumes that the label item with the underlined letter is the statement before the statement for the dialog box item selected by that underlined letter. This means that the statement for a text box should be immediately *after* the statement for the label that identifies the text box. When you create a dialog box with the Dialog Editor, the statements are recorded in the order they are created. If you did not create the labels immediately before the items selected by the underlined letters in the labels, the dialog box statements are not in the correct order.

Tech Tip: The order of the statements for dialog box items also determines the order that you move from one to the next when pressing TAB and SHIFT+TAB.

To fix this problem, you need to rearrange the statements in the macro. The drag and drop method works well for rearranging the lines. Move the Text statements to come before the statements for the dialog box items. Figure 16-5 shows some statements that are in the wrong order. The lines are drawn so you can see which statements the Text statements should precede. When you rearrange these statements, the revised version looks like Figure 16-6.

How do I get a dialog box back into the Dialog Editor so I can change it?

When you want to alter a dialog box, you can copy the statements that create the dialog box and paste them into the Dialog Editor. For example, you can take the statements shown in Figure 16-3 and copy them to the Clipboard. When you start the Dialog Editor and use its Paste command in the Edit menu, you will see the dialog box that these statements create. You can edit this dialog box and then replace the old statements used to create the dialog box with the new statements.

How do I set up a subroutine?

A subroutine can be set up either in the same macro as the main routine macro, or as a separate macro.

An example of a macro that calls another macro is the AutoNew macro used by most wizards. This macro contains the following statements:

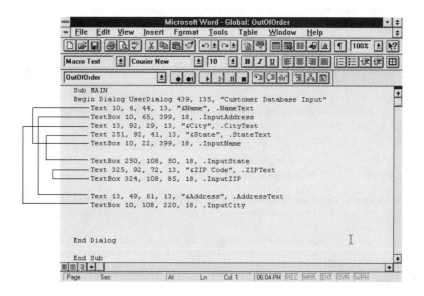

FIGURE 16-5   Statements for a dialog box in the wrong order

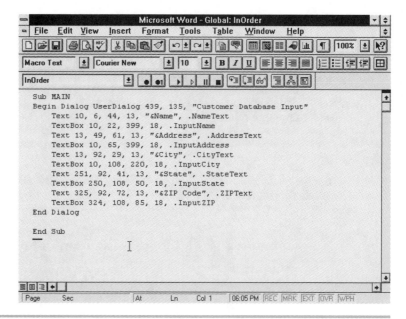

FIGURE 16-6   Rearranged statements for a dialog box

```
Sub MAIN
   StartWizard
End Sub
```

This macro calls the StartWizard macro. When StartWizard is completed, Word performs the next statement in this macro—End Sub, in this case.

If you want the subroutine in the same macro as the main routine, you will put the subroutine after the End Sub statement for the main subroutine. A macro like this might look like:

```
Sub MAIN
'    Here are the statements to perform
     DisplayNextItem
'    Here are more statements to perform
End Sub
Sub DisplayNextItem
'    Here are the statements that the DisplayNextItem subroutine performs
End Sub
```

Tech Tip: Set overtype mode on or off in a macro to indicate whether your entries replace or add to an entry. Your macro may exhibit different behavior as it operates on document text depending on whether or not you are in Overtype mode.

Working with Applets and Other Applications

Word comes with several miniapplications, or *applets*, that you use can use to enhance your Word documents. Their capabilities go beyond the scope of word processing and let you complete tasks that would otherwise be difficult, if not impossible, to perform within Word. Many Windows applications, such as Word, Excel, or Access, can use these applets to embellish their files.

A Complete installation of Word adds these three applets to your system:

- MS Graph, with which you can create a wide variety of graphs to insert into your Word document based on data in the Word document

- WordArt, which you can use to create and manipulate text with special effects

- Equation Editor, which lets you easily create complex scientific and mathematical equations

The applets that come with Word cannot create files of their own; their data is stored as embedded objects in Word documents or files created by other host applications. Except for the Equation Editor, you cannot start applets by themselves, but only as a part of a host application such as Word. You can edit these embedded objects within Word, just as you can edit others created with independent applications.

In addition, Word includes other tools to help you exchange data with various applications. For example, Word uses ODBC drivers to access database files that you can insert into a document or use for a mail merge. Word can also work with your electronic mail applications to send your documents to other users on a network.

FRUSTRATION BUSTERS!

Word's applets can make easy work of tasks that seem daunting or even impossible without them. The following table indicates some of the applets' possible uses and results. The next time you face a challenge in Word, you might find that one of the applets can streamline the process for you!

Applet	Potential Use	Sample
MS Graph	Data for annual reports, transparencies for a presentation	
WordArt	Logos, letterheads, flyers, newsletter mastheads	second Sight House Painters
Equation Editor	Term papers, technical specifications, government reports, lab reports	$S_x = \sqrt{\dfrac{1}{n-1}\left\{\sum_{i=1}^{n} x_i^2 - n\bar{x}^2\right\}}$

Tech Tip: See Chapter 8, "File Management," to learn more about OLE, the feature which lets you embed objects in another application's document.

What types of objects can I bring into Word 6.0?

Word 6.0 comes with several applets, or supplementary applications, that you can use to insert objects into your Word documents. To find out which applets are installed on your system, choose <u>O</u>bject from the <u>I</u>nsert menu and examine the contents of the <u>O</u>bject Type list box. Assuming that you have not deleted any of the Windows Accessory applications, the

Paintbrush Picture, Package, and Sound options should appear. If you performed a complete installation of Word 6.0, these applets will also display in the list:

- Microsoft Word 6.0 Picture
- Microsoft WordArt 2.0
- Microsoft Graph
- Microsoft Equation 2.0

The list also displays any other applications installed on your system from which you can insert objects into Word. Such programs can include Microsoft Excel, PowerPoint Presentation, and Ami Pro.

Sometimes WordArt or Equation Editor opens by replacing Word's menus and toolbars, and other times they open in their own windows. What controls the way applets open?

When you insert an object created with WordArt or Equation Editor, the applet's appearance depends on whether field codes are displayed. If you have field codes turned on, the applet opens in its own window, as shown in Figure 17-1. If the field

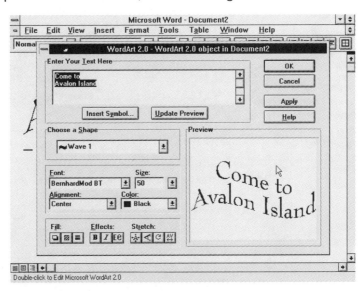

FIGURE 17-1   Applets can appear in their own windows

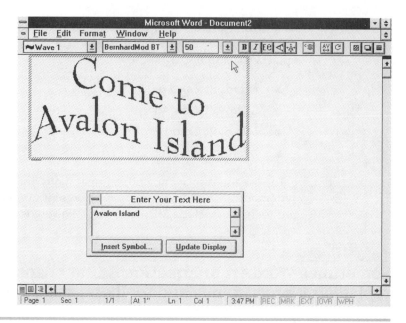

FIGURE 17-2   Applet toolbars and menus can replace Word's

Tech Tip: Microsoft Graph always opens in its own window regardless of the field code settings.

codes are not displayed, then the applet's menu and toolbar replaces Word's, as shown in Figure 17-2. In either case, you have complete access to all of the applets functions and features.

To display or hide the field codes:

1. Choose Options from the Tools menu.

2. Click the View tab.

3. Select or clear the Field Codes check box.

4. Click OK.

You can open an applet in its own window to edit an object when field results are displayed by simply selecting the object, choosing Object from the Edit menu, and then choosing Open.

Can I use any of the applets that come with Word 6.0 by themselves?

The Equation Editor is the only applet that comes with Word 6.0 that can be run by itself.

I use Equation Editor and WordArt frequently. Is there a shortcut I can use to open them?

Word provides toolbar buttons that you can use to start the Equation Editor and WordArt applets. To add these buttons to a toolbar:

1. Display the toolbar on which you want to the Equation Editor and WordArt buttons to appear.

2. Choose <u>C</u>ustomize from the <u>T</u>ools menu.

3. Click the <u>T</u>oolbars tab.

4. Choose Insert from the <u>C</u>ategories list box.

5. Drag the WordArt and Equation Editor buttons from the Buttons section in the dialog box to the toolbar. The two icons look like this:

WordArt ————  ———— *Equation Editor*

6. Click Close.

You can now open the desired applet by clicking its toolbar button.

Can I use my Word 2.0 applets with Word 6.0?

If you prefer, you can use these earlier applets with Word 6.0. If they are not currently on your system, you can run a Custom installation of Word 2.0 and add just the applets. You then launch the Word 2.0 applets from Word 6.0 in the same way you do the newer applets. When you choose <u>O</u>bject from the <u>I</u>nsert menu, you will see two versions of WordArt in the Object Types list box. You will also see Microsoft Draw, which is built into Word for Windows 6.0, and Microsoft Graph and Equation, which were not updated.

How can I add special effects to my text?

The WordArt applet lets you add text with special effects to your Word documents. With WordArt, you can change the shape, font, style, justification, rotation, width, height, and units of this text. You can also make the text all uppercase or add enhancements such as outlines, fills, and shadows. Figure 17-3 shows some of these effects.

Follow these steps to add text embellished with WordArt to your documents:

1. Choose <u>O</u>bject from the <u>I</u>nsert menu.

2. Select Microsoft WordArt 2.0 in the <u>O</u>bject Type list box and click OK.

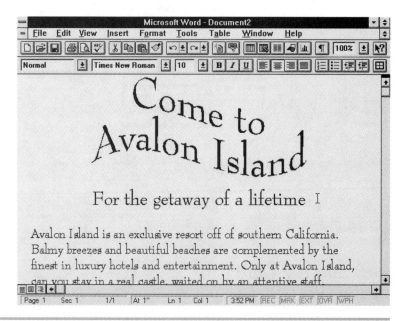

FIGURE 17-3   Document with text enhancements created in WordArt

3. Enter your text in the floating Enter Your Text Here dialog box.

4. Use the buttons on the WordArt toolbar, as shown here, to apply the desired embellishments:

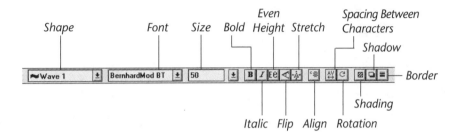

5. Click anywhere in the Word document outside the WordArt object to close WordArt and return to Word.

 ## In Word 2.0, WordArt contained a unique set of fonts that Word could not use. Can I use them in Word 6.0's WordArt?

No, you cannot use the fonts from Word 2.0's WordArt applet in Word 6.0's WordArt applet. The fonts in WordArt 1.0 (the version of WordArt that shipped with Word 2.0) are internal to the applet and unavailable to any other application. WordArt 2.0 (the version that ships with Word 6.0) uses the TrueType fonts installed in Windows. This gives you the advantage of using the same fonts in both your WordArt objects and the text in your Word documents.

Tech Tip: You can use WordArt 1.0 to insert a piece of word art into Word 6.0 if you want to use the fonts available with that applet. To do so, just follow the steps for adding a WordArt object, but remember to select WordArt 1.0 instead of WordArt 2.0. If you deleted WordArt 1.0 when installing Word 6.0, you need to reinstall it now.

Can I update the image in my document to reflect the changes I'm making while I'm still working in WordArt?

You can keep the image in your document up to date by clicking Update Display in the Enter Your Text Here dialog box.

I'm trying to remove a border around a text box that I created with Draw. The Borders and Shading command on the Format menu doesn't get rid of it. What can I do?

The border around a text box is formatting set by Draw (which is now built into Word 6.0), not by the Borders and Shading feature. To remove this border, you need to edit the text box as a drawing object. To do so:

1. Display the Drawing toolbar by clicking the Drawing button on the Standard toolbar.

2. Select the text box.

3. Click the Line Style button on the Drawing toolbar.

4. Click More at the bottom of the pop-up menu to open the Drawing Object dialog box.

5. Click the Line tab.

6. Select the None option button and then click OK to remove the border.

After I draw them, I can't see the drawing objects I've created in my document. What's going on?

If you can't see the drawing objects you created using Word's Draw feature, you are probably displaying your document in normal view, which does not show drawing objects. If this is the case, simply choose Page Layout from the View menu or click the Page Layout button next to the horizontal scroll bar to see your drawing objects.

It's also possible that you used the color white when you drew the object or set the line style and fill to None. To check these settings and modify them, if necessary:

1. Select the drawing object you can't see by clicking the Select Drawing Objects button on the Drawing toolbar and dragging across the area in which the object should appear. When the object is selected, small black boxes, or *handles*, display, even though you cannot see the object itself.

2. Choose Drawing Object from the Format menu.

3. Click the Line or Fill tab and confirm your line style and color settings. Modify them, if necessary, to make the drawing object visible, and then click OK.

In Word 2.0, I could zoom in the Equation Editor to see my equations better, but I can't find this option in the Word 6.0 version. Is there any way to do this?

The method you use to set the magnification of an equation depends on the way in which the Equation Editor is currently displayed. The Equation Editor can either appear as part of the Word window or in its own separate window, as shown in Figure 17-4.

When the Equation Editor displays within the Word window, you cannot change the zoom with the Equation Editor itself. Instead, you must specify a different magnification before you start the Equation Editor by choosing Zoom from Word's View menu, selecting the appropriate level of magnification, and clicking OK. When you open the Equation Editor, the equation appears with the appropriate zoom.

When you open the Equation Editor in its own window, you can change the zoom by choosing one of the magnification options from the View menu. You can also set the zoom percentage by double-clicking the current zoom percentage that appears on the status bar.

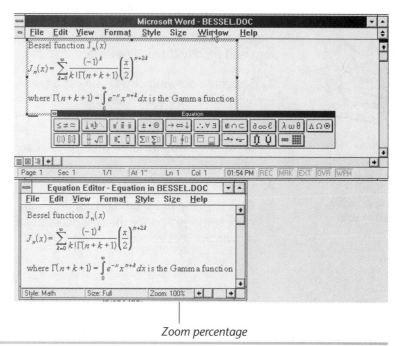

Zoom percentage

FIGURE 17-4   The Equation Editor as part of the Word window (top) and in a separate window (bottom)

What do each of the buttons on the Equation Editor toolbar do?

Because the Equation Editor toolbar doesn't display ToolTips as Word does, it can be difficult to tell which symbols you can enter using each of the buttons. When you click any of the Equation Editor's toolbar buttons, a *palette* presents you with a grid of possible choices. These palettes display specific, related types of information. Some palettes include a series of single symbols; others display a group of mathematical symbols with empty slots, called *templates.* You fill in a template's blank spaces with numbers or other variables. Table 17-1 briefly describes the types of symbols and templates available on each palette.

Button	Name	Inserts
$\leq \neq \approx$	Relational Theory	Relational symbols, such as ≠ (not equal) or ≈ (approximately)
	Spaces and Ellipses	Spaces and ellipses
	Embellishments	Embellishments, such as primes and arrows
$\pm \bullet \otimes$	Operators	Mathematical operators, such as × and the division sign
$\rightarrow \Leftrightarrow \downarrow$	Arrows	Arrows
$\therefore \forall \exists$	Logical	Logical symbols, such as ∴ and ∀
$\notin \cap \subset$	Set Theory	Set theory symbols, such as ∩ and ⊆
$\partial \infty \ell$	Miscellaneous Symbols	Miscellaneous symbols, such as ∞ (infinity) and ° (degrees)
$\lambda \omega \theta$	Lowercase Greek Characters	Lowercase Greek letters, such as φ or λ
$\Lambda \Omega \Theta$	Uppercase Greek Characters	Uppercase Greek letters, such as Φ and Ψ
(□) [□]	Fences	Template to enclose entries in parentheses, braces, or brackets
$\sqrt{\Box}$	Fractions and Radicals	Template for fractions and radicals
	Subscript/Superscript	Template for superscript and/or subscript slots
$\sum_{\Box}^{\Box} \sum_{\Box}$	Summation	Template for summation with possible superscript and/or subscript slots
$\int_{\Box} \oint_{\Box}$	Integrals	Template for integrals with possible superscript and/or subscript slots
□ □	Overbars/Underbars	Template for underbar and overbar slots
→ ←	Labeled Arrows	Template for under-arrow and over-arrow slots
$\bar{\Pi} \bar{U}$	Products and Set Theory	Template for products and set theory expressions
▯▯▯ ▦	Matrices	Template for matrices

TABLE 17-1   Palettes in Word's Equation Editor

Are there any shortcut keys I can use for the Equation Editor?

Word's Equation Editor provides many shortcut keys that can make creating equations easier. Since the Equation Editor has so many key assignments, you will probably memorize the few that you use most often. Table 17-2 lists the shortcut keys that you can use instead of Equation Editor commands. Table 17-3 shows the shortcut keys for inserting symbols. Table 17-4 displays the shortcut keys for templates. Table 17-5 indicates the shortcut keys for embellishments

Tech Note: These shortcut keys are indicated using a specific format. When a key is shown alone, just press that key. When two keys are combined with a + (plus sign) you press those keys simultaneously. When two keys are combined with a , (comma) you press the first key, release it, and press the second. When there is more than one shortcut key for a single option, each shortcut key combination appears on a different line.

Command	Shortcut
Update on the File menu	F3
Exit and Return to Document on the File menu	ALT+F4
Copy on the Edit menu	CTRL+C
Clear on the Edit menu	DEL
Cut on the Edit menu	CTRL+X
Paste on the Edit menu	CTRL+V
Select All on the Edit menu	CTRL+A
Undo on the Edit menu	CTRL+Z
100% on the View menu	CTRL+1
200% on the View menu	CTRL+2
400% on the View menu	CTRL+4
Redraw on the View menu	CTRL+D
Show All on the View menu	CTRL+Y
Left on the Format menu	CTRL+SHIFT+L
Center on the Format menu	CTRL+SHIFT+C
Right on the Format menu	CTRL+SHIFT+R
Math on the Style menu	CTRL+SHIFT+=
Text on the Style menu	CTRL+SHIFT+E
Function on the Style menu	CTRL+SHIFT+F
Variable on the Style menu	CTRL+SHIFT+I
Greek on the Style menu	CTRL+SHIFT+G
Matrix-Vector on the Style menu	CTRL+SHIFT+B

TABLE 17-2   Shortcut Keys for Equation Editor Menu Commands

Symbol	Shortcut Keys
∞	CTRL+S,I
T	CTRL+S,A
∂	CTRL+S,D
≤	CTRL+S,<
≥	CTRL+S,>
×	CTRL+S,T
∈	CTRL+S,E
∉	CTRL+S,SHIFT+E
⊂	CTRL+S,C
⊄	CTRL+S,SHIFT+C

TABLE 17-3 Shortcut Keys for Inserting Symbols

Symbol	Template	Shortcut Keys
(⬚)	Parentheses	CTRL+9 CTRL+0 CTRL+T,(CTRL+T,)
[⬚]	Brackets	CTRL+[CTRL+] CTRL+T,[CTRL+T,]

{⬚}	Braces	CTRL+{
		CTRL+}
		CTRL+T,{
		CTRL+T,}

⬚ fraction	Fraction	CTRL+F CTRL+T,F
⬚/⬚	Slash Fraction	CTRL+/ CTRL+T,/
⬚⬛	Superscript	CTRL+H CTRL+T,H
⬚⬛	Subscript	CTRL+L CTRL+T,L
⬚⬛	Joint super/subscript	CTRL+J CTRL+T,J

TABLE 17-4 Shortcut Keys for Equation Editor Templates

Symbol	Template	Shortcut Keys
	Integral	CTRL+I CTRL+T,I
	Absolute value	CTRL+T,I
	Root	CTRL+R CTRL+T,R
	nth Root	CTRL+T,N
	Summation	CTRL+T,S
	Product	CTRL+T,P
	3 × 3 matrix template	CTRL+T,M
	Underscript (limit)	CTRL+T,U
Embellishment	**Shortcut Keys**	

TABLE 17-4   Shortcut Keys for Equation Editor Templates (*continued*)

Overbar	CTRL+SHIFT+-
Tilde	CTRL+~ CTRL+"(on some keyboards)
Arrow (vector)	CTRL+ALT+-
Single prime	CTRL+ALT+'
Double prime	CTRL+" CTRL+~(on some keyboards)
Single dot	CTRL+ALT+.

TABLE 17-5   Shortcut Keys for Equation Editor Embellishments

After installing a new printer, my Equation Editor equations don't print correctly. What can I do?

To print the equations created with the Equation Editor correctly, your printer must be capable of printing TrueType fonts. You can use either the TrueType fonts installed with the Equation Editor or with another application. After installing a new printer, you may have to reinstall the Equation Editor. You can run a Maintenance installation of Word to reinstall the fonts so they will work with the new default printer.

Do I have to use data from a Word document with the Graph applet?

You do not have to enter the data in a Word document beforehand. You can bring the data directly into Graph, create the graph, and then insert it into the Word document. For example, if you are creating a sales report and all of your sales data appears in an Excel spreadsheet, you can import it straight into Graph and then insert the graph you create into Word.

You can import files in any of these formats into the Graph applet:

- ASCII or text-only files with fields separated by commas or tabs (.CSV or .TXT).

- Lotus 1-2-3 version 1A and Microsoft Works (.WKS)

- Lotus 1-2-3 version 2.0 (.WK1)

- Lotus Symphony (.WR1)

- Microsoft Excel worksheet (.XLS)

- Microsoft Multiplan, Microsoft Excel, and other symbolic link files (.SLK)

When I import data from a spreadsheet into the Graph applet, some of it doesn't show up. What can I do to fix this problem?

Graph can only import up to 256 columns and 4,000 rows of data from a spreadsheet. Many spreadsheets can be much larger than this; they may have more rows, more columns, or multiple sheets in a single file. If your spreadsheet is larger than these specifications, you cannot import it all at once. To bring in all of the data you need for your graph, you can select it in the spreadsheet, copy it to the Clipboard, and then paste the data into the Graph applet.

I have an Oracle ODBC driver. Can I use it with Word 6.0?

Word 6.0 cannot work with multiple-tier databases drivers such as Oracle or SQL. Word 6.0 only supports *single-tier drivers*. Single-tier drivers are those commonly associated with data sources that don't require the source application in order to view the data, such as a text-only file or a Microsoft Access file.

How do I install an additional ODBC Driver?

To install an additional ODBC driver:

1. Open the Windows Control Panel by double-clicking its program-item icon, which is usually found in the Main group of the Program Manager.

2. Double-click the ODBC icon in the Control Panel or choose OD<u>B</u>C from the <u>S</u>ettings menu.

3. Click D<u>r</u>ivers and then click <u>A</u>dd.

4. Enter the path and filename of the driver file in the text box that appears in the Add Driver dialog box and then click OK.

5. Select the driver you want to install in the Available ODBC <u>D</u>rivers list box and then click OK.

6. Click Close twice.

7. Choose E<u>x</u>it from the <u>S</u>ettings menu.

The driver you selected is now installed and available for use as a data source.

How can I use part of an Access database as a data source for a mail merge in Word?

There are two ways in which you can use selected data in an Access database as a data source for a Word mail merge. The option you should choose depends on whether you have Access installed on your system and, if so, whether you know how to use it.

If you are comfortable using Access and have it installed on your system:

1. Create a query in Microsoft Access that returns just the data that you want to use in Word.

2. Open to your main document in Word.

3. Choose Mail Merge from the Tools menu, or display the Mail Merge toolbar and click the Mail Merge Helper button.

4. Click Get Data and choose Open Data source from the drop-down menu.

5. Select the Confirm Conversion check box.

6. Select your Access database file in the File Name list box and click OK.

7. Select MS Access Databases via DDE (*.MDB) in the Open Data Source list box and click OK.

8. Click the Queries tab and select your particular query.

9. Click OK.

If you don't have Access installed on your system or do not feel comfortable creating an Access query:

1. Choose Open Data Source from the Get Data drop-down menu in the Mail Merge Helper dialog box, as you normally would to open a database.

2. Select the Confirm Conversions check box.

3. Select your Access database file in the File Name list box and click OK.

4. Select MS Access Databases via ODBC (*.MDB) from the Open Data Source list box and click OK.

5. Click the Query Options button (If you have Excel 5.0, you will be asked if you want to use MS Query. If so, select No.)

6. Select the field for which you want to set a criterion and then enter the criteria.

When I try to open my Paradox 4.5 database, I get a message that says I cannot access the file and that Word cannot open an unkeyed Paradox table. What does this mean and what can I do?

The message you see probably looks like this:

```
File Access Denied
ODBC error: [Microsoft][ODBC single tier driver][ODBC file library]
File access denied SQL state:4200 return code SQL_Error.
Can't open unkeyed Paradox Table.
```

Word 6.0's Paradox ODBC driver can only open files from Paradox 3.5. To open your Paradox file, you must first save the Paradox database table in a format supported by Word 6.0's converters or ODBC drivers. These formats include dBASE, Excel, and Paradox version 3.5.

Tech Tip: A converter converts data into Word's format so that you can modify it in Word, whereas an ODBC driver lets you manipulate the data in its native format.

Does Word 6.0 support electronic mail?

Yes, Word 6.0 supports two electronic mail interface protocols:

- MAPI (Messaging Application Programming Interface), which is used by Microsoft Mail
- VIM (Vendor Independent Messaging), which is used by Lotus cc:Mail

As long as your electronic mail application supports one of these protocols, you can mail Word documents electronically.

I installed Word 6.x on my workstation, but the command to send a document as an e-mail attachment isn't on the File menu. What went wrong?

There are several reasons why the File menu might not display the Send command. To determine the source of the problem, check the following items:

- *Is Word set up to mail documents as attachments?* To enable this feature, choose Options from the Tools menu, click the General tab, select the Mail as Attachment check box, and click OK.

- *Does Word 6.0 support the mail system you are using?* Word only supports certain mail systems with this feature. For example, you will only get this menu command if you are using version 3.0 or later of MS-Mail, since Word 6.0 cannot create a menu option for earlier versions.

- *Does the [Mail] section of your WIN.INI. file include the statement MAPI=1?* Open this text file (which is usually located in the WINDOWS directory) in Word 6.0. If MAPI=1 does not appear in this section, add this line and resave the file as a text file with the same name.

- *Was the mail system installed before Word?* If the mail system was installed afterwards, the Send command will not appear on the File menu. To correct this problem, restart the Word Setup program from the WINWORD directory by double-clicking the Word Setup program icon in the Word for Windows program group, or by using the Run command from the File menu in the Program Manager. Use Word Setup to the actual Word program file. Start Setup the same way and reinstall the Word program file.

- *If you are using Lotus cc:Mail, does the CCMAIL directory appear in your Path statement?* Open your AUTOEXEC.BAT file in the root directory of your hard drive and examine the line that beings with PATH=. If necessary, add the CCMAIL directory to the statement and resave the file as a text file. When you reboot your system, any changes you made to AUTOEXEC.BAT take effect. You also must uninstall and then reinstall Word for Windows 6.0 to display the Send command.

Index